Hundreds of miles from its supply center in Chihuahua and just freed from the grip of Spain's mercantilist colonial policies, New Mexico was ripe for foreign commerce when the first of the Missouri traders arrived in Santa Fe in 1821. For the next forty years trade flourished between Americans hawking anything that would sell, often at incredible profit, and New Mexican buyers hungry for all types of manufactured goods. But the frontier moved inevitably westward, goods became more readily available and consequently less expensive, and the railroad at last replaced the mulewhackers who had long plied the Santa Fe Trail.

Broadcloth and Britches is the first account to synthesize an abundance of primary source material—the reminiscences of traders, the impressions of journalists and soldiers, the unpublished manuscripts of both literate and semi-literate observers—and serious scholarly journal articles and monographs of the Santa Fe Trail and trade. In this detailed and lively narrative, the authors trace the origins, development, and decline of the trade: the early expeditions; the route and its hazards; transport, financing, and profits; the effects of complex political shifts in Spain, Mexico, Texas, and the United States; and the economic consequences of increasingly efficient supply to a relatively fixed market.

Broadcloth and Britches

Broadcloth and Britches

Britches

THE SANTA FE TRADE

By Seymour V. Connor
  and Jimmy M. Skaggs

 Texas A&M University Press COLLEGE STATION AND LONDON

Library of Congress Cataloging in Publication Data

Connor, Seymour V
    Broadcloth and britches.

    Bibliography: p.
    Includes index.
    1. Southwest, New—History. 2. Santa Fe Trail.
3. Southwest, New—Commerce—History. I. Skaggs,
Jimmy M., joint author. II. Title.
F800.C66   979   76-17978
ISBN 0-89096-022-4

Manufactured in the United States of America
FIRST EDITION

*This damned book
is dedicated to
Odie B. Faulk*

Contents

List of Illustrations

Preface

This book was generated by our friend Odie B. Faulk, to whom it is dedicated, who several years ago conceived the idea of a pair of companion volumes on the Gila and Santa Fe trails. The original design was for Faulk and Connor to coauthor both books because they had had so much fun working together on *North America Divided* (1971). A change in plans made Faulk responsible for the Gila Trail study and Connor for this one. Faulk published his manuscript in 1973, but work on the Santa Fe Trail suffered so many delays and setbacks that Skaggs was called on to coauthor the work.

Our research was facilitated by several persons at numerous institutions. The Texas Tech University Library, and especially Mrs. Gloria Lyerla of the Interlibrary Loan Department, saved us much legwork. The Southwest Collection at Texas Tech had most of the material we needed, and its director, Sylvan Dunn, patiently tolerated our slovenly work habits and (impatiently, we sometimes thought) listened to our problems with the book. The Huntington Library is a delightful place to work; if we could have remained in San Marino longer we would have finished the book sooner. Everyone on the staff was helpful and encouraging, and the general ambience is intellectually nourishing. We have recorded our debt to the late Dale Morgan in the bibliographic notes. At Wichita State University we have special obligations to Michael D. Heaston, former curator of Ablah Library's Special Collections, and to James B. Taylor, the business librarian; both facilitated our work by locating obscure material and imprints. Professor Ross McLaury Taylor, of Wichita State's American Studies Department, unselfishly opened his voluminous personal library to our use and made many valuable suggestions. And at Topeka, the staff of the Kansas State Historical Society greatly assisted us in locating graphic material for use as illustrations.

Broadcloth and Britches

Broadcloth and Britches

Santa Fe: Isolated Outpost

Governor Facundo Melgares must have been of anxious and unsettled mind that November day in 1821. Word had reached him that a small party of Americans had entered New Mexico illegally and were encamped at the village of San Miguel del Vado, not two days' journey from Santa Fe. Unquestionably they would soon arrive at the capital. Who were they? What was their purpose? Were they but simple trappers who had lost their way in the mountains to the north? Or were they members of the American army? Or agents and spies?

No matter their identity, the question of how to receive them and what to do with them was of vital concern to Governor Melgares. Law and precedent called for their arrest and imprisonment; in such stern fashion had his predecessors dealt with foreigners. But there were factors influencing him in 1821 that had not affected earlier governors. Melgares, a career officer of the Spanish crown, undoubtedly realized that his treatment of this party would have multiple ramifications. And as he pondered the problem, he probably reflected on the background of his empire's relations with the upstart young nation to the north.

For nearly half a century and through all of Melgares' lifetime, those Anglo-Americans had, in one way or another, caused difficulties for Spanish colonial officials. First had been their revolution against England, for no loyal Spaniard could condone the principle of separatism. The thought that colonies could revolt against the nation that had borne and nurtured them was abhorrent, and the idea that they could rightfully form a new government based on republican theories was even more repugnant. Yet tempering the intensity of this feeling toward American separatism was a pervasive dislike for Britain. Spain had suffered defeat, along with her Bourbon ally, France, in the Seven Years' War. The ignominy of her loss of Florida to the arrogant British in the Treaty of 1763 was but little offset by France's compensatory gift of the uncharted Louisiana wilderness west of the Mississippi. Spanish officials were ready to support any war against Britain, and some Spaniards, with thinly veiled secrecy, had actually supported American independence. Although the principle was disturbing, the result had been of some benefit to the empire, for Britain was constrained to return Florida to Spain in the Treaty of 1783.

This had brought the boundaries of colonial empire into juxtaposition with the new United States along the length of the Mississippi River and along the undetermined northern boundary of Florida. In 1795, somewhat to the surprise of many international observers, the Spanish crown had granted the Americans equal navigation rights on the great river as well as the right to deposit and transship their goods at New Orleans without duty and had conceded the 31st parallel as the northern Florida line. Soon Americans were trickling across the unmarked and unguarded Florida frontier, into New Orleans, and even west across the Mississippi. Personal and business alliances with French-descended frontier enterprisers led them into lucrative trapping and fur trade. Some few entered Spanish domains as permanent settlers, such as Moses Austin, who obtained permission to mine lead ore and founded a town southwest of St. Louis. Wilder men, like Philip Nolan, had received passports to hunt or to capture horses on the Texas prairies.

It was not, however, the aggression of American frontiersmen that caused a major change in the northern frontier, but rather the impotence of the Spanish crown. Under unrelenting pressure from Napoleon Bonaparte, who had dreams of reestablishing the French colonial empire, Spain returned Louisiana to France in 1800, secretly agreeing to continue administering the territory. Alarmed at this new ownership of the west side of the Mississippi and afraid of its effects on the developing river traffic, the new American president, Thomas Jefferson, quickly initiated efforts to purchase the mouth of the river. It was an accident of history that Napoleon, after ignoring American ministers for nearly two years, offered the Americans the whole of Louisiana rather than the Isle of Orleans. Thus, by chance alone and not by any hint of imperialism or expansionism or manifest destiny did the United States make its first and largest territorial acquisition.

Some serious historians have implied, however, that the Louisiana Purchase was the first step of a greedy and imperialistic nation toward domination of its continent, and they have asserted rather anachronistically that Spanish officials immediately became hotly suspicious of all moves made by Americans toward the west. There is some vague truth in this, but the reasons for Spanish attitudes are not so simplistic. For one thing, the authorities were suspicious of all foreigners near their empire's borders—certainly more so of the French a half century earlier than of the Americans at this time. Melgares probably did not consider this party from the new nation east of the Mississippi as a territorial threat at all. It is extremely doubtful if he even thought of them in those terms.

He had three far more immediate and important reasons for concern. One was the fifty-year-old Indian policy on the frontier; a second was the unsurveyed boundary between Spain and the United States; and the third was the revolution in Mexico. Recent events had complicated the life of a royal governor. He would definitely have to interrogate these Americans. He gave orders for the leader, William Becknell, to be brought before him.

Spain's Indian policy was a matter of importance to a frontier governor and military man such as Melgares. It had evolved during the eighteenth century and had become more or less fixed by the 1780's. The northern plains tribes, particularly the Comanches, were a constant menace. Spanish policy was to placate them with presents, coax allegiances from them, and, if possible, use them against the Apaches, who were not much less hostile. The policy dated back to the report of a frontier inspector, the Marqués de Rubí, in 1769 and the Royal Regulations of 1772.

Rubí's suggestions regarding the northern tribes had been implemented by various commandants of the *Provincias Internas*, or Interior Provinces—a new administrative agency created in the latter part of the eighteenth century to make frontier governance more effective and efficient. Hugo O'Conor, a military commander on the frontier, and Alejandro O'Reilly, governor of Louisiana after its acquisition by Spain in 1763—both Irish Catholics in Spanish service —apparently conceived the idea of using Frenchmen from Louisiana as Indian agents. The plan was endorsed by the first official commandant of the Interior Provinces, Teodoro de Croix, himself a French officer who had spent his lifetime in the service of Spain's Bourbon kings.

The most important such agent was Athanase de Mézières of Natchitoches, a capable man who could speak several Indian tongues and could read and write Spanish, French, and Latin. De Mézières, acting for O'Reilly, made several trips up the Red River between 1770 and 1772, winning the allegiance of several of the northern bands, including many of the Comanches. Croix appointed him governor of Texas in 1778, and De Mézières then cemented alliances with other Comanche bands, apparently provoking them to war against the Lipan Apaches. By 1780 Lipan leaders sued for friendship with Spain and an uneasy truce was established along the frontiers of Texas and New Mexico.

Almost as important as De Mézières was another apostate Frenchman, Pierre (or Pedro) Vial. This intrepid adventurer assured the continued success of the policy by traveling through Comanche country during the 1780's and distributing gifts to Comanche chiefs. He also tried to link isolated Santa Fe with other frontier settlements by exploring routes to San Antonio in 1786, to Natchitoches in 1787, and to St. Louis in 1792. This last was the first authorized and recorded exploration between Santa Fe and Missouri, but the difficulties of the proposed road prevented that venture's leading to the development of any trade.

Shortly after Vial's trek to St. Louis, Indian hostilities erupted. Governor Melgares remembered this well, for he had been personally involved as a young officer in the Spanish army. New Mexico's northern settlements were temporarily deserted and almost devastated. Melgares himself led an expedition that reestablished the alliance with the Comanches. The friendship of the northern tribes and the satisfactory status quo on the frontier again seemed in danger of being upset after the transfer of Louisiana to the United States in 1803. The renaissance-like curiosity of that new nation's third president led him to send out explorers to determine the nature of the vast territorial acquisition. Thus the famed Lewis and

Clark expedition went up the Missouri River and across the continental divide to the Pacific Ocean. Of more immediate concern to Spanish frontier officials were the visits of Dr. John Sibley to Indian tribes on the Red River, the search for the Red River's source by Thomas Freeman, and the expedition of Captain Zebulon Pike to the headwaters of the Arkansas in 1806.

It was Pike's expedition that caused the greatest alarm in New Mexico. It was also to give Americans their first direct knowledge of the terrain between Missouri and Santa Fe as well as of the interior of the northern Spanish provinces. Although Pike denied it, Spanish officials suspected him of attempting to woo the Comanches and other northern tribes from their shaky allegiance to Spain. Governor Melgares also remembered this well, for he had spent much time with Pike after his capture. Melgares had just returned to Santa Fe from an expedition against the Pawnees in 1806 when rumor of Pike's appearance at the head of an armed band of American troops reached New Mexico. A detachment was dispatched and took Pike and his men prisoner while they were ostensibly proceeding from the Arkansas in search of the headwaters of the Red River. It is little wonder that Melgares and others in New Mexico believed Pike had been tampering with the Indians.

To increase their suspicions was the behavior of Dr. John H. Robinson, who had detached himself from Pike and preceded the Americans into Santa Fe. Pike at first denied knowledge of Robinson. Then there was the fact that Pike was under the orders of General James Wilkinson, a man of intrigue and unknown objectives. Melgares could no more have understood Wilkinson than a modern historian can. Wilkinson was known to be in the pay of Spain as an agent, yet he was the ranking American army officer in command of the Louisiana Territory. He also was known to have been in communication with Aaron Burr in the plot to overthrow the United States in the Mississippi valley, yet when the Burr conspiracy was revealed, Wilkinson mustered American forces to oppose him. Likewise, he was known to have once employed Philip Nolan in his home, yet when Nolan was killed in Texas, he denied any connection with him. Wilkinson's son, also an army officer, had accompanied Pike on the first stages of the expedition. Pike's relationship to Wilkinson thus has created an enigma for historians.

In spite of feeling uneasy about Pike's activities among the Indians, Melgares evidently liked Pike and the feeling was reciprocated. Melgares, who questioned Pike thoroughly and went through his belongings and his papers, treated the American captain with respect. And it was Melgares who escorted the Americans to Chihuahua to be interviewed by the commandant of the eastern Interior Provinces. There further interrogation failed to yield any evidence that Pike was an Indian agent of any kind. He was released and sent back to the United States across Texas in 1807.

Yet the feeling persisted that the Americans might somehow have induced their Indian allies to forsake Spain. An answering expedition into the plains was called for. It was to be the last of the dying empire's glorious frontier *entradas*. Five companies of troops from Texas, Coahuila, and Nuevo León were assembled in San Antonio the following year, 1808, under the command of Francisco Amangual. He was ordered to make a leisurely trip across the Llano Estacado to Santa Fe, visiting Comanche bands and distributing presents to their chiefs. He was particularly instructed to look for any evidence of American activity among the Indians. Amangual returned with his expedition from Santa Fe in the spring of 1809 and reported that he could find no indication that Pike or any other Americans had disturbed Spain's alliances.

Nonetheless, as the years passed and as more and more Americans began penetrating the plains in search of furs, jealousy over the Indians lingered. The Americans could hardly be considered trespassers, since the boundary between Spain and the United States (of the Louisiana territory) was then unsurveyed. In fact, Spain's Indian allies themselves probably roamed much of the time on American soil. The problem was that Louisiana had never had a definite western boundary. France, because of La Salle, had claimed the lands drained by the Mississippi and then later, also because of La Salle, had established a vague claim to Texas after the establishment of Fort St. Louis on Matagorda Bay. Spain had been at great pains to eradicate this latter claim, burning the French fort to the ground and permanently colonizing Texas. Once France gave western Louisiana to Spain in 1763, there no longer was a need to define its western limit. And when Napoleon had wrenched it back from Spain, the treaty had simply specified vaguely that it had its original boundary. The abrupt transfer to the United States in 1803, then, gave the United States whatever claim France might once have had west of the Mississippi. Some Americans, including Thomas Jefferson, believed this could extend across Texas as far as the Rio Grande.

For a decade and a half diplomats casually pondered the question. There was no urgency in Washington or in Madrid to define the boundary, since the territory involved was largely unoccupied and unexplored. Only in East Texas was there any immediate need, and this was resolved informally and unofficially by generals Simón de Herrera for Spain and James Wilkinson for the United States in 1806 in what became known as the Neutral Ground Agreement. Wilkinson may have felt constrained to make this negotiation at the time because of the pressure of Burr's nefarious activities. It was thus established that the area between the Sabine River on the west and the Arroyo Hondo on the east would be a buffer zone occupied by neither Americans nor Spaniards and subject to the laws of neither nation. It became incidentally a refuge for outlaws and brigands.

The official boundary was finally set by the Treaty of 1819, sometimes called the Adams-Onís Treaty and, sometimes, the Florida Purchase Treaty. By its terms, Spain transferred Florida to the United States and in return the United States abandoned its pretensions to Texas and agreed to assume the claims of American citizens against Spain for depredations by the Florida Indians, long a bone of contention. The boundary between Spain and the United States was fixed as follows: up the west bank of the Sabine River from its mouth to the 32nd parallel; thence due north to the Red River; thence up the south bank of the Red River to the 100th meridian; thence north to the Arkansas; thence up the Arkansas to its source; thence directly north or south (for the location of the source was not then known) to the 42nd parallel; and thence due west to the Pacific.

Ratifications of the treaty were exchanged between Spain and the United States in February, 1821, but Melgares probably had not learned of this when he was pondering the appearance of William Becknell. It mattered little that the Americans were trespassers on Spanish territory. What did matter to Facundo Melgares was the

Indian policy that he had grown up supporting and a second, probably more important question, the possible role of these Americans in the Mexican independence movement.

On this issue the governor must have felt wary and anxious. For ten years all of New Spain had been in a turmoil of revolution. In Mexico the fighting had started with the *Grito de Dolores* of Father Miguel Hidalgo on September 16, 1810. It had been an uprising of the rabble, of the peons crying for economic reform and social justice, virtually a revolt of the long-subjugated Indians against their creole masters. The initial movement had been put down but not entirely suppressed. Again and again guerrilla leaders of the Hidalguistas had thrown themselves against royalist forces with negligible success. The movement lacked any concerned leadership, and it lacked financial support.

The real leadership in Mexico, the wealthy landowners and mine operators—those creoles who considered themselves pure-blooded Spaniards—would not support the peons' effort for reform. There was no middle class in Mexico: only the very rich and the very poor. In the early nineteenth century, the *ricos* grew increasingly dissatisfied with Spanish rule. A liberal constitution was being forced on the Spanish monarchy. The administrators sent over from Spain, the *gauchipines*, were but third-rate bureaucrats, many of them insultingly incapable of governing and none of them competent to maintain the privileges of the aristocracy in Mexico.

Thus, two inimicable forces of discontent arose in Mexico, the one demanding social and economic reform, the other desiring an independent monarchy in Mexico for the protection of its own class. To both, separation from Spain was the initial step. And it was this that brought them together ultimately in 1821. But for a decade after the death of Father Hidalgo in 1811, the Hidalguista reformers struggled along.

Insurgencies had broken out in scattered places all over Mexico, Melgares knew. What no doubt bothered him as he pondered the presence of the American party in New Mexico was the role Americans had played in this movement, especially in neighboring Texas.

The revolutionary movement had gained quick and ready sympathy in the United States. Not only did it contain the elements of republicanism, but it also adopted the American theme of separation from the mother country. With the initial collapse of the Hidalgo movement, many of his followers fled to the United States, some by ship across the Gulf and others overland across Texas. In Texas, far removed as it was from Mexico City, the revolutionaries almost took root. Hidalgo himself was headed north and might have reached Texas had he not been caught.

In San Antonio, one of his followers, Juan Bautista de las Casas, had provoked an uprising and taken over the capital in Hidalgo's name. Many people in the sparsely settled province of Texas sympathized with Hidalgo's goals. But there were not enough of them. A relatively well-to-do rancher, Juan Zambrano, organized a counterrevolution and harshly suppressed the Las Casas movement. Had Hidalgo lived and brought even a part of an army to San Antonio, the story might have been different. Las Casas, too, was caught and killed, but some of his followers escaped across the Sabine to the safety of the United States, where Natchitoches and New Orleans were becoming centers of the Mexican revolution.

One man who was to figure prominently during the decade had left his home in Tamaulipas to join Hidalgo but when the priest was captured had turned to San Antonio. Like a cat with nine lives, Bernardo Gutiérrez de Lara was to escape capture again and again. After the failure of Las Casas he slipped into Natchitoches and from there visited Philadelphia and the American capital at Washington. Although he was not officially received as an ambassador of the Mexican revolution, the American government officially having adopted a neutral posture, he was cordially welcomed unofficially by many important personages. Armed with letters of introduction and apparently some financial support, he returned to Louisiana to mount an invasion of Texas in 1812 in the name of Mexican independence.

Gutiérrez was not the only Mexican liberal in the United States stirring up sympathy and support for the revolution, but the example of his activities must have particularly perturbed Melgares. For Gutiérrez was highly successful in involving Americans in his work. The fascinating story of his American schemes and intrigue does not belong here and was probably not known to Melgares, but the simple fact of American volunteers' participation in revolutionary affairs in Texas was common knowledge and must have been of considerable concern to the governor of New Mexico. In 1812, accompanied by an American officer who had resigned his commission in the United States Army and several hundred American volunteers, Gutiérrez invaded Texas to overthrow Spanish authority there. The expedition gained temporary control of the province, and the people of Texas once more celebrated their independence from Spain, albeit somewhat cautiously and, for some, half-heartedly. A royalist army from Coahuila defeated the insurgents in April, 1813, suppressed the uprising, and executed many of its leaders.

Gutiérrez escaped and returned to Louisiana to help organize a new liberation movement. After the end of the War of 1812 and Andrew Jackson's successful defense of New Orleans, other Americans joined in the movement, some from purely idealistic motives but many for outright filibustering. A series of unsuccessful ventures followed, all bearing, in varying shades, the colors of the revolution. Luis d'Aury occupied Galveston Island; Francisco Mina invaded Tamaulipas; Jean Lafitte moved into Galveston Island; Charles Lallemond established a short-lived French settlement off Galveston Bay; and James Long of Natchez twice invaded Texas. Gutiérrez was involved in all but one of these undertakings, and every one of them had its origins in the United States, without official sanction, of course, but with individual American supporters. The appearance of Americans in New Mexico was just cause for concern.

The most recent of the American-based invasions were those of James Long in 1819 and 1821. Their inception and underlying motivation was the angry reaction on the part of some Americans to the Treaty of 1819, the same treaty that had settled the Louisiana boundary between the United States and Spain. Some Americans thought it was a New England sell-out by Secretary of State John Quincy Adams. Thus, Long started out to "reclaim" Texas but soon became entwined in Gutiérrez' schemes for Mexican independence. Even though the Long fiascos were nominally in the name of Mexico, Melgares surely knew of American unhappiness over the boundary line, although he did not know the accord had been ratified.

To the north and west of Texas, in the area roughly considered

New Mexico, the treaty line cut off from the United States a considerable amount of territory American fur trappers considered theirs. Those who had paid any heed to the question of the international boundary had been operating on the assumption that the United States had acquired the French claim to the watershed of the Mississippi with the purchase of Louisiana. A glance at a map will show how much prime fur region south of the Arkansas River was given up to Spain. The governor of New Mexico certainly had to consider whether the American visitors—harmless fur trappers, so they were reported—were perhaps incipient James Longs.

But when he learned of the American party at San Miguel, Melgares' overriding consideration must have been the revolution in Mexico. The two factions in Mexico, both desiring independence but each for different, almost diametrically opposite reasons, had finally united in February, 1821. Their agreement, called the Plan de Iguala, was one of the strangest in North American history. The *ricos* of Mexico, the wealthy creole class, having grown totally dissatisfied with Spanish rule, turned to the Hidalguistas for the manpower needed to overthrow the viceroy. And the reformers, disorganized and without real leadership or funds, embraced them. Both parties agreed to a compromise that was fundamentally unacceptable to either: separation from Spain and the establishment of a limited constitutional monarchy in Mexico. They could act in concert to achieve separation; they were doomed to split over the limited monarchy, for the reformers wanted a republic and the *ricos,* an absolute monarchy and an autocratic government.

But the Plan de Iguala temporarily united all of Mexico under the leadership of creole leader Agustín de Iturbide. Native-born soldiers in the royal Spanish army quickly followed their leaders in defecting to the new plan for independence. Iturbide himself had been a general in the royal army. By the end of the summer, with very little actual fighting, the royal banners had been struck and the viceroy had abdicated. Spain's three-century hold on Mexico was broken. Throughout the country during that summer of 1821 royal officials were in a quandary. Should they side with the Plan de Iguala or remain loyal to the crown? Most had little difficulty in deciding for the revolution. Antonio Martínez, the royal governor of

Texas, was almost rabid in his zeal for the new cause (once it was successful). "God and Liberty," he blatantly signed his correspondence.

In New Mexico, Melgares was less fervid and possibly more reluctant to change his allegiance. There is no extant evidence of what must have been the turmoil in the mind of this official who had for so long been in royal service. But convert he did, quietly and without fanfare. He was later to turn to Americans in Santa Fe for instruction about how to celebrate independence. But that was later. It was now November 17, 1821, scarcely two months after Iturbide's victory had been proclaimed. And Governor Melgares, troubled by divided loyalties and disturbed by the presence of unwanted foreigners, was forced by circumstances to receive William Becknell cordially rather than order his arrest. Who knew what these Americans' involvement in the revolution might be? More important, God alone could predict what the stance of the new government would be toward the United States. Melgares, who had liked Zebulon Pike, bowed to the times.

CHAPTER 2

Origins of the Santa Fe Trade

Little is actually known of William Becknell's reception by Governor Facundo Melgares. It is safe to infer that it was cordial, because the great and occasionally lucrative commerce between Santa Fe and Missouri developed directly out of it, Becknell having been generally credited as the originator of the trade. But this is inference. There is no record in the Spanish (or Mexican) archives of New Mexico of that meeting. There does exist a dubious report in what is known as the "Journal of Captain Thomas [sic] Becknell," first printed in the little frontier newspaper at Franklin, Missouri, the *Missouri Intelligencer*, April 22, 1823: "The day after my arrival [in Santa Fe on November 16, 1821] I accepted an invitation to visit the Governor, whom I found to be well informed and gentlemanly in manners; his demeanor was courteous and friendly. He asked many questions concerning my country, its people, their manner of living, etc.; expressed a desire that the Americans would keep up an intercourse with that country, and said that if any of them wished to emigrate, it would give him pleasure to afford them every facility."

One must look askance at this purported journal. Becknell's description of the courteous governor is cast in almost the same educated and courtly words that Zebulon Pike had used a decade earlier. Further, Melgares almost certainly did not invite American immigration. He had not the authority to do so and probably lacked the inclination. He was much too cautious a man to jeopardize his relations with the new government being formed in Mexico City by such a rash move. Finally, there is convincing evidence that Becknell did not write the "journal" published in the *Intelligencer*. The

excerpt below, taken from a manuscript in Becknell's own hand
(now in the Huntington Library) to Melgares' successor on October
24, 1824, demonstrates this conclusively.

His Exelinnce
governor of
New mexico
Bartola Ma Barker
                                        Sir I Have recd the
Lisance you granted me by the onnabel preste of
santa Cruse. . . . tha is 10 of us to gether all
amiarican those men at tous I have nothing to dew
with what tha ar going to dew I know not . . . I
cante say wheather tha ar (goin to trape) ar not
tha have sum trapes with them if any cums with in
my notis I shal give you notis . . . your Exlantance
wishes me to send you sum medison   I send you sum
Rubarb and sum Campher the Rubarbe you Can take
at any time what will Lyan the pinte of apockit
in sum shuger and a spunful of cold warter you may
Eaight or drinke any thing & hot or cold the best
time to take it is of anight when you go to Bed
it is not specli agentil purge and wil fritufy
the stumak . . .

Pretty clearly, the editor of the *Intelligencer* interviewed Becknell in 1823 and put the plainsman's grammarless account in his
own graceful journalistic style. But almost as clearly, Becknell was
on friendly terms with Governor Bartolomé Baca, so he probably
had the same relationship with Melgares and as cordial a reception
as the *Intelligencer* reported.

There is additional mystery about this 1821–1822 trip that
opened the Santa Fe trade. The newspaper "journal" does not describe the sale of any merchandise in Santa Fe, and nowhere is any
extant information to be found about trade on this initial expedition. Yet the editor implied that Becknell and others brought back
to Franklin over $10,000 in specie. An oft-repeated legend has it
that when Becknell and his companions returned to Franklin they
triumphantly ripped open their saddle bags to pour gold and silver
coins upon the dusty street before a large crowd of eager onlookers.
One must turn again to inference about this first venture. It indu-
bitably sparked other trade ventures, and Becknell himself bought

three wagons, loaded them with merchandise, and returned promptly to Santa Fe. Obviously he had discovered a market there, whether he had profited greatly from the trip or not.

Yet still a third mystery attaches to Becknell's first visit. What prompted it? What were his motives and intentions? Again, there is scant factual data upon which to base any conclusions. Becknell and a company of men, number unknown, left Missouri in September, 1821, and arrived in New Mexico in November. They had only pack horses, no wagons. They apparently had some variety of trade goods. Because of the fortuitous timing of their arrival, it does not seem likely that their original destination was Santa Fe, for they could not have known in advance of Iturbide's success or of Melgares' acceptance of the revolution. There is some evidence that they intended to trade with the Indians for furs but that somewhere near the Arkansas they either met a party of dragoons from New Mexico or heard rumors among the Indians of the change of government. Even so, it is still curious that Becknell and his party should assume, first, that they would be welcomed in New Mexico, and second, that there would be a market for their commodities— if they had trade goods with them when they got to New Mexico, and there is only inferential evidence of this. They took considerable risk entering New Mexico openly and illegally. Spain and Spanish frontier officials were notoriously hostile toward all foreigners. Becknell certainly had knowledge of several parties that had simply disappeared behind the prairie curtain before him.

Yet push into New Mexico he did, for reasons that will forever remain obscure. He was welcomed, for reasons examined in the previous chapter. And he did find a ready market, for reasons rooted in the history of Santa Fe, its geographical isolation, the logistical support that had been accorded New Mexico, and the economic philosophy of the Spanish colonial system.

In 1598, Juan de Oñate had established Spanish control over New Mexico, and his successor founded the capital city of Villa Real de la Santa Fe de San Francisco de Asis in 1609. There was little in New Mexico to attract active colonization—a persistent but unfulfilled dream of a city of gold and a dozen or so sedentary Indian villages scattered along the upper Rio Grande. As there were no mines to work, the labor the Indians might provide was of little value. But there were souls to be saved, and so the religious establishment became the most important aspect of early New Mexico.

For three-quarters of a century brown-clad Franciscans, supported by Spanish muskets, forced the benefits of Christianity onto peoples who had a fairly complex, well-developed, and workable religious system of their own. Then, as the reward of a remarkably well-organized conspiracy, the Pueblo Indians overthrew their masters and in a bloody massacre panicked the surviving Spaniards out of the area. A reconquest by Spain came under Pedro de Vargas in 1692, and by the eighteenth century New Mexico had settled into the somnolent pastoral existence that became its chief characteristic. The eighteenth century records no event that materially affected New Mexico's history. The most significant thing about the province was its insignificance—and its romantic isolation.

During that period Santa Fe was the most remote civilized spot on the globe. Nearly in the heart of the yet-unexplored North American continent, it was inaccessible by water. Quebec, founded the year previous to Santa Fe, and the tiny French settlements in Canada were in constant and relatively easy communication with the mother country because of the St. Lawrence River and its network of waterways. The British settlements—Jamestown was founded two years before Santa Fe—huddled along the Atlantic coast and were in such regular touch with England that they were in reality little more isolated than Old Sarum.

But Santa Fe could not be reached by ships, and the Rio Grande provided no such waterway as the St. Lawrence. It was six hundred rugged miles down the Mexico City trail to Ciudad Chihuahua, the nearest settlement of any consequence. It was a thousand virtually impossible miles over unknown territory to the frontier outposts in East Texas and Louisiana. To California, which was not established until the latter part of the eighteenth century, it was a similar impractical distance.

A few indefatigable *coureurs de bois* found their ways into Santa Fe. The Mallet brothers, Paul and Pierre, are usually recognized as the first to make a round trip from French territory. Their route in 1739 was circuitous and is but vaguely known: up the Mississippi from New Orleans to the Missouri; up the Missouri to the vicinity of the Platte; southward to the Arkansas; then up the Arkansas, probably to the Purgatoire; then probably along the way that later was established as the mountain branch of the Santa Fe Trail to New Mexico. They returned following the Canadian part of the way and then going down the Arkansas to the Mississippi.

The Mallet brothers had more than merely wandered along what eventually became the Santa Fe Trail, for the foresighted Frenchmen carried with them a wide assortment of consumer goods suitable for trade. The bell in the tower of the mission San Miguel rang out on July 22, announcing their arrival in Santa Fe. The Mallets were warmly greeted, generously feted, and comfortably lodged in the humble community's most commodious homes. Their few wares were eagerly snapped up by local buyers, who seldom had the opportunity to spend their money for manufactured goods. While the Frenchmen lingered in Santa Fe for nine months, the governor hastily dispatched a messenger to Mexico City to beg the viceroy's permission to establish regular commercial relations between New Mexico and French Louisiana. The reply was negative. The Mallets were to be deported at once. New Mexico was to remain closed to international trade.

But after the transfer of Louisiana to Spain in 1763 and the organization of the Interior Provinces, Spanish officials made an effort to link New Mexico with Louisiana and Texas. Employed for the purpose was Pedro Vial, a New World Frenchman who, like many of his fellows, had transferred his allegiance to Spain. After heroic explorations from San Antonio to Santa Fe and from Santa Fe to Natchitoches, in 1792 he was ordered to open a route from Santa Fe to St. Louis. Although he kept a diary, copies of which are extant, his journey is difficult to trace with any measure of accuracy. Yet it is the first recorded travel between Santa Fe and what later became Missouri.

Vial went from the New Mexico capital to the Pecos pueblo, turned northeast, and crossed the Gallinas Creek to reach the Canadian. He followed it into the present Panhandle of Texas and then turned north to the Arkansas. There, in present Kansas, he was captured by a party of Kansa Indians and taken to their village at the juncture of the Kansas and Missouri rivers. After his release, he canoed down the Missouri to St. Louis. He returned by boat up the Missouri to the vicinity of the present Nebraska boundary, then overland across the prairies in what appears to have been a south-westerly direction, crossing the Kansas River and various of its tributaries to reach the Arkansas in central Kansas, possibly near Hutchinson. Continuing southwest he crossed the plains to an un-identified river, possibly the Cimarron, which he followed for sev-eral days before turning again to the southwest to reach the Canadian, along which he traveled to connnect with his outgoing route and to return to Santa Fe. Vial's routes, both going and return-ing, lay considerably to the east of the later Santa Fe Trail and can-not be considered its predecessor. Nor did Vial's journey change Santa Fe's isolation; it simply emphasized it.

Thus, like the bloom on a yucca stalk, Santa Fe was precarious-ly supported and sustained at the end of the long thin road from Mexico City via Chihuahua which traced essentially the same route taken by Juan de Oñate in 1598. It went south down the Rio Grande from the Santo Domingo pueblo to the approximate location of to-day's Elephant Butte Reservoir, about midway between modern Socorro and Truth or Consequences. There the road cut south away from the river, which swung out to the west in a large bend. It was normally a two-day journey through the desert—the *jornado del muerto*—to rejoin the Rio Grande near present Las Cruces. From there the road continued along the east bank to the foot of Franklin Mountain, where it crossed the river and headed almost due south, again through desert country to Ciudad Chihuahua. Chihuahua was linked by several routes to the heart of Spanish North America in Mexico City.

From Santa Fe to Chihuahua was approximately six hundred miles. It took Oñate's wagon train a little over four months to make the trip. In 1609, with the founding of Santa Fe, a regular supply service was established from Mexico City, about 1,500 miles away. Eighteen months was allowed for the round trip—six months from Mexico City to Santa Fe, six months in New Mexico to distribute supplies and recuperate, and six months to return. Then, a year and a half later, another caravan was supposed to make the journey. In other words, the colonial government's plan was to supply Santa Fe and the New Mexico missions every three years. The provision serv-ice was supported by the government and was nominally for the maintenance of the mission outposts. In point of fact, however, trade goods were regularly carried by the caravans for the benefit of civil settlers while authorities looked the other way—the typical pragmatic response of the regulation-bound colonial administration. Without such pragmatism, which usually involved a change of ownership of a pocketful of *reales*, much of colonial Spain would certainly have been strangled to death with bureaucratic red tape.

Although the supply caravans were scheduled every three years, their regularity was also subject to practical adjustment. During the seventeenth century the supply caravans reached Santa Fe on the average of every six or seven years, which created a condition of perennial hardship in New Mexico. In the eighteenth century, after the Pueblo Revolt and the subsequent reconquest, logistical support caravans plied the route more frequently but continued to be irregular. By the middle of the eighteenth century, they had begun to operate on a more or less annual basis, probably carrying fewer goods because the service was shifted from ponderous ox-drawn wagons to mule trains. Additional sporadic mule trains worked north from Ciudad Chihuahua to Santa Fe. Shortly after the establishment of Chihuahua, commercial intercourse began on an unofficial annual basis with Santa Fe. The four months' time it had taken Oñate's wagons to roll from Chihuahua's site to Santa Domingo was reduced to an average of forty days, which seems to have remained the customary time for the journey, although in the nineteenth century mail runs were made more rapidly.

An important change in the logistical support of New Mexico came after the establishment of Ciudad Chihuahua in 1709. Located in a rich silver mining district, the new community grew relatively rapidly and became the focal point for the supply of the missions and settlements to the north. A few merchants in Chihuahua virtually monopolized the trade to New Mexico. Apparently these businessmen profited handsomely, if not exorbitantly, at the expense of a handful of Santa Fe traders who stayed almost constantly in debt to their Chihuahua suppliers. Excessive costs were passed on, of course, to consumers in New Mexico.

Historian Max Moorhead (*New Mexico's Royal Road*) has described this as a "vicious circle of swindles" growing out of the

"unscrupulous policies" of "pure extortion" followed by the Chihuahua merchants. Because of a complex system of monetary values
and because the New Mexico businessmen normally operated on
barter, a typical transaction often netted Chihuahua merchants
profits ten times and more of their original outlays. In effect, a yard
of woolen textile which retailed for about twenty cents in Chihuahua
might be sold in New Mexico for fifty bushels of corn that were
worth a total of two and a half dollars back in Chihuahua. Thus,
the commercial system, growing out of the isolation of New Mexico
and its complete dependence on Chihuahua, caused goods in Santa
Fe generally to cost many times their value.

Whatever may have been the motivation of Becknell's first visit
in 1821, it was this inflated price structure that caused him to return
immediately with three wagonloads of goods the following year. It
was an obvious economic fact: entrepreneurs from Missouri could
sell manufactured articles in Santa Fe much cheaper than the going
rates and still make huge profits. During that first year of the trade,
1822, according to an oft-quoted table of values compiled some
twenty years later by Josiah Gregg, the great chronicler of the
Santa Fe trade, some $15,000 worth of American goods were taken
by several parties into New Mexico.

One further factor contributed to the competitive edge enjoyed
by Missourians, a factor that kept the Missouri–Santa Fe trade
alive even after the back of the Chihuahua monopoly had been
broken, that indeed enabled New Mexico merchants, together with
Missourians, to turn the tables on the Chihuahua quasi-cartel and
to sell goods cheaper in Chihuahua than the Chihuahuans themselves could. From the very beginning in 1822, a large portion of
the Santa Fe trade from Missouri found its way south into northern
Mexico, which greatly enhanced the Missouri trade; for Chihuahua
itself, like all of Mexico, was enmeshed in the antiquated economic
policies and philosophy of the decadent Spanish empire.

Spain's officials had always viewed the colonies from within a
mercantilistic economic framework. In short, the colonies existed
for the sole purpose of enriching the mother country. To implement
this policy, Spain had imposed an increasingly heavy burden of
taxes on the colonies and their New World citizens. Then, to ensure

that only Spain would profit from Spanish colonies, a system that jealously prohibited foreign trade was imposed. All commerce was funneled through Mexico City to Veracruz. Veracruz was for all practical purposes the only Atlantic port-of-entry in Spanish North America, and it was virtually closed to all European commerce except that from Spain. This created on a grander scale the same kind of vicious circle that had enthralled the trade in New Mexico. Monopoly, corruption, and unscrupulousness were the governing themes of Spanish colonial commerce.

A striking example of Spain's stifling economic policy can be seen in the cattle trade in Texas. Soon after the Treaty of Paris of 1763 by which Spain acquired Louisiana, Texas cattlemen were permitted (for the first time) to sell their livestock in Louisiana. There followed a cattle boom in microcosm, and for the first time in a century Spanish Texans began to prosper. For about a quarter of a century ranchers from the San Antonio River area were allowed to drive herds to market in Louisiana, which was in fact the only market they had. Thousands of head of livestock were trailed along incredibly difficult paths through heavy timber and across broad rivers to be sold for profit. Almost at once the government began levying taxes on the trail herds, but even this did not stop the profitable movement of livestock. Then, in 1803, with the United States' acquisition of Louisiana, Spanish officialdom absolutely forbade the continuation of the trade. It was a stupidly short-sighted move by the government but thoroughly in the economic tradition of the empire: no foreign trade. Texas lost the only economic base it had ever had and its brief-lived prosperity quickly died, leaving the area stagnant, depopulated, and vulnerable. One can only speculate about what a cattle trade allowed to thrive might have done for Spain's hold on Texas.

It was similar selfishly narrow policies that inhibited commercial development in Mexico and created a corrupt, overly taxed, and overly regulated economy. It was within the framework of this two-century-old system that merchants had learned to function. And it was within this system that all of northern Mexico, including Santa Fe, was trapped at the end of the Spanish era. Little wonder that as soon as a crack appeared in the restrictive wall of Spanish policy,

American goods could be traded profitably and Missouri traders welcomed warmly. Santa Fe, because of its isolation, the weakness of its logistical support, and the inhibitory economic policy, was ripe for the opening of foreign commerce. The market was almost like a vacuum waiting to be filled.

CHAPTER 3

The First Rush Southwestward

A few men seem to have anticipated the opening of the Santa Fe bonanza and acted prematurely. The treasure trove would not be unlocked until after Mexican independence in 1821. But between the American purchase of Louisiana in 1803 and the end of Spanish rule in Mexico at least a half-dozen American parties had reached New Mexico. Some of them were fur trappers, apparently lost or at least aimless in their movements; others were definitely intent on trade.

Commerce was the clear purpose of the first of these adventurers, although it is less clear whether Santa Fe or the western Indian country was the primary objective. A merchant of Kaskaskia, Illinois, named William Morrison employed a pair of experienced trappers and Indian traders in July, 1804, and sent them out ostensibly to trade with the Indians. Conflicting newspaper accounts exist. One states that Morrison sent a trade party to Santa Fe; the other, later, is a denial by Morrison. However, whether Morrison aimed at then-forbidden Santa Fe or not, it seems to have been in some men's minds. Two merchants of Shelbyville, Kentucky (A. and R. Steele), that same year took a different approach and asked Senator John Breckenridge to obtain permission from the Spanish ambassador for them to sell wares in New Mexico. Permission was not received, but the request is evidence that at least some sensed the potential of the Santa Fe trade even that early. Perhaps Morrison had.

His pair of rascals (for such they seem to have been) were Jean Baptiste Lalande and Laurent Durocher. Morrison never heard from them again, but the pair reached Santa Fe in 1805, where they announced their intention of becoming Spanish subjects and sold his goods for their own profit. They guided a Spanish expedition into Pawnee Indian country that year and the following year were encountered in Santa Fe by the American explorer Zebulon Pike. Durocher faded from recorded history after that, but Lalande became a sufficiently prominent resident of Santa Fe that his death was mentioned by the New Mexican chronicler, Pedro Bautista Pino. After Morrison learned that Lalande had taken up residence in Santa Fe, he tried to file a claim against him for the misappropriated trade goods.

There is wholly unsupported evidence that Morrison's plans may have reached beyond sending Lalande and Durocher to trade with the Indians. The last Spanish governor at St. Louis, Carlos Delassus, noted in 1804 that another French trader named Jeanot Metayer was with Lalande when he passed through St. Louis, that Metayer had several boatloads of goods belonging to Morrison, and that Metayer was scheduled to meet with one Joseph Gervais up the Missouri. Gervais was to be accompanied by Jacques d'Eglise, another fur trader, and an American named Nicholas Cole. There is some ambiguous evidence that these three did reach Santa Fe in 1805.

That year, without any doubt or ambiguity, another American did reach Santa Fe—James Purcell. A carpenter from Bardstown, Kentucky, Purcell had left St. Louis in 1803 with two companions to trade with Indians. Somewhere out on the plains their horses were stolen, but by means of a canoe they had started back to St. Louis when they met another trading party on the Missouri River, which Purcell decided to accompany. He then wandered about the plains for several months before he went as an emissary for a band of Sioux Indians to Santa Fe in June, 1805. He remained there and once more took up his trade as a carpenter but returned to Missouri in 1824. All that is known about him in Santa Fe comes from the journal of Zebulon Pike, who seemed to have become well acquainted with him in Santa Fe.

There are hints of intrigue and mystery connected with Pike's own venture into the western wilderness and misadventure into Santa Fe in 1806. On the surface, Pike was an officer in the United States Army sent on a mission by the president of the United States,

Thomas Jefferson, to explore the headwaters of the Arkansas River. Since Jefferson authorized several explorations of the newly acquired Louisiana territory, a serious historian must accept the Pike expedition as fundamentally what it purported to be. It is less than frivolous, however, also to note some of the curiosities about the expedition.

Zebulon Montgomery Pike was selected to lead the expedition, not by Jefferson, but by the enigmatic General James Wilkinson. Wilkinson, former Revolutionary quartermaster under George Washington, was the ranking officer in the American army in the West. A one-time associate of Aaron Burr's, he had been linked with the Burr conspiracy. He was also involved with innumerable schemes relating to westward expansion. Neither the extent of his operations nor his motives and objectives have ever been firmly delineated. He certainly acted as a double agent, accepting pay from Spain, but he reported also to the U.S. secretary of war. Some historians suspect anything Wilkinson was associated with and thus eye with jaundice Pike's appointment by Wilkinson.

But in the extant orders to Pike there is absolutely nothing sub rosa. The protagonist of the mystery appeared a month later in the person of Dr. John H. Robinson, a surgeon whom Wilkinson attached to the Pike party in July, 1806. Robinson may have had secret instruction from Wilkinson to explore the way to Santa Fe. He did in fact carry with him William Morrison's claim against Lalande, which some consider as prima facie evidence that Robinson intended from the beginning to enter Santa Fe.

Pike, with two subalterns (one a Lieutenant James B. Wilkinson, the son of the general), Dr. Robinson, and sixteen men, left St. Louis in July. Then-lieutenant Facundo Melgares left Santa Fe in June with orders to explore the Pawnee country and to intercept an American party rumored to be on the Arkansas. Melgares returned empty-handed; Pike crossed his trail, followed it a way, and turned westward to reach in December the mountain that bears his name. Then, in mid-winter, after sending Wilkinson's son home with dispatches, Pike sallied forth to find the source of the Red River. With his men suffering from privation and cold, he built a stockade and winter quarters on a tributary of the Rio Grande. Had he deliberately penetrated Spanish territory, or was he lost? In any event, the western boundary of the Louisiana Territory between Spain and the United States had not at that time been determined.

Pike then sent Robinson to Santa Fe, as he himself wrote, "to gain a knowledge of the country" under the guise of "seeking the recovery of just debts." The scenario in Santa Fe thenceforth is clouded with unexplained circumstances. Robinson apparently convinced the governor that he was what he claimed to be—a bill collector—and he denied knowledge of Pike. Pike and his men surrendered to Spanish dragoons a week later and were marched to Santa Fe. The governor received him with so much hostility that Pike believed, so he said, that Spain and the United States were at war. Hoping to protect Dr. Robinson, the explorer denied any knowledge of him. Each person who reads Pike's journal of those events and the happenings in New Mexico will interpret it for himself. Everything that transpired, including the misdirections and appearances of intrigue, could have happened as innocuously as Pike explained it. Or, if one looks for a double meaning, that too can be found.

Pike was asked to go to Chihuahua to be interviewed by the commandant there. On the way, he was escorted by Facundo Melgares and rejoined by Robinson. Melgares ("as urbane as a Frenchman," Pike wrote) and the young explorer became quite friendly on the journey. After the interview in Chihuahua, Pike and his party were escorted across Texas back to the United States. Although a trunk containing many of Pike's papers had been confiscated, his journal and Robinson's notes on the courses and distances the expedition had followed survived. Pike's report was published in 1810, and Robinson drafted and published an inaccurate but important map of western Louisiana. Despite inferences that he was an anachronistic disciple of Manifest Destiny involved in nefarious plans for the conquest of New Mexico, Pike's motive, taken at the very worst, could not have been anything more than reconnaissance of the forbidden country.

In Santa Fe Pike had seen Lalande and James Purcell. He noted the presence of several American deserters and named Solomon Colly, who acted as an interpreter for the Spaniards. In Chihuahua he encountered John P. Walker, who was serving as an en-sign in the Spanish army. It is obvious that a few Americans, some known to history and some unrecorded, already had begun making their ways to Santa Fe.

There is ambiguity regarding the next parties to venture the trek. The well-known fur traders Jacques Clamorgan and Manuel Lisa formed a partnership which James Wilkinson believed was determined to open commercial intercourse with Santa Fe. They did employ a trapper-trader named Louis Baudouin, who subsequently was arrested in New Mexico in October, 1807, by the ubiquitous Lieutenant Facundo Melgares. Baudouin and his trade goods, which belonged to Clamorgan and Lisa, were taken to Santa Fe. The curtain of obscurity then closed behind him.

In December, 1809, according to newspaper reports, three Missourians named James Patterson, Joseph McLanahan, and Reuben Smith left St. Louis guided by a New Mexican named Emanuel Blanco with the presumed objective of trading in Santa Fe. They were arrested near the headwaters of the Red River, taken to Santa Fe, and then sent to Ciudad Chihuahua in irons. According to McLanahan's later statement, they were separated and sent into the interior of Mexico but later allowed to make their way back to Chihuahua. In 1812 they were released and soon returned on their own to the United States. While they were gone a report circulated in Missouri that they had been killed, and the editor of a newspaper tried to whip up sentiment to organize an expedition to Santa Fe for the purpose of releasing or avenging them.

The next American party to Santa Fe did indeed suffer a harsh fate. Apparently believing that the Hidalgo uprising in Mexico had been successful, James Baird and Robert McKnight organized a party to cross the plains for the express purpose of trading in Santa Fe. There were ten men in the party; Baird, McKnight, Samuel Chambers, Benjamin Shreve, and Michael McDonogh were proprietors of merchandise purchased at McKnight's brother John's store in St. Louis. They set out in April, 1812. Captured at Taos in July, they were imprisoned in Santa Fe and their goods were confiscated and sold at public auction. Sometime thereafter they were taken to Ciudad Chihuahua where they were released on bond but forced to remain in the city. In 1815 they were tried and convicted of participation in the Hidalgo revolt and again imprisoned. James Baird was taken to Durango to work in a mine, from which he escaped. Recaptured, he was put in solitary confinement in Durango.

When word of the capture of the Baird-McKnight party reached the United States, Edward Hempstead, Missouri's territorial delegate to Congress, implored the State Department to obtain their release, as did Baird's wife, Jane, but apparently no effort was made in that direction. In 1817 Secretary of State James Monroe brought the prisoners' plight to the attention of Luis de Onís, the Spanish minister in Washington. This request was pursued the following year by John Quincy Adams, and the House of Representatives passed a resolution demanding their release.

It is doubtful that these efforts in Washington helped, but in the spring of 1820 the prisoners were allowed to return home. With them were two men who had been captured with Philip Nolan and one who had been with Zebulon Pike. All of the Baird-McKnight party of 1812, however, did not return to the states. William Mines remained in Chihuahua as a clerk in a store; Robert McKnight stayed on for a short time in Guarisame (Durango), where he seems to have had part interest in a mine; Thomas Cook had died; and Michael McDonogh had joined a monastery in Zacatecas.

While the Baird-McKnight party were awaiting their trial in Chihuahua, another group of Americans had stumbled into trouble in New Mexico, more or less inadvertently. Unlike the Baird-Mc-Knight group, which had gone purposefully to New Mexico to trade, Jules DeMun and Auguste P. Chouteau were fur trappers who tried to avoid difficulties with Spanish authorities. In 1815 Chouteau and DeMun joined Joseph Philbert, another trapper, who was returning with supplies to a party of trappers he had left the previous year on the upper Arkansas.

When they reached the rendezvous they learned from Indians that the trappers, desperate for supplies, had gone into Taos. There DeMun, who was sent after them, found the refugees. He then bravely proceeded south to Santa Fe to explain their presence in New Mexico. He was well-received by Governor Alberto Maynez, who granted permission for them to continue trapping in the Sangre de Cristos (in present southern Colorado). But Maynez was soon succeeded by Pedro de Allande, who ordered the Americans out of

Spanish territory. They moved their operations to the eastern slope of the mountains, which they thought to be American soil. But that winter of 1815–1816 there was in fact no boundary yet in existence. Allande, however, believed they were in Spanish territory, and he had troops to support his belief. The trappers were arrested in May, 1816, and taken to Santa Fe. They were held in prison for a month and a half before they were tried. By DeMun's account, Allande was a vicious tyrant who had not even accepted the fact of the American purchase of Louisiana. They were better treated, however, than the Baird-McKnight party had been. Their goods—some $30,000 worth of furs—were confiscated, but they were allowed to return to Missouri. They reached St. Louis in September, 1817, and Chouteau promptly filed a claim with the State Department against the Spanish government. It was among those settled after the Treaty of 1819.

One more American adventurer is known to have been in Santa Fe before the epoch-making visit of William Becknell. David Meriwether was captured with a party of Pawnee Indians somewhere near the Arkansas and hauled into Santa Fe in 1819. Melgares had just become governor, and although Meriwether thought the governor was hostile, Melgares released the adventurer and his black servant and sent them back to the United States. A quarter of a century later Meriwether would return to Santa Fe as the American territorial governor of New Mexico.

Of the preceding parties reaching Santa Fe, only one, the Baird-McKnight entourage, is indisputably known to have gone there for the express purpose of trading. Yet the commercial prospects in New Mexico must have been fairly common knowledge on the Missouri frontier. Full circle, then, back to the motivation of Becknell's first trip: trade in Santa Fe or trade with the Indians? Becknell had proposed the expedition through the columns of the *Missouri Intelligencer*, set the rendezvous at Ezekiel Williams' home at Boone's Lick, and even published proposed articles of association. The party, a paltry five in number, left for Santa Fe on September 1. Cordially received by Melgares, Becknell rushed back to Missouri to organize a trading expedition in the spring of 1822. The opening of the Santa Fe trade followed hard on his heels, and he is thus credited with being the "Father of the Santa Fe Trade."

But there were two other expeditions that reached Santa Fe practically at the same time as Becknell. One party was led by Thomas James and John McKnight, the other by Hugh Glenn and Jacob Fowler. Either of these groups has almost equal claim to beginning the trade, as in fact does James Baird, who returned from Chihuahua in 1821 and promptly organized a new trading expedition to Santa Fe the following year.

The account of the James-McKnight party rests primarily on James' book, *Three Years among the Indians and Mexicans*, published twenty years later and written from an apparently somewhat faulty memory. James left St. Louis on May 10, 1821, accompanied by John McKnight, who was going to New Mexico to seek the release of his brother, and by a dozen other men. James said he had about $10,000 worth of supplies with him. Somewhere on the Canadian River they were attacked by Comanches, who stole most of the trade goods. During a second attack they were rescued by a group of New Mexicans and taken to Santa Fe. There James sold the remnant of his supplies for about $2,500, with the permission of Governor Melgares. This was in December, 1821, and it is unlikely that James did not encounter the other American then in Santa Fe, William Becknell. Yet James' account does not mention Becknell and Becknell's journal does not mention James. An enigmatic statement in Becknell's journal may explain this: ". . . we left [San Miguel] December 13, on our return home, in company with two other men who had arrived there a few days before by a different route." The two other men may have been unidentified members of the James-McKnight group. Although there is no doubt that James and McKnight reached Santa Fe, there is some doubt that they were there in December. In a statement written ten years before his book (but ten years after his visit to Santa Fe), James said that he had a Spanish passport to visit New Mexico and implied that he had arrived there in 1822.

On the way to Santa Fe, near the site of later Fort Gibson, the James-McKnight party had encountered another trading party headed by Hugh Glenn. According to James, Glenn refused to travel with James' party. The chronicle of the Glenn-Fowler expedition is the *Journal of Jacob Fowler*. Fowler left Fort Smith, Arkansas, on September 6, 1821, joined Glenn and about twenty trappers on the

Verdigris River, and with them spent several months wandering across the plains. At one time, on November 28, Fowler said they were within six days' travel of Taos. Glenn went into Taos in January, 1822, and Fowler and the rest of the party joined him there early in February. They continued to trap for furs in the mountains around Taos until June.

Hugh Glenn visited Santa Fe before they left for the States and returned to his party with John and Robert McKnight, James Baird, and Thomas James. Together they all headed back to Missouri. James and Glenn, who came to dislike each other, evidently quarrelled most of the time. Glenn was carrying back a profit in furs; James had lost his merchandise to Indians. Perhaps the most significant thing about their return, however, was not their quarrels or their losses but the fact that they spotted the ruts made by wagon wheels on what had previously been a trackless prairie. It is a little difficult for the modern mind to picture their astonishment at the sight. It would have been almost as if Neil Armstrong had seen footprints in the moon dust.

The wagon tracks had been made by three ox-drawn wagons belonging to William Becknell and twenty-one men as Becknell hurried back to Santa Fe to capitalize on the trade possibilities he had found. His company has been organized at Arrow Rock, Missouri, and had left from there on May 22. By the time Jacob Fowler spotted his wagon tracks in July, Becknell was already in Santa Fe. His company had been joined on the Arkansas River by John G. Heath from Boone's Lick, who was leading a small group of mounted men and pack animals. Heath was later to make several trips over the trail and eventually to settle on the north side of the Rio Grande at El Paso.

Becknell's return from his first trip had aroused sufficient interest in the market at Santa Fe that a second party, commanded by Benjamin Cooper, had been formed to trade there. The Cooper venture, consisting of twelve men including Braxton and Stephen Cooper, nephews of the leader, took pack animals rather than wagons and apparently left Missouri about the same time that Becknell's second party did.

James Baird, who had returned to St. Louis in July, 1822, with the Glenn-Fowler expedition, fell in with an old compadre of his

1812 trip, Samuel Chambers, and the two of them promptly organized an expedition to return to New Mexico. Financed by some St. Louis merchants and joined by twenty new adventurers, the Baird-Chambers group left St. Louis the last week in August, leading a pack train of sixty mules laden with merchandise for Santa Fe.

Due to some confusion in contemporary newspaper accounts, it is not clear whether a fourth party made the trip in 1822. Virtually all accounts of the history of the Santa Fe Trail give only the three 1822 expeditions: Becknell, Cooper, and Baird. But the *Missouri Republican* of August 27, 1823, indicates that there was a fourth expedition consisting of forty men led by a Mr. Bartow which left St. Louis on August 22, 1822. And the *Missouri Intelligencer* of September 2, 1822, stated: "Since the revolution [in Mexico] four or five parties have gone [to Santa Fe]." Josiah Gregg, in the classic *Commerce of the Prairies*, gave the total number of men going to Santa Fe as seventy but did not indicate how many separate ventures were involved.

The year 1823 saw only two or possibly three groups make the trip; Gregg reported a total of fifty men. One of these groups was the Stephen Cooper–Joel Walker party of thirty men, each with two pack horses carrying an average of $200 worth of goods. It left from Arrow Rock about May 6. Most of the company's horses were stolen by a band of Osage Indians near the Arkansas River. Undaunted, Cooper went back for additional horses and led his men safely into Santa Fe. They returned to Missouri in October, 1823, with over four hundred "jacks, jennies, and mules." Some historians credit this trip as the beginning of the famous Missouri mules. There is a vague reference in the *St. Louis Enquirer* of November 10, 1823, to the return from Santa Fe of the McGannegle-Anderson company. And finally, the famous Antoine Robideaux received a permit in December and led six men through the Indian country to Santa Fe. Since the permit was signed at Fort Atkinson, Robideaux and company were probably en route at the time, although winter travel was highly unusual.

By 1824, then, the trade with Santa Fe may fairly be said to have begun. During the previous three years there had been eight to ten expeditions and 150 to 200 men who had made the round trip. Although the adventure of crossing the plains and entering long-forbidden Santa Fe was glorious, the profitability of such a trip was not yet firmly established. Becknell seems to have been quite successful, but the legend about the rawhide packages of silver dollars he dumped on the street in Arrow Rock should be associated with his second venture, not his first. Hugh Glenn made some money on furs rather than by trading. James lost heavily. Stephen Cooper made his profits by bartering for mules and furs which he brought back to St. Louis.

The Santa Fe adventurers had used horses, mules, and ox-drawn wagons, but horses and pack-trains of horses predominated. They had found their way across the plains by a variety of routes, but a definite trail, with modifications, was beginning to emerge across the prairie vastness.

CHAPTER 4

The Route

Santa Fe was separated from Missouri by what was known and labelled on contemporary maps as the "Great American Desert." The term is often attributed to Stephen Long, but its origins rest in reports of early nineteenth-century explorers, such as Zebulon Pike, John Sibley, and others, who conducted the first examinations of the Louisiana Purchase. Accustomed to the humid eastern woodlands, these men were struck by the aridity of the western region.

It was not a desert, of course, but most of the area over which the Santa Fe Trail was to pass had an average rainfall of only ten to twenty inches a year, whereas eastern Kansas and western Missouri ranged from twenty inches to an occasional high of forty inches. However, in the summer months, when travel was practical, the intense heat, which frequently exceeded 100°, rapidly dried up creeks and streams and evaporated the residual snowmelt and rainfall that had collected in ponds and playa lakes. Evaporation rates in the area of southwestern Kansas and southeastern Colorado, through which the trail was to pass, have been measured by agricultural experiment stations at more than sixty inches during the six months from April to September. Thus, to the eastern overland traveler the region certainly seemed like a desert, and many persons suffered hardship and even privation. They clung to the live water in the major rivers that traversed the area and crossed from one watershed to another with understandable fear and trepidation.

Indeed, on the unmarked plains the rivers and their tributaries served as the principal landmarks. With few exceptions, these watercourses were all a part of the great Mississippi drainage system. The route from Missouri to Santa Fe first had to cross northward-flowing tributaries of the mighty Missouri River, often flood-swollen, and then southeast tributaries of the Arkansas before reaching that great river. The Arkansas River was the major feature of the eastern part of the trail. Born of melting snow in the Rockies and augmented by live springs along the way, it ran an eastward course to what was known as the Great Bend in central Kansas, where it swung sharply northeast and then back southeast to plunge toward the Mississippi. Its principal tributary was the Canadian, which very roughly paralleled its course about 150 to 200 miles farther south. It was in the semiarid western reaches of the area between Missouri and Santa Fe that travelers would have to find a way to cross from the Arkansas watershed to the Canadian. Two characteristics of these plains rivers and streams were unlike eastern waterways and created major problems for travelers. One was quicksand; the other, the steep, sometimes almost vertical, cut banks which the erosion of cascading flash floods over the eons had carved. Consequently, the larger streams could be crossed with ease or safety only at certain places.

Weather also created hazards. There was the scorching heat in the summer, and in the winter there were heavy snows and blizzards. Temperatures often dropped to zero and below, with wind-chill temperatures far lower than that. Summer and winter, winds blew almost constantly, sometimes approaching tornadic strength. The area has almost twice the average hourly wind velocity of any other part of the continental United States.

The extremes of temperature, the cutting winds, and the aridity of the region are characteristic of its geographical environment as part of the Great Plains of North America. It was, before American settlement, virtually treeless except along the streams and rivers and without distinctive topographic features. The land ranged from rolling prairies in western Missouri and Kansas, covered with tall wind-waved grasses whose deep roots created a firm sod, to the flatter plains country to the west where short grasses usually protected the soil from rising with the winds. At the western extremity of the region towered the forbidding Sangre de Cristo Mountains.

It was a natural habitat for grazing animals, such as deer, antelope, and buffalo, that could feed on the nutritious grasses while they found their ways from watering place to watering place. Especially in the short-grass country in the western part of the area, the buffalo roamed in uncounted numbers, and the plains were furrowed with their trails. Ranging in large herds, they often cut parallel paths that to some travelers looked deceptively like wagon roads. These grass eaters were the economic basis of human life on the plains before the coming of the white men and remained the mainstay of Indian life until the 1870's.

The earliest men in the area crossed by the Santa Fe Trail were quite primitive stone-age Americans (Paleo-American stage) equipped with flint-pointed throwing sticks and crude bows and arrows. They wandered in small, clan-like bands in a never-ending search for food. Since their weapons were at the best lightweight and since there were no horses or other mounts, which forced them to travel and hunt on foot, they were generally limited to small game, when they could get it, and to wild fruits and nuts. Frequently they were reduced to rooting and grubbing for insects. Gradually over the centuries aboriginal man passed into a more advanced cultural stage (Archaic), typified by more sophisticated weapons and improved hunting techniques, such as the "surround." They were able to bring down an occasional buffalo and, less frequently, fleet-footed deer and antelope. They remained nomadic, and still they traveled on foot.

Generations passed. On the margins of the plains some bands adopted agricultural practices from their more sedentary eastern woodlands neighbors and curtailed their ceaseless wandering. It was in this cultural stage (Neo-American) that Francisco Vásquez de Coronado, the first European to cross the plains, found them in 1541. He was not impressed. They were unmounted, unwarlike, and generally docile. Indeed, they were clearly over-awed by the mounted and steel-armed and armored Spaniards. But contact with the Spaniards, in the passage of time, was to change completely the Indian (for so they must now be called) way of life. During the next century and a half horses lost and stolen from the *ramudas* of Spanish expeditions found their ways into Indian hands. It is difficult to imagine the emotions of the native American as he first climbed upon a horse's back, found that he could ride him, and suddenly discovered that, mounted, he was the equal of four-footed creatures who grazed the plains. The acquisition of horses brought a major social and economic revolution to the plains Indians. Riding bareback, they became probably the greatest horsemen of all time. By the eighteenth century, the region was peopled, not by weary, half-starved, footsore, humble bands, but by fierce, hostile, mounted warriors, skillful in both hunt and battle.

By Spanish accounts a people known as Apaches emerged to dominate the southern plains, displacing or driving away the less savage Indians who previously had hunted there. Then the wild and terrible Comanches swept out of the foothills of Wyoming, splitting the Apache domain and claiming the South Plains for themselves. Other strong tribes appeared, some having successfully made the conversion to the new way of life, others moving in from the margins of the plains.

By the time of the opening of the Santa Fe Trail, the region it traversed was occupied, albeit sparsely, by the fiercest native tribes North America had ever known. Although the tribes had no fixed geographic boundaries and although many of them were constantly on the prowl, a few generalizations may be made. At the eastern end of the trail were Indians who both hunted and practiced agriculture, living in semipermanent villages. Chief among these were the Osage, the Kansa, and the various bands of Wichita. (But, illustrating the mobility of even these less nomadic Indians, there had been an Osage raid on Santa Fe during the eighteenth century.) Farther west, approaching the plains, the trail moved into Kiowa and Kiowa Apache country. On what was to be called the mountain route, Cheyenne and not infrequently Arapahoe were encountered, as well as occasional parties of Pawnee. The Cimarron cutoff ducked through the western edge of Comanche territory. In what is now eastern New Mexico both routes were plagued by southern Utes, as well as by Kiowa Apaches and Comanches.

Even when these Indians were not openly hostile to caravans passing through their hunting grounds, they were always a potential menace and a constant nuisance. They stole horses, mules, and oxen. They openly plundered camps whose defenders frequently suffered this in preference to outright battle. And they arrogantly demanded food and gifts from many frightened travelers. Through the early years of the traffic over the trail, the Indians became increasingly hostile. Thus, both the natural environment and the native Indians made the Santa Fe Trail the most forbidding and dangerous major pioneer route in American history.

To the first parties over the trail, the hazards of nature and the unknown were the greater of the two. Such geographical knowledge of the region as did exist may have been worse than none at all. Early maps twisted the topography, distorted the courses of streams and rivers, and belied distances. These maps grew out of indirect third- and fourth-hand reports and legends of some of the first daring trips across the region, such as that of the Mallet brothers in 1739 and Pedro Vial in 1792. Vial's diary and the inaccurate maps of his explorations contributed to the cartographic jumble.

Although there were other Spanish explorations into the Indian country north and east of Santa Fe (and two American parties, Jean Baptiste Lalande and James Purcell, reached Santa Fe), the next fully recorded journey was Pike's in 1806, after the American purchase of Louisiana. Pike followed the Arkansas to its headwaters, turned south across country, was arrested by a detachment of Spanish dragoons, taken to Chihuahua, and ultimately released to make his way back through Texas in 1807. His observations provided the most accurate knowledge of the course of the Arkansas River up to that time, although he had not followed it for a portion of the way through Kansas. His popular account, published in 1810, was of some value to later travelers, although maps of the 1820's did not have the location of the Arkansas accurately designated in relation to other water courses. His companion, Dr. James Robinson, published a map of the region that was used by some but was so inaccurate as to be worthless—probably even dangerous.

Pike's circuitous route from Missouri to Santa Fe made no contribution to the development of the later Santa Fe Trail. Nor did the 1809 trip by Patterson, McLanahan, and Smith. The route they followed is unknown except for a comment in McLanahan's letter of 1812 which gave the location of their capture as the headwaters of the Red River. It is of interest, however, that they were guided by a Spaniard from New Mexico, which suggests that a few unrecorded plainsmen may have traversed the trackless prairies.

The route followed by the Baird-McKnight party of 1812 is largely speculation. They did have Pike's published account with them, and they are known to have passed through Fort Osage on the Missouri River headed southwest for the Great Bend of the Arkansas as described by Pike. Most probably they followed Pike's advice and ascended the Arkansas to the mountains, working their way south from there to Taos.

The DeMun-Chouteau-Philbert expedition clearly followed the Arkansas, for it was near the head of that river that Philbert had left his trappers a year before. And it was from Huerfano Creek near present Walsenburg, Colorado, that DeMun went south to Taos. Their meanderings through the mountains cannot be traced, and their embittered return route from Santa Fe after their release is not known. It would seem probable that they went back via Taos to the head of the Arkansas and followed that river.

Because of the publication in the *Missouri Intelligencer* of Becknell's alleged journal, his route on his first visit is better known. His party left from Arrow Rock on the Missouri River, cut across the Petit Osage prairie for about thirty-five miles to Fort Osage on the Missouri, and then turned southwest, crossing the Osage River to strike what was probably the Neosho. Two days later they were on the main Arkansas, east of the Great Bend. They meandered upstream to what Pike had called the forks of the Arkansas, and then followed the left fork, Purgatoire River, into the mountains. By Becknell's account, they climbed some very steep cliffs, broke out onto a plain, and two days later reached the Canadian. They probably went through Raton Pass, along or near what later came to be known as the mountain branch of the trail. From the Canadian the group struggled southward until they struck a path. There they encountered New Mexicans who guided them into San Miguel. Becknell's return route to Missouri is unidentifiable, but it seems very unlikely that he crossed the so-called Cimarron desert on this trip, as some historians have speculated.

The Thomas James–Robert McKnight route to Santa Fe in 1821 made no contribution to the trail. That party, using barges, descended the Mississippi from St. Louis to the Arkansas, which they ascended to somewhere near the mouth of the Cimarron. There they abandoned their barges because of shallow water and continued on horseback. They moved up the Cimarron, cut across what is now the Oklahoma panhandle to the North Canadian, where they were attacked by Comanches, and then found their way southwest across New Mexico into San Miguel.

As stated earlier, neither James nor Becknell mentioned the other in his account, but Becknell said he was accompanied on his return on December 13 from San Miguel by "two other men who had arrived there a few days before, by a different route." The last phrase, "by a different route," has led some historians to believe Becknell meant that he returned to Missouri by a different route, to wit, the Cimarron route.

The Glenn-Fowler party quite clearly ascended the Arkansas River into the mountains of Colorado, from which Glenn made his trip into Taos and Santa Fe. Since James returned with them, there are two hopelessly vague accounts of the trip back, which seems to have followed a route much north and west of the later trail.

The big development in breaking the Santa Fe Trail came in the summer of 1822 when Becknell, on his second trip with three loaded wagons, decided not to venture through the mountains. He obviously initiated the Cimarron cutoff on this trip, but his journal is too vague and incomplete to determine details. On his return he also crossed the Cimarron "desert" but followed a different course, "which considerably shortened the route," he said.

The path of the Benjamin Cooper party of 1822 is not known, but since they traveled with pack animals, they most likely followed the Arkansas into the mountains and then cut south into Taos, west of the mountain branch of the trail. The next year Cooper's nephew Stephen took another band of traders over essentially the same route. The 1822 Baird-Chambers expedition, also using pack animals, definitely went up the Arkansas and then south through the mountains to Taos. There is no indication whether they followed the Purgatoire to Raton Pass (which seems likely because it was shorter) or went farther upstream before cutting south.

Thus, by 1824, after the eight or ten expeditions of the three preceding years, two basic modifications of the trail to Santa Fe had begun to emerge. Both crossed the Kansas prairies to the Great Bend of the Arkansas and then went up the river (around the bend) to the vicinity of present Cimarron, Kansas. The most popular early route, known as the mountain branch, then continued up the river to the mountains and near what is now LaJunta, Colorado, and turned south through Raton Pass to the headwaters of the Canadian River in New Mexico. The Cimarron branch, or Cimarron cutoff, left the Arkansas near Cimarron and ran southwest across the semi-arid reaches of the Oklahoma panhandle and eastern New Mexico. But it was not until 1824 that a more thorough description was recorded by the largest and most important expedition yet to make the trek.

On March 20, 1824, an announcement by Robert W. Morris appeared in the *Missouri Intelligencer* that there would be a meeting at Shaw's Tavern, in the then-thriving village of Franklin, of all persons wanting to go to Santa Fe. The Shaw's Tavern meeting took place the end of the month. Alexander LeGrand was elected chairman, and the principal business was a discussion of pack animals versus dearborn wagons. It was decided that each individual should make his own choice, but that those taking wagons should also take two or three pack saddles and spare horses in case of a breakdown. Each individual was to provide himself with twenty days' supplies, a rifle, a pistol, four pounds of powder, and eight pounds of lead. A rendezvous was set for May 5.

Between eighty and a hundred men gathered, adopted rules, and elected officers for the expedition. Alexander LeGrand was elected captain, but the expedition is often called the Storrs party because of the prominence of Augustus Storrs, who was along. There are two conflicting reports on the size of the business venture that departed on May 25: seventy-eight men (eighty-one persons plus two servants), twenty-three carriages, wagons, and dearborns (two wagons, two carts, twenty dearborns), and about two hundred horses (two hundred horses and mules). One report said the party had a small cannon. The total value of the goods to be carried to Santa Fe was in excess of $30,000.

A journal of this expedition kept by M. M. Marmaduke, later governor of Missouri, gives the best idea up to that time of the route followed to Santa Fe. The party left from Arrow Rock on the Missouri and followed a trail to the Osage mission (established in 1821) near the Kansas-Missouri boundary. Marmaduke mentions crossing

the Big Blue, the Marais des Cygnes, the Verdigris, and the Little
Arkansas before reaching the Arkansas proper after a distance of
about 350 miles. This part of their route was to become fairly
standard as the trail from the Missouri to the Arkansas. They followed the Arkansas for about two weeks over a distance that is not
clear, crossing it probably downstream from the well-known Caches,
where Baird and Chambers had buried their goods in 1822, and
struck southwest across the arid country. They almost became lost.
Obviously, despite the earlier travels, the Cimarron cutoff route was
not well-known at that time. Experiencing more fright than deprivation from lack of water, they finally reached the Cimarron River,
which they ascended for a few days before crossing over to the
North Canadian. Marmaduke does not indicate that they followed
a known pathway across eastern New Mexico nor does he mention
any of the land forms that later became known as Rabbit Ears Peak,
Round Mound, Wagon Mound, and so forth, but he did pass through
country of "stupendous knobs and points" on the way to the ranch
of Juan Pena at the site of modern Las Vegas, New Mexico. From
there the way to Santa Fe via San Miguel was well-established. The
expedition arrived in Santa Fe on July 28, 1824. Marmaduke estimated the distance from Franklin to Santa Fe to be 931 miles.

The party broke up in Santa Fe, some going south to El Paso
del Norte and Ciudad Chihuahua and a few even farther, into Durango. Some went to Taos and into the mountains to trap for beaver
on their way home. Of the latter fourteen or fifteen men, two were
reported killed by Indians and one by "Spaniards," according to
William Huddart, who returned to Franklin in April, 1825. William
Christian, who got home the next month, had gone south and had
first attempted to return by way of "precetynorth" (apparently the
presidio on the Rio Grande across from present Presidio, Texas), but
because of an Indian attack in which two men were killed, turned
back all the way to Durango and then crossed Mexico to the Gulf.
It is unfortunate that Christian left no journal or diary of what must
have been amazing adventures.

The main portion of the LeGrand-Storrs-Marmaduke party returned directly to Missouri, apparently by their out-going route.
According to unconfirmed reports they had with them $180,000 in

furs—a highly profitable undertaking. It was unquestionably their success that aroused national interest in the trade with Santa Fe. The expedition is important also because it led directly to the attempt of the federal government to survey, map, and mark the road to Santa Fe.

CHAPTER 5

The Federal Survey to New Mexico

Tales of the Santa Fe trade had not gone unnoticed by the enthusiastic Missouri senator, Thomas Hart Benton. Benton quite clearly understood that his state was the gateway to the West, and he intended to do all he could be promote it. Trade with Santa Fe was as much a part of his vision as were the fur trapping companies that ascended the Missouri into the vastness of the western Louisiana Purchase. The politician analyzed the needs of this infant commerce shrewdly: the Santa Fe traders needed protection from hostile Indians, a well-marked road, and consular representation in the Mexican provinces. To him such activities were in the proper sphere of the federal government.

The appointment of a United States consular agent in Santa Fe required no special congressional action; the procedures already existed, and it remained only to make an appointment. However, the other two items would require legislation. So Benton introduced a bill in the Senate to provide for them. As they were somewhat novel, if not wholly without precedent, he had to demonstrate to Congress in considerable detail the propriety of such government actions. The road would have to be laid out by government surveyors across Indian territory and then into Mexico, and a right-of-way as well as promises of safe conduct would have to be obtained by treaties. To carry weight no doubt with other congressmen, Senator Benton implied that he derived the idea from former President Thomas Jefferson during a Christmas Eve visit with him in 1823. According to Benton, Jefferson had told him that during his second administration Congress authorized the building of a road of about two hundred miles from Georgia to New Orleans, part of which passed through Indian territory and part through what was then Spanish West Florida. It seemed a perfect precedent for a road from Missouri to Santa Fe through Indian country and across the foreign soil of New Mexico.

Benton found further precedents in other federal roads through Indians lands and leaned heavily on the protection given to ocean commerce by the government. Indeed, was there such a great difference between protecting ships at sea and wagons on the prairies? His point was well taken, for that very session of Congress had appropriated half a million dollars for the suppression of piracy on the Caribbean.

To answer questions raised about the value and potential of the prairie commerce, Benton called on Augustus Storrs, who had just returned from Santa Fe with the LeGrand expedition, to testify. The Storrs deposition, written answers to Benton's queries, was presented to the Senate in January, 1825. Its optimistic and enthusiastic tone greatly influenced the passage of Benton's bill. Storrs touched on a number of significant points and made several recommendations. Chiefly these involved the nature of the trade at that time, its value and future potential, the problem of Indian hostility, the need for a well-marked route, and the usefulness of consular agents, especially at Santa Fe and Chihuahua.

About the route, Storrs was somewhat confusing. He indicated that the country between the Missouri River and the Arkansas was easily traversable, although beset with Indian dangers. The Arkansas could be crossed at almost any point (which did not prove to be be so) but its bottom was quicksand. Storrs had not seen the Cimarron River charted on any maps and emphasized its importance. Although there had been virtually no water in the Cimarron when his outbound party had reached it, they had been able to obtain water by digging no more than eighteen inches into its sandy beds. On the return, the Cimarron was found to be flowing with a strong current. Where the river went, Storrs did not know but supposed that "it loses itself in the sand." After crossing over to the North Canadian, the expedition went to Taos, according to Storrs, but Marmaduke's journal clearly shows that the route led southward to San Miguel. Storrs urged that a road be laid out to intersect creeks and streams at the most advantageous crossings; that, where necessary, laborers chisel away steep cut banks; and that the route be marked with mounds of earth at appropriate distances.

Like Benton himself and other senators, Storrs seems to have recognized the international complications of surveying the route through Mexican territory. Some senators believed that Mexico should mark the trail south of the Arkansas, while others insisted that the new government in Mexico, then struggling for its very existence, would be unable to pay the costs of laying out a road. Benton's bill provided vaguely for United States surveyors to mark the way south of the Arkansas only with the consent of the Mexican government. This was to be a point of considerable difficulty when the survey was made.

The bill passed easily through the Senate and, with a smaller margin, through the House (which had to appropriate funds). It was approved by President Monroe on his last day in office, March 3, 1825. Benton's road, which he later stated somewhat grandiosely had "remained a thoroughfare of commerce between Missouri and New Mexico, and all the western internal provinces ever since," was about to become a reality. Ten thousand dollars were appropriated for marking the route and twenty thousand for securing a right-of-way and safe passage through the Indian country. On March 16, 1825, incoming President John Quincy Adams appointed three commissioners to fulfill the terms of the new statute: George Champlin Sibley and Benjamin Reeves of Missouri and Pierre Menard of Illinois, who resigned and was replaced by Thomas Mather, also of Illinois.

For over thirty years Menard had been a merchant in Kaskasia, Illinois, growing wealthier and more prominent each year. He begged off, graciously, on the grounds that the long absence required by the assignment would be detrimental to his private affairs. His replacement, Mather, was also from Kaskasia and was also a merchant, although much less eminent than Menard. A descendant of Cotton Mather, he was a member of the Illinois legislature. Reeves had served in the Kentucky legislature before migrating in 1819 to Missouri, where he rose quite rapidly in public office; he was lieutenant governor at the time of his appointment to the commission. Sibley, though of a distinguished family, was the least prominent man appointed; however, he was to become the most important member of the commission before its work was ended.

The son of the famous Dr. John Sibley, he had been for twenty years nothing more than a government trader (or factor) to the Osage Indians. Stationed at Fort Osage, he had witnessed the inception of the trade with Santa Fe and was also, naturally, well acquainted with the Indians of the vicinity. He was a knowledgeable and zealous public servant whose devotion to duty was probably responsible for what success the commission was to achieve. But his personal affairs were in some disarray. He had overextended himself financially, particularly in land purchases, was in debt, and had little means of staving off bankruptcy. When the posts of government factors to the Indians had been abolished two years earlier, he had been thrown upon his own meager financial resources. This new position was welcome, not only because of the remuneration, but also because it opened new opportunities to him.

Although rumors of his appointment had reached him while he was on his way to St. Louis on a business trip in early April, 1825, Sibley did not receive official notification until he arrived in that city. Assuming an initiative that was to make him the tacit leader of the commission, he wrote to Benjamin Reeves at Franklin, Missouri, suggesting a prompt meeting of the three commissioners in St. Louis. That meeting did not take place until May 10, however, because Reeves was delayed in leaving Franklin. Meanwhile, Menard had resigned and his replacement, Thomas Mather, was unable to come to St. Louis. Thus circumstances thrust further leadership on Sibley. It was to him that scores of applications were made for the key posts of surveyor and secretary, as well as for other positions on the survey. Also it was to Sibley that Thomas Hart Benton wrote with several suggestions about the work of the commission. Most notable of these was that Sibley keep a diary, which he did; it has become the single most important source for the history of the survey. Benton also thought additional funds could be obtained if the appropriation of $30,000 was exceeded.

Sibley had apparently done a good bit of the organizational groundwork and had made up his mind about most of the personnel of the expedition by the time Reeves arrived for the May 10 meeting. Sibley's lifelong friend, Joseph C. Brown, was named surveyor, and Sibley's brother-in-law, Archibald Gamble, who had previously served as Brown's assistant, was given the post of secretary. There was a small amount of furor in Missouri when these appointments were announced, and charges of nepotism were made against Sibley. But in fact Brown probably was the best and most experienced man available for the job, and it was not at all illogical that his former assistant be chosen as well.

There may have been a private agreement between Sibley and Reeves, for Reeves was allowed to name the captain of the expedition. He chose Stephen Cooper, who by that time had made several trips to Santa Fe as a trader. Thirty men were hired to make up the party, including such experienced frontiersmen as William S. ("Old Bill") Williams, Joseph Reddeford Walker, his brother Joel P. Walker, and Andrew Broadus. The men were to be paid twenty dollars a month, to furnish their own equipment, and to depend on their hunting skill for their food. "We do not want a party of Gentlemen Coffee Drinkers who cannot even cook their own Victuals or Saddle their own Horses," wrote Sibley in his journal.

Reeves returned home within a few days after his arrival in St. Louis, but Sibley remained to complete the organizational details, which included the purchase of supplies and six wagons to carry them. This took longer than anticipated, and the expedition did not leave St. Louis until June 25, arriving at Franklin on July 2, where Reeves joined the party. They still did not know who was to replace Menard on the commission but decided to proceed without him. Thomas Mather, with his credentials, caught up with them on July 11 at Fort Osage. Sibley, who had been gone from his home there since April 12, remained behind for three weeks while the expedition began its survey over a fairly well-known route to Council Grove.

Actually, Council Grove was unnamed at the time. It was a beautiful motte or copse of oak and other fine trees on a branch of the Neosho River, surrounded by excellent pasturage in the tall prairie grasses. It was to become a common camping place on the trail and ultimately a substantial city in Kansas. Sibley gave the place its name and had it carved in the bark of a large oak tree. He called it Council Grove because it was there that he and the other commissioners met with a party of Osage chiefs to negotiate the first of two Indian treaties they had been authorized to make.

Benton's bill had charged the commission with two primary responsibilities: to survey and mark a route to the boundary of New Mexico (and on to Santa Fe if permission from the Mexican government could be obtained), and to make necessary treaties with the Indians to permit the safe passage of traders along the route.

The territories claimed by the seminomadic Indians had no specific boundaries, of course, but two major tribes, the Osage and the Kansa, then dominated the region through which the route would pass to the Arkansas. Neither tribe was as hostile as the Comanche, the Pawnee, the Kiowa, or even the Ute, but those bands usually roamed farther west and south of the Arkansas, in Mexican territory. Treaties with the plains Indians were generally rather ineffective, regardless of the band, partially because they had no organized central tribal government (in the white man's sense) that could require enforcement; partially because the plains Indians were highly individualistic and moved and hunted in relatively small groups, following their own separate leaders; and partially because the Indians had little concept of land ownership or tribal boundaries. The commission distributed presents and negotiated the Osage treaty at Council Grove on August 10 and six days later, at a camp on Sora Kansa (or Sora Conista) Creek seventy-five miles farther west, concluded a treaty with several Kansa chiefs. The two accords were identical.

The chiefs of the two tribes granted permission for the expedition to survey the route through their respective territories, guaranteed unmolested passage along the route and for a reasonable distance on each side of it to citizens of the United States and Mexico, and agreed to render aid and assistance to travelers between Missouri and Santa Fe. This last, particularly, must have given a good laugh to cynics among both Indians and the survey crew. Nevertheless, it would look good to congressmen and stay-at-home easterners who had no notion of plains Indian behavior. In return for these dubious promises, the commission was to pay eight hundred dollars (in merchandise) to the head of each tribe. Sibley distributed three hundred dollars' worth of presents at the conclusion of the negotiations; the remainder was to be obtained by the Indians when and where they might choose. But according to Sibley's diary, the Osage were to trade with Auguste Chouteau, to whom Sibley gave a draft on the government, and the Kansa with the firm of Curtis and Ely. Since all the men involved had reputations for fairness, it would seem likely that the Indians received fair value for the stipulated sum. However, Sibley recorded that some of the Indians were dissatisfied because they believed their own chiefs did not distribute the largess equitably. It was this kind of personal disgruntlement that often led to treaty violations on the plains.

The expedition then set out to complete the second part of its mission—the survey to the Arkansas. Sora Kansa Creek was a branch of the Arkansas, the main stream of which they reached three days later. They then traveled up the Arkansas without incident to a point 418 miles from Fort Osage. Here Surveyor Brown estimated they had reached the 100th meridian. This was significant because south of the Arkansas the 100th meridian marked the boundary between the United States and Mexico. Brown, however, was uncertain about the accuracy of his observations (in fact, he was surprisingly close).

Brown based his estimate on his instruments, on the distance measured from Fort Osage, and on contemporary maps and observations. His instruments were crude by modern standards: magnetic compasses, one of which may have been mounted on a Jacob staff (tripods not then being in use), and a single sextant. Compasses had been used to chart the bearings of the route but were of no value in locating the meridian. Nor was the sextant (for celestial observation) much more satisfactory. The distance had been measured by chain—a heavy and awkward device four rods (or sixty-six feet) long, made up of one hundred straight steel links joined at the ends by loops. Brown suspected that his chainmen had probably miscounted their stations while traversing some of the rough territory through which they passed. Compounding these problems was the almost total lack of recorded cartographic data. Brown's report does not mention which of the early maps he may have had with him, if any. Probably the best known of the time was John Melish's 1820 map, which traced the course of the Arkansas River over a hundred miles southwest of its actual channel. Sibley had purchased John H. Robinson's map of 1819 to take along on the journey; it too shows the Arkansas and the other principal waterways a considerable distance south and west of their actual locations. Brown also knew of Stephen Long's observations, which placed the 100th meridian about forty miles downriver from his location. Little wonder the surveyor was doubtful!

No matter, Sibley wrote, "we have not yet trespassed upon Mexican territory, let the line be where it may," for the commission remained on the north side of the river. It was the question of whether to cross into Mexico and continue the survey that brought the first and only serious dissension to the expedition. By the terms of their enabling act they could not proceed without the expressed permission of the Mexican government. Sibley argued that they should camp on the Arkansas for another month waiting for the desired authority to reach them via Washington and that, if it did not arrive, a part of the expedition should go on informally to Santa Fe and spend the winter, thus reconnoitering the country and being prepared to make a proper survey on their return. The other two commissioners believed this would exceed their authority and proposed to return at once to Missouri.

A compromise was reached after several days of argument. The party remained at its supposed 100th meridian camp from September 11 to September 21. Then Reeves and Mathers with most of the expedition decamped for the return journey. Sibley, with Brown and ten other men, proceeded toward Santa Fe. Meantime, a small party of traders who had accompanied the expedition, weary of the delay and uncertainty, crossed the Arkansas and headed for Santa Fe by way of Taos. Sibley entrusted them with delivering to Augustus Storrs his commission as the first United States consul in Santa Fe.

Sibley's bold judgment in the controversy was sounder than that of the other commissioners. The task would not be completed until a route had at least been explored, if not surveyed, all the way to the ancient New Mexico capital. The friendly relations that existed between the United States and the new government in Mexico, as well as the cordial person-to-person relations between Missourians and New Mexicans that had been evident since Becknell's first visit, seemed to assure that permission to continue the survey would be forthcoming.

Sibley and his men pushed on up the Arkansas about forty miles

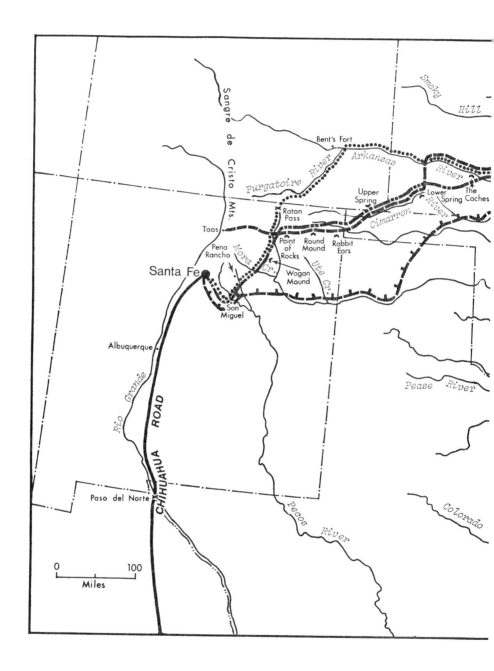

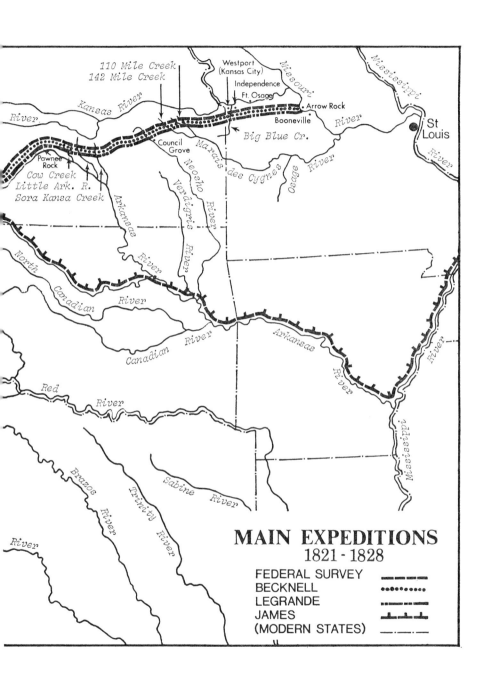

110 Mile Creek
142 Mile Creek
Westport
(Kansas City)
Independence
Ft. Osage
Arrow Rock
Booneville
Big Blue Cr.
Kansas River
River
Missouri
Mississippi
St Louis
River
River
Council Grove
Manais des Cygnés
Osage River
Neosho River
Verdigris River
Pawnee Rock
Cow Creek
Little Ark. R.
Sora Kansa Creek
Arkansas River
North Canadian River
Canadian River
Arkansas River
River
Mississippi
Red River
River
Brazos River
Trinity River
Sabine River
River

MAIN EXPEDITIONS
1821 - 1828
FEDERAL SURVEY
BECKNELL
LEGRANDE
JAMES
(MODERN STATES)

to a crossing known to one or more of the party (probably Bill Williams, who acted as interpreter) and then followed the south bank a few miles farther before they turned south into New Mexico and the somewhat forbidding Cimarron desert. Despite the lack of authorization, Brown continued to record the compass readings and the distances of their march. When they reached the Cimarron, about forty miles due south, they followed it upstream, roughly approximating the route of what was later to be known as the Cimarron cutoff. Like later travelers through this desolate country, they experienced shortages of good water and forage and used buffalo chips (dried dung) for firewood. They passed the Lower and Upper Cimarron Springs, Rabbit Ears, Round Mound, and Point of Rocks to reach the Canadian River. There they had to decide whether to turn southwest to San Miguel on the road to Santa Fe or to continue westward to Taos. On the advice of two of the men who had made the trip before, they determined on Taos, and Sibley sent ahead for some mules to carry the baggage over the mountain pass. They arrived at Taos on October 30, five weeks after the expedition had split.

CHAPTER 6

Completion of the Survey

At Taos, Sibley found a letter awaiting him, dated July 4 and carried by a group of traders, who, unencumbered by the paraphernalia of the survey, had followed a shorter route. The letter informed him that Joel Poinsett, the United States minister to Mexico, had been instructed to forward Mexican authorization for the survey as soon as it was obtained through Mexican channels to Santa Fe. Thus, Sibley's decision to pursue the journey on into New Mexico was justified.

But the operation was to be held up by several snags. In the first place, winter was coming on, and travel in the mountains of northern New Mexico was severely restricted by blizzards, cold, and heavy snow. In the second place, and far more important, the expected Mexican authorization had not arrived. Indeed, the alcalde (chief administrative and judicial officer) of San Fernando de Taos called on Sibley for an explanation of his presence there—"a little arrogantly," Sibley noted, but quite satisfied by the explanation. From that time on, through what was to prove to be a frustratingly extended stay in New Mexico, Sibley's relations with the officials and the people of New Mexico were friendly and cordial, although he did later remark privately in his diary that the alcalde was "as thoro' going a Scoundrel, I believe, as I ever came across."

Sibley rented quarters in Taos and purchased supplies for the winter, planning to leave his men there but to go to Santa Fe himself, with Brown, to stay the winter. He began fretting almost at once that no word had been received from Mexico regarding the survey. Had he known then how long the protracted delay was to be, he might possibly have essayed the return to Missouri in the

face of the coming winter storms. He postponed for a week notify-
ing the governor at Santa Fe of his arrival, hoping the weekly mail
would bring a message. It did not. He then shot off letters to the
governor and to Joel Poinsett (via Mexican channels). He demanded
that Poinsett reply at once. "At once" was a long interval for an im-
patient man. Poinsett's answer, dated December 3, did not reach
him until February 26, 1826, and then, disappointingly, informed
him that no progress had been made in securing permission from
Mexico. Sibley's vigil continued.

The situation in Mexico at this time was confusing and is often
misunderstood and misinterpreted. Poinsett, who was later to become *persona non grata* in Mexico, at that time enjoyed friendly
relations with the government. It was not because of any hostility
toward Poinsett or the United States that permission was delayed,
but rather because of the chaotic political conditions in the Mexican
capital and Poinsett's sometimes bumbling attempts to implement
Henry Clay's Mexican policy. Clay, the United States secretary of
state in the newly-formed Adams administration, had only vague
ideas about the realities of Latin American politics in general and
Mexico in particular. Among his instructions to Poinsett, who was
sent to represent the United States in Mexico, were two that directly
affected the survey. One was a presupposition—logical, of course,
but totally unrealistic—that the Mexican government would happily
bear the expense of laying out the route through Mexican territory.
The other—realistic, perhaps, but certainly illogical—was that the
new government in Mexico would be willing to negotiate a boundary
treaty that, as Clay sincerely viewed it, would be more "logical" for
Mexico than the line set by the Treaty of 1819, relieving Mexico of
territory in its hinterlands too difficult for administration and trans-
ferring to the United States the responsibility for the marauding
Comanches of the South Plains.

The Treaty of 1819, which had resolved the western boundary
of the Louisiana Purchase after sixteen years of controversy with
Spain, had not been ratified until 1821, the year Mexico gained its
independence. This accord and the national limits it set had been
made with Spain but were assumed to be binding on Mexico. However, it had been neither rejected nor accepted by Mexico, primari-

ly because it was not a major consideration in the post-independence turmoil. The revolutionary coalition formed by the Plan de Iguala which had overthrown Spain quickly split asunder. Agustín de Iturbide proclaimed himself emperor and in a travesty that lasted less than two years tried to establish an absolutist government. Followers of the cruelly executed priest, Father Hidalgo, who had started the independence movement in 1810, then forced the abdication of Emperor Agustín I, and during 1824 organized a republican form of government based on democratic principles.

An irreconcilable dichotomy then arose in Mexico between such Federalists, as they later came to be known, and the wealthy and aristocratic *criollos*, who adamantly demanded a centralized and autocratic government. A national election under the new Constitution of 1824 (modeled after the United States Constitution) put a remarkable Indian leader, Guadalupe Victoria, in the Mexican presidency. Guadalupe Victoria was still in the agonizing throes of trying to form a stable government when Poinsett arrived in Mexico on May 25. To establish even a semblance of stability or permanent policy in the presence of such diametrically and violently opposed factions as existed in Mexico was an impossibility, as proved by the scores of revolutions, uprisings, and insurgencies that plagued the first century of Mexico's history. Anyone who seeks to understand United States–Mexican relations during this time must realize that one part of Mexico, in political philosophy the disciple of the United States, was basically pro-American, and that another part of Mexico, committed by economic reasons as well as political heritage to an absolutist type of government, was fundamentally destined to be anti-American.

In what may have been a misguided attempt to create harmony, Guadalupe Victoria had named one of the most ardent men in the faction that was later known as Centralists to the post of minister of relations to handle foreign affairs. This was Lucas Alamán, who four years later engineered the Centralist coup d'etat and who authored the rabidly anti-American Law of April 6, 1830. It was through Alamán that Poinsett had to conduct his negotiations with the Mexican government. (It is only incidental to this narrative that Poinsett played into the hands of the Centralists by being unseemly active in domestic Mexican politics in support of the Federalists and that after the Centralist takeover Poinsett was asked to leave Mexico.)

Alamán insisted that any plans for the building of a road between Santa Fe and Missouri must await the settlement of the international boundary question. On this, of course, American diplomacy had been both naive and foolish. Relations with the Mexican government would have been much smoother had Poinsett requested only an affirmation of the line established by the Treaty of 1819. The suggestion of a new boundary merely awakened suspicions, especially in Centralists' minds but also to a lesser extent in others. And the influx of Americans into New Mexico along the Santa Fe Trail as well as the small tide that poured into Texas under Mexico's generous colonization policy did not go unnoticed by these suspicious minds.

Thus Poinsett's efforts to get Mexican authorization for the survey were thwarted at the outset. Ultimately Poinsett had to settle for a treaty confirming the boundary line of 1819, and he was not able to get even this crumb until January 12, 1828. Promptly ratified by the United States Senate, this agreement failed to be accepted by the Mexican congress before the two-year time limit had expired (partially because of the 1829 uprisings in Mexico), was renegotiated in 1831, and finally was ratified by both governments on April 5, 1832. In addition to the interminable delays in official recognition of the international boundary, Poinsett's negotiations for the survey were also frustrated by a change in Guadalupe Victoria's cabinet. In October, 1825, Manuel Gómez Pedraza, a man of indistinct and ambiguous political inclinations who was to be supported in the 1828 election by the Centralists, replaced Alamán as minister of relations. It was not until the following April that Poinsett finally secured a somewhat grudging and restricted authorization for the survey. Mexico would not participate, either with funds or with men, in laying out the route. The developing trade, of course, would be of great benefit to the northern provinces—but largely at the cost of merchants in central Mexico. The United States team in Mexico was to be limited to surveying only, were not to erect any markers on the route, and were not to make any improvement or do any kind of road building.

Meantime poor Sibley, his patience chafed between duty and delay, stewed helplessly in New Mexico. After settling his small party in Taos, he and Joseph Brown set out for Santa Fe on November 27, 1825. They rented a house and settled down to await both the coming of spring and word from Poinsett. At first the pleasant society of Santa Fe, so unlike the cruder frontier to which he was accustomed, assuaged his impatience and growing loneliness. He dined often with Governor Antonio Narbona. He attended candle-lit dinner parties and danced at fandangos. He went to weddings, to baptisms, and to funerals. And he obviously enjoyed his cordial contacts with the people of Mexico. More than three months passed after his arrival in Taos before he finally received the December 3, 1825, letter from Poinsett telling him that no progress had been made in the negotiations. He then cancelled a projected trip to Chihuahua and shortly returned to his men in Taos.

The long-awaited authorization, limited though it was to surveying only, reached him in Taos in mid-June, 1826. He and Brown then concluded that they should defer their departure for Missouri in the expectation that the other two commissioners, Reeves and Mather, would join them in Taos. When it was finally learned that they were not coming, Sibley and his party left Taos on August 24 for an apparently uneventful journey home. It was another year before the final report of the commission was submitted, on October 27, 1827, because of some corrections and relocations of the route in Missouri and what is now Kansas. The commissioners expressed pride in what they grandly called their "highway between nations" and congratulated themselves on their success "in locating and marking out a very direct and permanent highway across the immense desert plain that intervenes between the settlements of the Missouri River and those of the Rio Grande del Norte. . . ."

In truth, the commissioners perhaps gave themselves more credit than they deserved. A clue lies elsewhere in their own report in the phrase that the route "is sufficiently marked out . . . by the tracks of the numerous caravans that have passed on it. . . ." The Santa Fe traders had found and were continuing to find their way with little assistance from the government. Thus, the importance of the federal survey to the Santa Fe Trail was not great. Without the survey, the trade would quite probably have thrived in about the

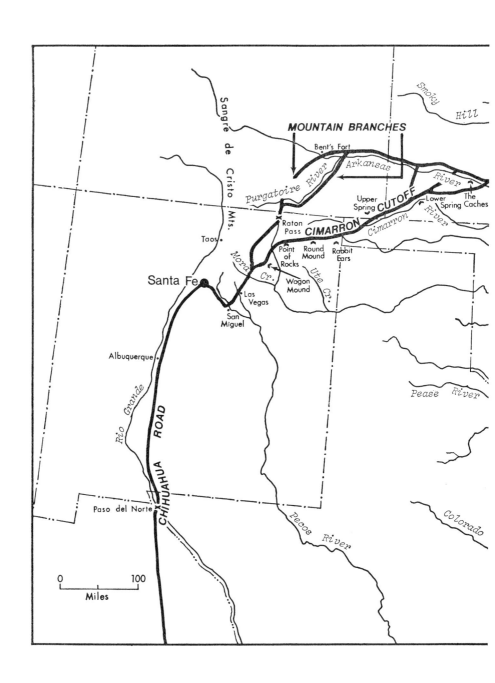

MOUNTAIN BRANCHES

Sangre de Cristo Mts.

Smoky Hill

Bent's Fort

Purgatoire River

Arkansas River

River

Upper Spring

CUTOFF

Lower Spring

The Caches

Raton Pass

CIMARRON

Cimarron River

Taos

Mora Cr.

Point of Rocks

Round Mound

Rabbit Ears

Ute Cr.

Santa Fe

Wagon Mound

Las Vegas

San Miguel

Albuquerque

Rio Grande

CHIHUAHUA ROAD

Pease River

Paso del Norte

Pecos River

Colorado

0   100
Miles

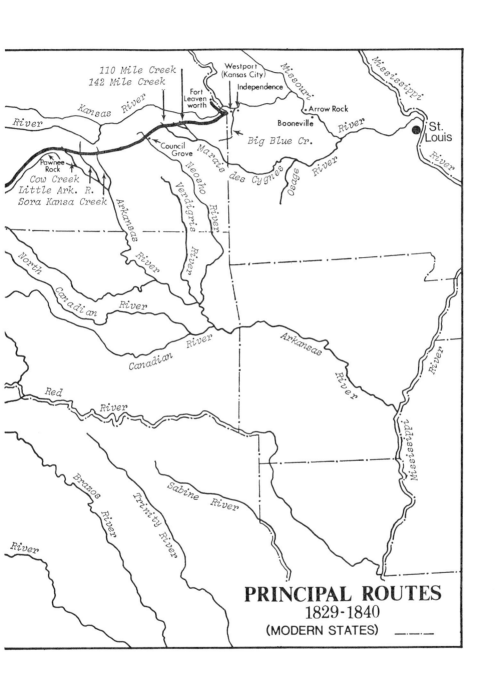

110 Mile Creek
142 Mile Creek

Westport
(Kansas City)
Independence

Missouri

Mississippi

Fort
Leaven
worth

Kansas River

River

Arrow Rock
Booneville

River

St.
Louis

River

Council
Grove

Big Blue Cr.

Pawnee
Rock
Cow Creek
Little Ark. R.
Sora Kansa Creek

Marais des Cygnes

Osage River

Neosho River

Verdigris River

Arkansas River

North

Canadian

River

Canadian

River

Arkansas

River

Mississippi River

Red

River

Arkansas River

Mississippi

Brazos River

Trinity River

Sabine River

River

PRINCIPAL ROUTES
1829-1840
(MODERN STATES)   —·—·—

same way it did. Likewise the treaties with the Kansa and the Osage would appear to have had minimal value. The real Indian problem was to develop with bands further west. But even if the commission's work was of only minor importance, the achievement should not be underrated. It was no small matter to measure by chain and compass course a distance of 750 miles through the relatively unexplored region and produce a fairly accurate chart. (Incidentally, before he left Santa Fe, Sibley gave Governor Narbona the Robinson map, with the comment that it was of no value.) Furthermore, the mounds the surveying team erected and the landmarks they described were unquestionably of assistance to the subsequent traffic over the trail. After all, there had been only a small number of caravans to make the Santa Fe trek before the survey, and many of these had followed varied and circuitous routes. The survey did help to standardize large segments of the trail for the thousands who came later.

The first starting point for the trail had been Franklin, from which Becknell had left, on the Missouri River. Early travelers cut across a bend in the Missouri to Arrow Rock, where a ferry carried them across the usually turbid river. From there they followed, normally without incident or difficulty, a well-established trail, sometimes called the Osage Trace, to Fort Osage. Here they turned southwest, still roughly paralleling the Missouri on its south side, to an established crossing of Little Blue Creek and then to a crossing of the Big Blue. A few miles farther they reached the site of present Independence. After the establishment of that town in 1827, it became the customary starting point for the trade. A few miles up the Missouri, Westport Landing (the progenitor of Kansas City) came into being to accommodate the river traffic.

It was from these adjacent places that the main trail swung southwest across the prairies toward Santa Fe. The various trails from Westport and Independence merged near present Gardner, Kansas, and there the route turned west to cross the branches of the Marais des Cygnes near their headwaters. A well-known location on this section was identified as the "Narrows"—the highland between the drainage of the Kansas and Marais des Cygnes. The trail followed this divide for about 15 miles to cross a creek that was named 110-Mile Creek because it was 110 miles from Fort Osage by the measurement of the federal survey, which had located and marked a good crossing. In the next 32 miles the trail crossed a half-dozen branches of the Marais des Cygnes to reach a favorite camping site on 142-Mile Creek. After Fort Leavenworth was established in 1827, a branch of the trail from the fort conjoined between these two streams.

About 20 miles farther west the trail crossed a main fork of the Neosho River at the Council Grove named by Sibley. The next well-known site was Diamond Spring, sometimes called the Diamond of the Plains although prosaically named Jones Spring by the survey. From Council Grove, past Diamond Spring, to Cottonwood Grove on the last branch of the Neosho to be crossed was a distance of 46 miles. The trail then, still heading generally westward, moved to the waters of the Arkansas River, crossing Sora Kansa Creek (where the Kansa Treaty was made), the Little Arkansas, Cow Creek, and others, to the Arkansas proper, about 270 miles from Fort Osage. This was near present Ellenwood, Kansas, just on the east side of the top of the Great Bend of the Arkansas. From Franklin, Fort Osage, or later Independence to the Arkansas can be considered the first and easiest stage of the trip. The next went along the Arkansas, and the third and hardest stage was the passage from the Arkansas into New Mexico.

In following the north side of the Arkansas west, Brown advised that "the traveller should not keep near the river, as 'tis sandy. Near the foot of the hills the ground is firm and the travelling better." There were a myriad of creeks and draws running into the river that the caravans had to cross as the trail moved southwest along the Great Bend. The first notable landmark passed was Pawnee Rock, about 325 miles from Fort Osage, near present Larned, Kansas. From here, some variations of the trail occurred as travelers sought better crossings of the Arkansas drainage. These merged again at the end of the Great Bend where the Arkansas channel ran slightly from the north.

At this point, near what was known as the South Bend, was the lower crossing of the Arkansas, where occasionally caravans crossed the river and headed into the parched and arid land in a more direct route toward Santa Fe. The main branch of the trail, however, continued along the north bank of the Arkansas, through present Dodge

City and Garden City. About midway between these two modern
cities was the middle crossing of the Arkansas, where a little-used
branch of the trail cut southwest to the Cimarron. The main crossing was farther upriver, about 480 miles from Fort Osage, near an
easily recognizable landmark—a large island in the river called
Chouteau's Island.

These three crossings, with the upper crossing the most frequently used, were variants of what was called the Cimarron cutoff. The mountain branch of the trail continued along the north side
of the Arkansas to Bent's Indian trading post near modern LaJunta,
Colorado, which is often referred to as Bent's Old Fort. It was about
120 miles from the upper crossing to Bent's Fort. Some caravans
forded the Arkansas near the mouth of Purgatoire River and others
a few miles upstream at Bent's Fort. The mountain branch of the
trail then, with these two minor variants, turned southwest, merging
near present Trinidad, Colorado, and turning south through Raton
Pass. The mountain branch joined the variants of the Cimarron cutoff near what is now Fort Union National Monument.

The mountain route was a somewhat easier journey because of
the availability of water, but it was farther and was not quite as
often used in the trade as the Cimarron route. From the lower crossing at the South Bend to Fort Union via the mountain route was
slightly over four hundred miles, depending on the variants followed. The lower crossing route to Fort Union after its establishment saved about seventy-five miles. The route by the middle
crossing and the Cimarron cutoff was about ten miles farther, and
by the upper crossing slightly farther still. But the upper crossing
to the Cimarron River constituted less than fifty miles of travel without fresh water, and this was the most frequently used route. Roads
from all three crossings came together at the Lower Cimarron
Spring on the Cimarron in the southeast corner of present Kansas.

What was to be the most often described section of the trail
led from there up the Cimarron, past Middle Cimarron Spring and
Upper Cimarron Spring, where the trail left the river and headed
across the barren wastes of the Oklahoma panhandle and northeastern New Mexico. Travelers sighted on Rabbit Ears Peak, near
the foot of which flowed an intermittent creek, then on past Round
Mound, Point of Rocks, and Ute Creek, and headed for the upper

waters of the Canadian River. From the crossing of the Canadian, east of present Springer, New Mexico, the next well-known landmark was Wagon Mound. It was then an easy journey on to Fort Union, the juncture with the mountain branch, and Mora Creek.

Travel from there to Santa Fe was through the foothills of the Sangre de Cristo Mountains. The trail swung to the south to circle the mountains, passing through the village of San Miguel del Vado and turning back northwest along the upper Pecos. It then crossed the mountains over Glorieta Pass, from whence it was only about twenty miles to Santa Fe.

CHAPTER 7

Broadcloth and Britches

The year 1825, the year of the survey, may be fairly said to mark the real beginning of the Santa Fe trade. The previous expeditions, although initiating some commerce, had generally been accidental, experimental or tentative, and exploratory. The LeGrand-Storrs-Marmaduke party that had gone to Santa Fe in 1824 and returned in the summer of 1825 was the first large trading venture, but even it had more an air of adventure than commerce about it.

Josiah Gregg's well-known table, which depicted the Santa Fe trade from 1822 to 1843, the basis of virtually all historical comment, is probably somewhat inaccurate for the first several years of the trade. Nevertheless, it shows a marked increase in the value of the goods taken from Missouri to Santa Fe in 1825—from $35,000 worth in 1824 to $65,000 in 1825, an increase of virtually 100 percent. Gregg's tally also indicates that ninety proprietors and forty employees made the trip in 1825. There is no way to check the accuracy of his figures, for only fragmentary records of the customs house at Santa Fe are extant today. Indeed, it is not at all unlikely that the records kept were themselves cursory and incomplete. And even if the data were complete, they would inevitably understate the true volume of the trade, for certainly at least some of the American businessmen would have disposed of their merchandise without going through the nettlesome formality of paying taxes on it.

A section of the Santa Fe customs book for January to July, 1825, is extant. It reflects what was apparently the arrival of one party in March, probably four in April, one in May, one in June, and two very large parties in July. The names of the traders, that is, those declaring merchandise, total fifty-seven. The aggregate value of the goods subject to customs was over 27,000 *reales*, but unfortuately the document does not state which of the three different kinds of money (that is, silver content) then in use in New Mexico was meant, so it is impossible to equate this with American monetary values.

The pages of the *Missouri Intelligencer* published at Franklin reflect a flurry of activity in 1825. For the first time Franklin merchants, such as "Ingram & Reilly," began advertising goods "well-adapted to the Santa Fe trade." When William Becknell returned from his second trip to Santa Fe, the editor gave his expeditions extensive and enthusiastic coverage. Stories repeatedly appeared in the newspaper about the organization of trading companies and their departures for Santa Fe. In addition to the Missouri parties, there was one reportedly organizing in Tennessee, another in Arkansas, and a third rumored to be assembling in Alabama. The Tennessee and Arkansas ventures did make the journey, but there was no further word on the Alabama group.

According to the newspaper, bands of traders usually assembled at Franklin and completed their final organization out on the prairies, often at Fort Osage. What was probably the largest group to make the trip that year gathered at Fort Osage in mid-May, 1825. A code of laws to govern the expedition while en route was prepared by a special committee. Since some of the businessmen had elected to use pack animals to carry their merchandise, they decided to split off, as a group, from the rest, and departed as an advance party on May 16. The principal advantage of the pack animals, mules and horses, was their relative speed on the journey. Moreover, they could negotiate difficult terrain and stream crossings more easily than the cumbersome wagons and thus with little difficulty could follow the better-watered mountain branch of the trail, which most of the pack caravans seem to have done. However, what was gained in speed and convenience was lost in efficiency, for fewer and smaller goods could be carried in pack saddles.

After the "packers" had left the rendezvous, the remaining "wagoneers," 105 in all, held an election. They adopted a code of laws and chose Augustus Storrs as their captain. Storrs, who had prepared the deposition for Senator Benton's use, was to be named the first American consul in Santa Fe, but he had not been informed of this at that time, his commission being delivered to him after his arrival in New Mexico. According to the newspaper report, there were thirty-four wagons in the party.

It is difficult to tell whether the stories in the *Missouri Intelligencer* under different dates refer to the same or to different expeditions. For example, May 14, 1825: "A company of 80 men left Franklin last week for Santa Fe. . . ." Was this the Augustus Storrs party that rendezvoused at Fort Osage, or another group? Of the half-dozen or more ventures reported leaving Franklin, how many were separate and discrete parties? Further, since the names in the customs book are different from those in the *Intelligencer*, should these be added to the total reported as having made the trip that year? It would appear that Gregg's often-used figures are considerably lower than the actual number, perhaps half too low. There must have been, at the very minimum, two hundred men who followed the Santa Fe Trail in 1825.

If Gregg's table is wrong about the number of men, it is also probably inaccurate about the value of their goods. For example, one company returning from Santa Fe that summer brought back $18,568 in silver, $182 in gold, $10,220 in beaver pelts, and $15,700 worth of mules, jacks, and jennets. Of course, profits must have been substantial, but even so, Gregg's estimate of $65,000 as the value of the trade in 1825 may have fallen far short of the mark. It must have been closer to $100,000 in U.S. dollar-value going out and nearly $200,000 coming back. In the long view of history, however, the actual dollar-value of the trade is relatively unimportant— it was enough to cause great excitement and stimulate far-ranging interest.

Among other problems in the early years was the "irregularity" of the customs levy by Mexican officials. Not only did the rate schedule appear to Americans to be "flexible," but also the collection seemed subject to negotiation. M. M. Marmaduke complained in 1825 that the 25 percent charged his party was too high. The *Intelligencer* reported an average levy that year of 28 percent. Another 1825 complaint was that the excise was totally unrelated to the invoice price of goods. A report in the Missouri journal stated that white cotton goods, which were in the greatest demand in Santa Fe, were assessed at better than 50 percent ad valorem. There was also a long list of commodities prohibited under an act of May 20, 1824, of which traders usually were unaware until they had arrived. The prohibited imports were extensive, encompassing a wide variety of goods from artichokes to monk's robes and other items that the Santa Fe merchants would not be likely to bring anyway. But the other wares on the list were common and profitable trade items. For example, all kinds of broadcloth were interdicted from trade, as were gloves for both men and women, britches of all kinds for men, and short cloaks for women. The list was obviously compiled for the benefit of merchants of central Mexico. To circumvent the restrictions, some traders avoided customs altogether, while others simply bribed the officials in Santa Fe, Taos, and San Miguel. It helped to be able to speak Spanish, one trader reported.

There was some gloom, even that first year of the trade. Stephen Cooper reported that a few businessmen were unable to sell their merchandise on their arrival in Santa Fe. One of the community's residents, who claimed that he was not involved in the trade, informed the *Intelligencer* that no one should expect enormous profits. Some Missouri merchants, quoted in that newspaper, found it hard to dispose of their goods at all. "Cash is scarce here, or rather, it is in the hands of a few, who are able to live without parting with it." Such a statement reflected what must, in truth, have been the basic economic scenario. New Mexico had never been a wealthy province; in fact, over the years it had been just the reverse. Once the trade vacuum created by years of extortionate commerce from Chihuahua was filled, Americans would need to search elsewhere for eager buyers. The editor of the *Intelligencer* sensed this as early as June 4, 1824: "We have no doubt that our persevering citizens will penetrate into the remotest provinces and seek new markets, and that the trade will not be abandoned until the whole country has been explored, and every source from which profit can be derived has been exhausted."

The bleakest picture of the incipient trade was presented by an anonymous informant in the pages of the newspaper in November. By his account, New Mexico was completely inundated: "Every village is crowded with goods. . . ." Many merchants were selling at a loss, and some were unable to dispose of their inventories at any price. "The little cash that was in the country has been expended."

As of August, more than two-thirds of the merchandise that had been imported was sold. He estimated the excess goods at an invoice value of about $60,000. "On the whole," he concluded gloomily, "it appears that there is little prospect of a successful trade being kept up between the United States and this province."

That was 1825; yet the trade continued and generally prospered for a half century. But it is obvious that the people of New Mexico were short on specie. Therefore, merchants frequently resorted to bartering for furs. Many ventured south into the interior of Mexico. Some, indeed, were to lose money. But the international commerce survived.

The next year, 1826, brought an apparent increase in the value of the trade, which continued in 1827, and then in 1828 jumped even higher—to $150,000 in terms of American embarcation evaluations, if Josiah Gregg's table can be accepted. In fact, as has been indicated, it may well have been an underestimation. For instance, Gregg reported a total of ninety traders going to Santa Fe in 1827. But an extant leaf from the New Mexico archives shows that one party alone, which arrived in July, 1827, numbered thirty-six, and the *Intelligencer* regularly reported each spring that several groups of eighty to one hundred persons each had departed for northern Mexico.

In 1827 the town of Independence was platted, thereby giving the Santa Fe trade its principal American terminus. It soon boomed. Franklin, the original jumping-off point, immediately was placed at a disadvantage. Navigation of the Missouri River was easily possible farther upstream at Independence. And Franklin's site was a poor one, for the surging river water continually eroded the embankment there, endangering the community. A change of location in 1828 to New Franklin (the present town) saved the village from destruction but did not save its important commerce, which in the next few years moved almost completely to Independence. The year 1828 was Franklin's last substantial year. In May, just a few months before the original townsite slipped ingloriously into the muddy Missouri, the editor of the *Intelligencer* wrote happily of the bustle of preparation in the new town for the summer's trade. Merchandise was being unloaded at the docks, wagons were rolling into town, stores were humming with traffic, and men were crowding the saloons, elbowing their way to the bar.

Several events of 1828 were of importance to the trade. The Mexican congress increased the tariff rates, but irregularities of collection remained the rule in New Mexico. American businessmen petitioned the United States Congress requesting a fort on the Arkansas and military protection from Indians along the trail; military escorts began the following year. Mexico passed a law on May 12, 1828, requiring foreigners coming to Mexico to obtain passports before entering. For a few months, at least, the enactment apparently was scrupulously observed in New Mexico, and the archives there reflect the applications of numerous traders who had not bothered to obtain passports until they reached Santa Fe or Taos. According to Josiah Gregg, the year also served as the apogee for the Santa Fe trade. Some two hundred men, eighty of whom were proprietors, brought $150,000 worth of American goods into New Mexico, a figure almost double that of the previous year. Newspaper accounts and the incomplete records available confirm that 1828 was indeed prosperous. But changes were in the offing.

Both the United States and Mexico held national elections in 1828. The outcomes had profound effects on each nation, which in turn affected the commerce between the nations. In the United States, Andrew Jackson won an overwhelming victory that ushered in the "Age of the Common Man," a government sympathetic to the frontier, and an era of expanded democratic participation. In Mexico, however, democratic government suffered a blow from which it was many years recovering.

In 1824 the liberal faction in Mexico had wrested control of the government from the Iturbidists and monarchists, had adopted a constitution modelled after that of the United States, and had elected an Indian as the first president of the Republic of Mexico. Guadalupe Victoria did not run for reelection. The leading candidates were Gómez Pedraza and Vicente Guerrero. Both were associated with the liberal faction, but Guerrero was an old-time Hidalguista, a hard-core, liberal reformer. The conservatives in Mexico, the wealthy *criollos*, rather than run one of their own faction, threw their support to the lesser of two evils, Gómez Pedraza.

It proved to be a disastrous move for the liberals, since it split their faction asunder.

It is only coincidental but nevertheless interesting that the political factions that year were known by the masonic rites to which the two leaders belonged. Gómez Pedraza had become a Mason through the Scottish rite (*Escosés*), which had been brought to Mexico by the British representative to the new republic, Lewis Pakenham. Guerrero was the newly elected grand master of the York rite (*Yorkinos*) lodge, which had been organized by the American minister, Joel R. Poinsett. The election marked the beginning of Poinsett's unfortunate involvement in Mexican politics. Had Guerrero won, Poinsett would not have been run out of Mexico, and the course of United States–Mexican diplomatic relations would have been smoother. Thus, it was the *Escosés* versus the *Yorkinos* in 1828.

The electoral body certified that Gómez Pedraza had won the election; the old guerrilla leader, Guerrero, declared that he had been cheated out of a victory by a corrupt election canvass. What an interesting parallel to the American election of 1824! That election had been thrown into the House of Representatives, John Quincy Adams was the victor, and Andrew Jackson cried "corrupt bargain." But there the parallel stops, and the inexperience of the Mexican people with democratic processes was revealed. Jackson gathered his forces, bided his time, and overwhelmingly won the next election. But in Mexico Guerrero gathered his forces, armed them, and took over the government by force.

Thus it was the leaders of the very faction that had established democracy in Mexico who overturned democracy when the results, corrupt or not, failed to please them. Precedent had been established, and there was not to be a peaceful election in Mexico for many years to come. Uprisings and open rebellions broke out everywhere, especially near the capital. The *criollos* or *Escosés* or soon-to-be Centralists still controlled large segments of the military forces and under the guise of supporting Gómez Pedraza actually began plotting to seize power. Their chance came in the spring of 1829. While Guerrero, with his military forces, was trying to stamp out the brush fires of revolution, Spain had launched an attempt at the reconquest of Mexico. It was a puny effort, more nominal than real, but there was an invasionary landing at Tampico. It was quickly repelled, but it caused Guerrero to divide his forces. The situation in Mexico became quite complex; it is an oversimplification to state that while Guerrero was thus weakened, the Centralists made their power grab, but this is essentially what occurred. Anastacio Bustamante, a *criollo* leader who had been declared vice-president of Mexico, led an army into Mexico City literally in the dead of night, captured the capital, and later executed Guerrero. Then, instead of installing (or reinstalling) Gómez Pedraza, Bustamante declared himself president of Mexico.

This new Centralist government under Bustamante was totally without authority or justification under the Constitution of 1824. It was a complete and illegal usurpation based solely upon force of arms. Although lip service was still rendered to the constitution, for all practical purposes the infant republic gave way to an authoritarian military dictatorship. Again Mexico was thrown into revolution. A new leader arose to take advantage of the situation— Antonio López de Santa Anna. He had previously put himself at the head of an insurgent force at Veracruz in support of Gómez Pedraza; he now became the leader of the Federalists. The Centralists were well-organized, in control of most of the government agencies, and in command of a trained and disciplined army. The Federalists were disorganized and generally without funds but appealed to much greater numbers of people. Many of their sympathizers supported the resistance movement covertly, at least immediately after the takeover, and apparently many of the troops were among those secret Federalists. Fighting between Centralist forces and guerrilla bands of Federalists sporadically spread throughout Mexico during the next three years.

New Mexico, however, was largely unaffected, either by the Bustamante coup or by the insurgencies that followed, though some instability naturally resulted from the rapid-fire succession of three different governors in 1828. These were governors in fact, although not in name. New Mexico had been joined in 1824 with Chihuahua and Durango into one state under the constitution. Its principal administrator, the *jefe político*, was appointive, but since the governors of New Mexico as a Spanish province had always been appointed, this created no problem. The people of New Mexico probably would not have known how to elect a chief executive had they been required to do so, and for practical purposes the *jefe político* filled the same functions that formerly the governors had. After the quick succession of three men in this office during 1828, the appointment went to Antonio José Chávez, a *rico criollo*, who held the post for three years. He did not seem to be particularly unfavorable either to the Americans in New Mexico or to the commerce that accompanied them.

However, according to Josiah Gregg, there was a sharp decline in trade from $150,000 worth of goods brought in from the United States in 1828 to $60,000 in 1829. The number of men Gregg reported making the trip dropped from two hundred to fifty and the number of merchant-proprietors from eighty to twenty. The next year, 1830, the trade climbed back almost to the 1828 levels, and in 1831 it doubled. A fear of Indians may be the explanation for the 1829 decline. The turmoil in Mexico may have discouraged one or two traders, but it seems unlikely that it thwarted many. No mention of it appears in contemporary accounts. The flood and relocation of Franklin and the establishment of Independence could have caused a slight interruption in commerce but could not have accounted for a major drop. Perhaps the most likely explanation was a rising danger of Indian attacks.

CHAPTER 8

The Indian Threat

In the early years of the trade, the Indians had not been as menacing as the frontier merchants had anticipated. Rather, they had been more of a nuisance. They would join a caravan encamped on the prairies, usually locating a site of their own nearby, and "visit" the traders, professing friendship. Obviously, the whites preferred amicable visits to hostilities, so they generally tolerated the procedure. The Indians would wander through the camp, staring, talking to one another, and picking up various articles to admire them, while their leaders attempted to converse in bad Spanish or worse English with the caravan captain and his lieutenants. They almost always begged for food and invariably offered to trade buffalo skins for clothing or ammunition. The behavior alternated between obsequiousness and rude arrogance. Usually the Indian parties were relatively small, but occasionally they substantially outnumbered the whites. It is easy to imagine the tension in the caravan when one of these large parties stopped them and began poking into wagons, tents, personal gear, and anything else in sight. Open confrontations were avoided, but the traders were always on tenterhooks. And when the visiting Indians left, numerous items inevitably left with them. As pilferers they had no match.

Some historians assert that as the caravans increased in size and number the Indians began to fear that the whites would drive them out of their hunting grounds and thus became more dangerous. Such a threat may indeed have been implicit in the advance of the white man's frontier, but it seems highly unlikely that any of the Indians were sophisticated enough to recognize such a sweeping socioeconomic concept. Indian depredations did increase along the trail, but probably more because the red men began to recognize the weakness and vulnerability of the overland parties than because they feared the imminent loss of lands. Such a concept of land sovereignty was outside their cultural background.

The 1822 caravans had encountered Indians but no hostilities. The whites, however, many of them former trappers, were constantly on edge about the possibilities. In 1823 a group led by John McKnight, whose purpose was trade with the Indians rather than in Santa Fe, was attacked on the Arkansas by a war party of Comanches. According to contemporary accounts, the McKnight venture had erected some fortifications with the plan of establishing a permanent trading post. The reason for the attack is not clear, but McKnight was killed and the few men with him fled. This served, of course, to spread alarm among the traders. When the Prince of Wertenberg visited the American West that fall, he was prepared to go no further than Fort Atkinson (in present Iowa) because of the hostility of the Indians. Other parties that year, however, encountered only the usual pilfering. One group had its horse herd stolen by Osage Indians, which created a considerable inconvenience. A few similar encounters took place in 1824, with one party reporting the loss of sixty mules to Indian thieves. This pattern of Indian-white encounters continued during the next two years, although in 1825 a group led by William Huddart was attacked by Arapahoes on the Cimarron and two of the traders were killed.

Thus, although robbery was an almost constant nuisance, actual death at the Indians' hands was in fact rather rare. Only three deaths resulted from Indian attacks in six years of activity along the trail. In part, of course, this was because the caravans were well armed and alert and organized to repel attacks. Also, the threat evidently was not as great as many believed it to be. But an incident in 1828 brought a feeling, if not the reality, of open warfare on the plains.

Daniel Munroe and a son of Samuel G. McNees (his first name is not known) were riding in advance of a major caravan returning from Santa Fe in the late summer. As they slept on the banks of a small creek (now called McNees Creek), they were murdered with their own guns by one or more Indians who sneaked up on them. Munroe lived long enough to tell the story when the caravan reached the site, but he did not identify the Indians. While the bodies of the two men were being buried on the Cimarron, a party of six or seven Indians rode up. Josiah Gregg speculated that they not only were innocent of the murders but did not even know of the attack. However, the inflamed traders opened fire and all but one of the Indians were massacred. By some accounts, this unfortunate episode triggered a "plains war," but the term is too grandiose because neither the traders nor the Indians were sufficiently organized to conduct a war. There does seem to have been an increase in depredations, however. The whites that killed the Indians in revenge for Munroe and McNees were attacked later on the Arkansas and suffered much fright and the loss of a reputed thousand head of mules and horses.

A second caravan returning from Santa Fe a few weeks later encountered a large band of Comanches at Upper Cimarron Spring. Uneasily attempting to ride through the Indians, the caravan was attacked. The leader, John Means, was killed in the fighting. The wagon train passed through without further loss of life but was harassed for several days by the Indians, who finally managed to run off the traders' horse herd. Stranded with their wagons and with no livestock to pull them, the traders divided up the silver bullion and coins, abandoned the wagons, and set out on foot across the prairie for Missouri. According to apocryphal accounts, the Indians burned the wagons but, strangely, did not attack the little column. A legend, widely believed but probably spurious, is that the men buried (cached) their silver on Chouteau's Island in the Arkansas before making their way into Franklin. Their tale was a wild one and of course grew with each telling. Three accounts were later written by men from this party: Milton E. Bryan, William Waldo, and William Y. Hitt, whose reminiscences were used by Henry Inman in his book about the trail. But the bare facts remained: the seriousness of the attacks in 1828 equalled the total of the six previous years.

The frontiersmen of western Missouri were outraged and indignant, and their reactions were echoed in the press and in the legislature. Editors wrote fiery statements about the need for protection along the trail. The governor of Missouri, John Miller, demanded protection in an address to the legislature. That body passed a resolution and sent a memorial to the United States Congress, requesting the federal government to ensure the safety of the trade. Two bills were introduced, one in the Senate calling for four companies of infantry to be stationed along the trail, the other in the House authorizing the president to raise militia companies for safeguarding the trade. Both bills died of inertia when Congress adjourned, but neither measure would have been effective anyway.

In the first place, it was ridiculous to send infantry troops against mounted Indians as skilled in cavalry tactics as the plains Indians. Second, the House proposal especially placed reliance on the mere authorization of militia companies. Third and most important, the attacks had occurred south of the Arkansas in Mexican territory. Nothing could be done by American troops to provide security on foreign soil.

So, without aid from the government, the caravans began to organize in the spring of 1829 at newly established Independence. Obviously the fear of a bloodbath on the plains was not going to frighten everyone away from the potential profits. "The fewer the traders the greater the profit," commented one of the men who made the 1829 trip. And the bolder and more daring among the frontier merchants showed their determination. The threat to the trade was real, however, whether the Indian menace was overrated or not. Fewer men laid their plans, fewer goods were purchased for Santa Fe, fewer wagons were outfitted.

In Washington, even though the bills for protection of the trade lay moribund, pressure for assistance did not. If the maritime trade of New England merchants could be protected by the government, why should the inland commerce with Mexico not receive like treatment? The West had its representatives and powerful supporters, such as senators Benton of Missouri and Richard Johnson of Kentucky, and the election of 1828 had brought to power the strongest supporter of all, Andrew Jackson, the new president. Just how Jackson's attention was directed to the problem is not clear, but he certainly was aware of it. At his request, through Secretary of War John Eaton, Major General Alexander Macomb ordered four companies of infantry detailed to provide protection as far southwest as the Mexican border on the Arkansas. Thus General Henry Atkinson at Jefferson Barracks ordered Brevet Major Bennet Riley and four companies of the Sixth Infantry to "proceed from Cantonment Leavenworth about the first of June on the Santa Fe road to the Arkansas River for the protection of caravans in commercial intercourse with the provinces of New Mexico."

Cantonment Leavenworth (present Fort Leavenworth) had been established in March, 1827, and would become the military terminus of the trail and probably the most important post in the middle American West. The Sixth Infantry was led by General Atkinson, who also was commander of the army's Department of the West. That there was no cavalry unit, indeed no regularly mounted troops at all, in the western department deserves caustic comment. Frontiersmen recognized, if the army did not, the futility sending foot soldiers to chase mounted Comanches and Kiowas.

Bennet Riley, who was given command of the two hundred infantry, was a competent and efficient officer. He was then forty years old, the father of five children, held the permanent rank of captain, and was a veteran of the War of 1812 and several Indian campaigns. Eleven other officers were detached to this special duty, all except the surgeon and one captain being West Point graduates. Among these, the second youngest officer, was Phillip St. George Cooke, whose deeds as well as whose pen made him one of the best-known names in the history of the American West. He was then just two years out of the military academy, where he had graduated near the bottom of his class. Cooke probably wrote both Riley's official report of the expedition and the commanding officer's journal.

The four companies were organized as a temporary battalion. The men moved on foot, armed with single-shot muskets and rifles, probably of the 1817 Harpers Ferry type. The equipment was carried on ox-drawn wagons. Cooke later stated in his autobiography that this was the first time oxen had been used to pull wagons over the Santa Fe Trail. They were slower than mules or horses, but they were cheaper—and, if it became necessary, more palatable. In all, the military command as it moved out of Leavenworth consisted of a dozen officers, about two hundred men, twenty-five wagons (six of which were two-wheeled carts), six dozen yoke of oxen, one six-pound brass cannon, and about a dozen horses.

At Round Grove the battalion rendezvoused with a caravan of

traders that it was to escort to the Arkansas: about seventy men and three dozen wagons commanded by Charles Bent. On June 13 the prairie parade rolled off down the road to Santa Fe; on July 9 it reached the crossing of the Arkansas at Chouteau's Island. The following day the traders continued on into Mexican territory, and the military bivouacked to await their return. Although a few Indian parties had been encountered, everyone knew that the real Indian danger lay further down the trail.

Bent, determined to proceed cautiously, sent out an advance party, a strategically sound plan that may have saved the caravan from ambush. Riding six or seven miles ahead of the traders, the three scouts stopped to water at a stream crossing. Bedlam erupted as some five hundred shrieking Kiowas swooped down on them. The scouts raced back to the caravan, but one, mounted on a mule, did not reach safety; it was said he was scalped while still alive. Captain Bent and his brother William heroically and almost single-handedly diverted the Kiowa charge while the caravan prepared to defend itself.

A courier rushed back to the military escort on the Arkansas a scant half-dozen miles away. It was certainly unauthorized and almost unprecedented for a United States military command to cross onto foreign soil. (Think of the trouble aroused by President Jackson when a few years earlier as a militia commander he had chased Seminole marauders into Spanish Florida.) Riley noted in his journal: "They were only six miles off, and the Indians were all around them, and if I did not go to their assistance [they would] be all killed and scalped." What would Riley have done if the attack had occurred fifty or one hundred miles into Mexico? Clearly the proximity made the decision easy.

It was dark when the infantry struggled across the Arkansas and one in the morning when Riley's command reached the embattled caravan. A massive Indian attack was expected at dawn, but it did not come. Gregg, either from imagination or hearsay, stated that a bugle call at reveille frightened the Indians away. The traders pleaded with Riley to escort them on into Santa Fe, international protocol notwithstanding. Riley agreed to accompany them until he believed them to be out of danger. Three days later, about thirty miles inside Mexican territory, Riley decided he had gone as far as he could. The military returned to their camp on the north bank of the Arkansas; Bent and the traders proceeded toward Santa Fe. Excitement was ahead for both groups.

The traders traveled under constant alert for over six weeks. Not allowed by their leaders to undress or even unboot at night, they bedded down under arms, rarely getting more than three or four hours sleep. An atmosphere of near-panic prevailed. Several times men awoke screaming and plunging their knives into the earth beside them. Then, exhausted, they would take to the trail and frequently fall from their saddles in moments of drowsiness. Along the route they were reinforced by a hundred-odd Mexicans who were to escort them through the canyons and mountains into Santa Fe. Rumors of a combined force of Indians in one of the canyons led to an attempt by Ewing Young and forty or more trappers from Taos to reinforce them. The mountain men did engage in one skirmish with unidentified Indians, joined the caravan, and led it into Taos. From there the traders reached Santa Fe without additional harassment.

Meanwhile, Riley and the infantry had returned to the Arkansas, camping for several days on the Mexican side because of high water. By the end of July no Indians had been sighted, supplies were running short, and the men were growing restless. Riley ordered daily drills to commence—the unquestionable bane of enlisted men anywhere, anytime. Four, whose enlistment had expired, demanded permission to return to Kansas. It seemed perfectly clear that there was nothing to be feared from Indians. Despite Riley's persuasion, they left on foot one morning but were back by nightfall. About eighteen miles from camp they encountered a band of Indians. One of the soldiers, George Gordon, was killed; the others were rescued by chance by a hunting party foraging out of camp.

Two days later the military encampment was caught by surprise by a mounted Indian charge. Riley rallied his men into defensive positions, drove the marauders off, and held them at rifle and musket range. It was an unequal contest between infantry and cavalry, but the U.S. troops were saved by the superiority of their weapons and the skillful tactics employed by Riley. Lieutenant Cooke distinguished himself in an attack that probably saved one of the rifle companies. Actual fighting lasted about forty-five minutes, but the Indians circled the camp for hours before leaving with much of the command's livestock. One soldier was killed in the fighting; twenty horses and mules and over fifty oxen were lost.

A few days later one of the most heroic but least heralded episodes in the history of the Santa Fe Trail ended. A single emaciated and thoroughly exhausted soldier walked into camp to the utter wonder and astonishment of all. He and another enlisted man had been dispatched from Leavenworth a month earlier with messages for Major Riley. A few days out of Leavenworth they had been attacked, both were wounded, and they lost their horses. They continued down the trail afoot, perhaps having no idea of the distance to the Arkansas, perhaps afraid to turn back, but certainly with much will to live. Nursing their wounds, they had lived on the decayed remnants of an army ox and on worms and grubs. When they heard the firing of the cannon in the Indian engagement, the least seriously wounded had pushed on alone. A rescue party was sent out for the second man, who died in camp several days later.

The day after the couriers' arrival there was another Indian attack. Actually the camp was under fairly continual harassment from what apparently was a large band of Kiowas during the entire time it was bivouacked on the Arkansas. On this occasion a hunting detachment led by a Lieutenant Joseph Pentland was attacked by a superior number of Indians several miles from camp. Pentland panicked and fled in fright, thus dissolving the morale of his command, all of whom fled helter-skelter to the banks of the river, where they were rescued by Lieutenant Cooke. Fortunately only one man, bugler Matthew King, was lost. Riley promptly placed Pentland under arrest, and he was court-martialed, convicted, and cashiered the following year for cowardice, misconduct in the face of an enemy, false reporting, and disobedience. In the raid, in addition to the death of King, more head of now very valuable livestock were lost.

By previous arrangement with the traders, Riley was to await their return until October 10. He gave them one day of grace and moved out—or rather limped out after destroying his useless wagons—on October 11. The timing seems incredible, but before noon that day advance riders from the traders' caravan caught up with the battalion.

Despite the many problems, the traders had enjoyed a profitable season in Santa Fe. A report in the *Western Monitor* of November 7, 1829 (probably exaggerated), stated they returned with $240,000 in silver. In addition, they had with them a dozen *gauchipines*, or Spanish-born families, exiled from Mexico under a decree of March 20, 1829, and a military escort of sixty Mexican troops commanded by the respected Colonel Antonio José Vizcarra. The government of New Mexico seemed unwilling to see the American trade endangered, and by William Waldo's account, Colonel Vizcarra had volunteered to lead the protective escort.

The returning caravan had sustained a dramatic attack on the Cimarron by about 150 Gros Ventres. Bravely ordered by Vizcarra to surrender their arms, the Indians agreed to do so to the Mexicans if the Americans were removed from camp. When this was done, however, the Indians attacked the Mexican force. Vizcarra's own life was saved by a Pueblo Indian who stepped in front of the Indian gun aimed at the colonel. The Americans immediately returned to the aid of the Mexicans, and the fighting that ensued was among the fiercest ever reported on the plains.

Unfortunately the sources for the history of this encounter are meager, and there are several curious aspects about which one can only speculate. Were the Indians truly Gros Ventres, whose customary range was much farther north? If so, what were they doing so far from home? And why did they seem to have an antipathy toward the Mexicans and not the Americans? And, finally, were the American traders as savage as the Mexican commander stated to Lieutenant Cooke? The Mexicans, themselves veteran Indian fighters and not noted for compunction, reportedly were appalled by the Americans' brutality. At least one Indian was scalped alive and several were skinned like wild animals. Cooke saw one of these skins tacked to the side of a wagon.

The reunion of Riley's command with the trading caravan and their escort on October 12 occasioned a gala celebration that lasted two days, the Americans feasting the Mexican command that night and Vizcarra and his staff honoring the American officers the next. Among the facts that impressed Cooke was that Santiago Abreau, an important official of the New Mexican government soon to be appointed governor of the province, had accompanied the returnees.

Cooke was also impressed by the large number of grave Spaniards "who had been exiled from Mexico; by the criollos—polished gentlemen, magnificently clothed in Spanish costume"; by the fact that "four or five languages were spoken . . . Frenchmen were there *of course*" [Cooke's italics]; and by the grand feast that Vizcarra spread for the American officers, complete with linen, silverware, and wine. Several days later the parties split, Vizcarra to return to Santa Fe and the Americans to Kansas. No major incident was reported on the return from the Arkansas.

Whether the military escort was a success is moot. One newspaper account said that without it the trading caravan would have been lost. Another called it "the auspicious revival of the trade to Santa Fe." But another commented: *"Four companies* of the *United States troops*, employed half a year to *protect* a trade the whole of which is only $120,000." The costs did indeed seem out of proportion, and the practice of providing regular military protection was not continued, although there were later escorts. One result was that the proved clumsiness of the infantry on the plains added to pressure already building for the creation of cavalry units. A mounted infantry bill passed Congress in 1832, and by the end of that year a "corps of mounted rangers" had come into existence. The report of the secretary of war for that year stated that this unit was used on the Santa Fe Trail, although contemporary accounts fail to mention it.

CHAPTER 9

The Decade of the Thirties

By all odds, the busiest man in the Santa Fe traffic for several years was Charles Bent, who had captained the 1829 caravan of traders escorted by Bennet Riley. It was Bent and his brother William who had courageously diverted the Indian attack south of the Arkansas by riding straight at the marauders. That was apparently Charles Bent's first trip to Santa Fe.

The first of eleven children in his family, Charles Bent was born in present West Virginia in 1799. His father had studied law, became a successful surveyor, and later entered the judiciary in Missouri, once serving on the territorial supreme court. Charles grew up in St. Louis during the exciting period of American exploration of the Louisiana Purchase. Although he spent a few years at an eastern college in Pennsylvania, his eyes were always on the West. He entered the fur trade, went up the Missouri, and soon was employed by Manuel Lisa's Missouri Fur Company.

Unfortunate ventures left Bent nearly bankrupt in 1828. Since the Missouri fur trade was dominated by large trading companies, often virtually at war with each other, Bent may have viewed New Mexico and the Santa Fe trade as an opportunity for a lone man to make a new start. He was apparently able to finance several wagons of trade goods for the 1829 caravan. During 1830 he evidently made three round trips from Independence, and, in 1831, an unbelievable five such journeys, one of these taking him into Chihuahua.

Newspaper accounts of the 1830 caravans are scarce. Josiah Gregg reported that the trade totalled $120,000 worth of goods taken by 60 proprietors and 140 men to Santa Fe. One of the proprietors that year was Ceran St. Vrain, who had made his first trip to New Mexico in 1825. St. Vrain seems to have been more interested in the fur trade than in the Santa Fe commerce, and he made Taos his headquarters. Then in December, 1830, Charles Bent and Ceran St. Vrain formed an important business association. Bent would handle the purchase of goods in Missouri and transport them to Taos; St. Vrain would undertake to sell them in New Mexico. Apparently it was a profitable arrangement, for it was during the next year, 1831, that Charles Bent made the alleged five trips between Missouri and New Mexico.

The year 1831 was a significant one for the Santa Fe trade. As mentioned earlier, Gregg reported its value at more than double the previous year. And his figures for 1831 were probably accurate, for that year Gregg himself made the first of his many journeys to Santa Fe. That year, also, Charles Bent took the first caravan of wagons to be pulled entirely by oxen to New Mexico. That year the famous explorer Jedediah Smith lost his life on the trail. And that year at the site of present Pueblo, Colorado, William Bent built a stockade, the forerunner of the famed Bent's Fort.

Josiah Gregg's name has become almost synonymous with the Santa Fe Trail, for between 1831 and 1840 he became one of the most important merchants in the Santa Fe trade. What is more important, he was a keen observer and had an inquiring mind. He mastered Spanish and spoke it fluently. He was curious: he pried and asked questions endlessly. Withdrawn and detached from the usual preoccupations of fur traders, although not unfriendly, Gregg moved about the frontier—Missouri, New Mexico, Texas, Chihuahua, and later Sonora and California—soaking up his experiences and pedantically recording them. His book, *Commerce of the Prairies*, published in 1844 and many times reprinted, is one of the genuine classics of American frontier history. Its popularity in its own time gave the Santa Fe trade the widest kind of publicity in this country and in Europe. And Gregg's observations are at the heart of any history of the trail and are an important source for all histories of the Southwest.

Born in Tennessee in 1806 to pioneer parents of Scotch and German ancestry, Josiah was the youngest of seven children. The family followed the frontier from Kentucky to Tennessee, Illinois, and eventually Missouri. There, in a frontier schoolhouse, Josiah fell in love with knowledge. He was an eager student with a quick intellect. In a different region or at another time he might have become a university professor. He learned surveying at the age of sixteen; at eighteen he opened a private school. At twenty he began the study of law, at which he was not successful. At twenty-four he fell seriously ill, suffering relapse after relapse from a mysterious ailment that was diagnosed as chronic dyspepsia and consumption. He was expected to die and grew so weak that he could not leave his room for days at a time. In desperation, Gregg's physician, having found no other remedy, prescribed a trip on the prairies. It would probably kill him, but recent reports had come in of the curative affects of the prairie air.

It is difficult today to realize how hopelessly ineffective mid-nineteenth-century medical science was. Indeed, it could hardly be called a science. Physicians had some knowledge of anatomy and some skill at setting broken bones or amputating mangled limbs. They knew nearly nothing else, although they "practiced" an amazing variety of "cures." Patent and packaged medicines abounded, most laced heavily with alcohol and some with hard narcotics. "Heroic" treatment was popular: it would not help unless it tasted bad, or stung, or hurt. One could not get well until his system had been cleaned out. Purgatives and nausea-inducing concoctions left patients weak and trembling. Some patients survived the treatment, which reinforced the doctors' belief in their bizarre techniques, but down deep in their hearts, doctors and patients alike knew the physician was generally helpless.

A new approach to medicine was beginning to germinate in the 1830's, one that did not reach bloom until after the Civil War, when it was known as "climatology." It was frequently observed that a change of climate often affected miraculous restorations to health. Thus sea voyages became a fad in Europe and the East, and prairie "voyages" were beginning to be recognized as possible cures for otherwise hopeless invalids. No one knew whether it was the restorative power of the open air or the rigorous discipline of a prairie trip, but some invalids experienced astonishing recoveries. Those who did not, of course, undoubtedly would have died anyway.

Gregg recovered his health, and thereafter hardly a caravan

left Missouri that did not have one or more health-seekers along. When Gregg had started his first trip in May, 1831, he was a pathetic invalid confined to a dearborn carriage. Such was the miracle of prairie travel that within two weeks he was strong enough to ride a pony. Before long he was entirely free of his sickbed and became an able-bodied member of the company.

He was employed for this first trip as a bookkeeper by Jesse Sutton, one of the merchant-proprietors. (So well did he master the essentials of the trade, including the Spanish language, that on his next trip in 1834 he went as Sutton's partner and was elected captain of the caravan.) Elisha Stanley was elected captain of Gregg's 1831 caravan, which Gregg said consisted of "nearly two hundred men without counting invalids" and carried nearly $200,000 worth of goods to Santa Fe.

At least two other caravans made the journey that spring, both smaller. One led by William L. Sublette left Independence about a month before Gregg's party. A second, led by Charles Bent, departed a week or two later. The first, the Sublette venture, became involved in one of the major tragedies of the trail's history. Sublette, David E. Jackson, and Jedediah Smith had formed a partnership in 1826 to purchase William H. Ashley's trading company. In 1830 they sold the enterprise to the Rocky Mountain Fur Company and decided to invest in the New Mexico trade. All were experienced frontiersmen, trappers, and mountain men. Smith was probably the greatest of the three and had certainly traveled more in the wilderness. He was also an important geographer and had reported on many of his explorations to the War Department. He had wandered through the Oregon country and explored the Snake and the Columbia rivers. He had been to San Diego and had journeyed the California coast with Ewing Young.

Although the prairies may have been new to many of the Sublette party that spring, the frontier was not. Twenty new wagons laden with trade goods and some eighty men made up the caravan. Unaccountably these veterans got lost while trying to follow the Cimarron cutoff. For three days they were without water, and the deprivation told heavily on men and animals alike. Sublette sent some of his hardiest men out in various directions to search for water. Smith, sturdy frontiersman that he was, went out alone. He reached the Cimarron, and his fate there was related later by Mexican traders who found his body. He had scooped a small water hole in the sands of the Cimarron bed and while quenching his parched throat was surprised by Comanches. It is not clear whether he was pierced by a lance or an arrow, but before he died he pistolled two of his attackers.

Sublette's party was led to the scene shortly afterward by the Mexican traders who had found Smith's body. Having buried him, they were proceeding toward Santa Fe when they encountered a large band of Indians referred to by Gregg as Blackfeet and Gros Ventres. Sublette's experience with Indians got them through what was described as a perilous adventure. Gregg's party, following also the Cimarron cutoff, encountered large bands of Comanches and Blackfeet, who gave them several suspenseful days and nights but did not molest the caravan. Bent's party, about a fortnight behind, also passed through the dangerous Indian country safely. It must be supposed in the absence of any record that Bent followed around the bend of the Arkansas to take the mountain route, since he was headed for his partner's post at Taos.

For Bent it must have been a hurried trip. He was reported to be back in St. Louis in August outfitting a new caravan. This one produced yet another first for the trade; as noted before, all the wagons in the small train were drawn by oxen. Two years earlier Bennet Riley had demonstrated the usefulness of the heavy bovines when he had used them to haul his military supplies. In time oxen were to predominate the plains drayage. For the Santa Fe traders oxen had three advantages over mules (or horses, for that matter). They could pull heavier loads. They were not coveted by the Indians as were horses and mules and thus were less likely to attract raids and thefts. And, if the need arose, they doubled as an emergency source of food. Mules were faster, more sure-footed, and perhaps easier to handle. Although Bent probably took the mountain route to Taos with these ox-drawn wagons, the sure-footed mules were usually more popular on that part of the trail. Among the thirty-odd men with Bent on this trip was the young Albert Pike, who later added to the literary history of the plains.

Bent's younger brother, William, who had accompanied him on the first trip to Santa Fe, had gone on to adventures of his own while Charles was almost flying back and forth along the trail during 1830 and 1831. In the winter of 1829–1830, William joined a small party of trappers at Taos bound for the Rockies in present southern Colorado, where they wintered in a crudely built stockade on the upper Arkansas. There William Bent hid two Cheyennes from a band of Comanches and initiated a friendly rapport that had important bearing on later developments.

After returning to Santa Fe, William Bent joined three other adventurers in the summer of 1830 for an expedition to present southern Arizona. At a winter camp on the Gila they turned back an Indian attack that enhanced the reputations of all four. Then only twenty-one, William Bent had already emerged as a potent leader on the southwestern frontier. The next winter he returned to the upper Arkansas and at the mouth of Fountain Creek at the site of present Pueblo, Colorado, he built a stockade. Its purpose was different from the one where two years earlier he had befriended the Cheyenne. This one was not merely to protect him while he trapped; instead, it was to serve as a trading post. Here he stockpiled goods hauled up from Taos and traded with the Indians for the furs they had taken.

Charles Bent, accompanied by two other brothers, George and Robert, visited William's stockade trading post in the summer of 1832. Probably Charles took the lead in expanding William's plans, for Charles had seen similar large operations on the Missouri. Such a post for the Indian trade would the Bent brothers build on the Arkansas. It would be large, to accommodate many people and to store quantities of trade goods and animal pelts. It would be as formidable as a fortress to protect the traders and discourage Indian raids. And it would be an oasis of civilization in the wilderness. Tradition in the Bent family ascribes a Cheyenne chief with the suggestion that the location be changed from the foot of the mountain downstream to the open plains.

Thus by the spring of 1833 work was begun on the Southwest's most important trading post—Bent's Fort on the Arkansas, located between present La Junta and Los Animas in Colorado. When completed, Bent's Fort was the most impressive sight between Independence and Santa Fe. Built of adobe bricks, with walls three feet thick, it rose two stories high and was approximately 140 by 180 feet in size. Tower bastions 21 feet in diameter reached another 6 feet into the air on the northeast and southwest corners. A six-pound cannon was swiveled on each of these. One broad wooden entry faced south toward the river with a guard post above it.

Various storage rooms and living quarters were built on the inside perimeter of the walls, and in the middle was a commodious plaza 80 by 100 feet. In time the fort housed a carpenter shop, a blacksmith shop, a council or meeting room, a billiard room, and a large dining room that was also used for entertainments. A protected wagon yard and corral were attached outside to the south and east walls.

The Bents brought scores of laborers from New Mexico to make the mud adobe bricks and build their prairie castle. It was perhaps an omen that during construction smallpox struck the encampment. St. Vrain was sent back to Taos on a mule litter; William Bent had a light case but was pox-marked the rest of his life. Bent's Fort began with an epidemic; it ended with a plague. Cholera moved into the impregnable structure in 1849. William Bent burned down what he could and abandoned the site, moving about forty miles downstream to build what is called Bent's New Fort in the Big Timbers in 1852. But the new post was never as successful as its predecessor.

When Charles Bent visited the site of William's stockade in the summer of 1832, he probably envisioned its potential success—an insight based on his past experiences and present acumen. The tradition that the actual location was suggested by a Cheyenne chief has a touch of the mystic or the occult about it. But no one made any claims of divine inspiration. On September 22 of that year, however, one Joseph Smith did claim divine revelation about another site. His revelation, unlike Bent's, led to failure and near disaster. Independence, Missouri, said Smith, was to become the "New Jerusalem" for his "Saints."

This was just two years after Smith had formally organized the Church of Jesus Christ of Latter-Day Saints in Fayette, New York, although for a decade prior to that time Smith had been receiving visions and revelations, had been visited by the angel Moroni, by

God, and by Jesus Christ, and had experienced all sorts of other miracles, including the finding of the tablets of gold on which were inscribed the Book of Mormon. A year before the revelation of the site of New Jerusalem, Smith and his followers had moved to Kirtland, Ohio, near Cleveland.

During the winter of 1832–1833 a small stream of Mormons moved into Jackson County, Missouri. Purchasing a site of about twenty acres on the southern outskirts of the new village of Independence, they also moved into vacant lots and acreage and talked vaguely of taking over other property in the name of the Lord. They were sanctimonious, aloof, and unsociably fanatic. In a matter of months resentment among the frontiersmen in Independence began to boil. In July, 1833, a mass meeting erupted against the outsiders. A mob attacked a Mormon store and newspaper and tarred-and-feathered a couple of the pious Saints, one of whom claimed to be a bishop. It was the beginning of a small reign of terror at that terminus of the Santa Fe trade.

The *Western Monitor* demanded that the Mormons leave Jackson County. Elsewhere in town the citizens began to work themselves into a frenzy. Threats were made to horsewhip all Mormons, to destroy their crops, and to ravish their daughters. The Mormons called down the wrath of God on their tormentors and, more practically perhaps, petitioned the governor for aid. Ultimately the state militia was called out to bring peace. It did so, temporarily, by helping Independence drive the Mormons entirely from Jackson County during the first week in November, 1833.

In Kirtland, Ohio, during the months that followed, Joseph Smith organized an "Army of God" to punish Independence and to take possession of New Jerusalem. The march of the Army of God against Missouri began on May 7, 1834. In Jackson County, rumors of the forthcoming attack interfered with the organization of the spring caravans for Santa Fe and provoked the creation of vigilante bands. In June an armed mob from Jackson County crossed the Missouri and met the Army of God head-on, almost routing it. Smith lost considerable prestige among his followers and, temporarily at least, abandoned his pretensions to a New Jerusalem. Mormons continued to move into Missouri, causing trouble wherever they went, and the legislature decided to create Caldwell County for their special benefit in 1836. In 1838 they were expelled from that area.

Although the so-called Mormon wars were not a direct threat to the Santa Fe trade, the unrest did create some problems at the eastern terminus. Several men prominent in the trade's history became involved, including Lilburn W. Boggs, who as lieutenant governor and governor forced the expulsion of the Mormons, and Alexander Doniphan, who served briefly as Joseph Smith's attorney. Perhaps the most interesting aspect of the Mormon trouble is the fact that none of the Mormons entered the trade or followed the Santa Fe Trail west.

Josiah Gregg, who had become a temporary resident of Santa Fe, returned to Missouri at the beginning of the Mormon wars in the fall of 1833, but he was more concerned with Comanche trouble on the prairie than with the clash between religious fanaticism and bigotry. Repeated rumors of threatened Comanche attacks on the wagon trains in the spring of 1834 caused the traders to organize more carefully and resulted in the offer by the military of an armed escort to the Mexican boundary. The traders gathered at Franklin and elected Gregg captain of the out-going caravan. Gregg had become a full partner of Jesse Sutton, the man who had first employed him as a clerk. Lieutenant John H. K. Burgwin, later to distinguish himself in the Taos Rebellion, brought the army's offer of assistance to Gregg, who of course accepted it.

The military escort was commanded by Captain Clifton Wharton, Company A, First Dragoon Regiment. In a generalized way the dragoons were predecessor to the famed cavalry troops of the West. They were for the most part mounted, unlike the clumsy escort of 1829 under Bennet Riley. Gregg's caravan started for Santa Fe near the end of May; Wharton's column rode from Fort Gibson to intersect the Santa Fe Trail on June 3 near the Neosho River. The traders reached them a few days later, and they moved down the well-known route toward the Arkansas.

The traders' anxiety about Indian attacks became evident on June 17 when a friendly party of Kansa Indians were sighted. It was all Wharton and Gregg could do to keep some of the inexperienced men from opening fire. But the two leaders knew of the 1825 treaty and calmed their men. The Indians, however, were a nuisance, and some pilfering was reported, which did not leave the traders happy. Then a few days later a band of Comanches was encountered near the Arkansas.

The Comanches made signs of peace; Captain Wharton, who had no idea of their numbers, decided to risk a visit to their en- campment under a flag of truce. The Indians apparently were a raiding party, but through interpreters they agreed to hold peace talks the following day. No more than five of the whites were to meet with Comanche leaders across the river the following day. The traders were unhappy with Wharton's arrangements, and many wanted to open fire on the Indians, but Wharton believed it would be possible to negotiate. Gregg's attitude is unknown, but the next day, before Wharton was aware of it, Gregg himself met with the Comanches, taking four of his own men with him thus to exclude the military officer from the talks.

Wharton was incensed. Neither Gregg's later book nor his cor- respondence explains this usurpation of authority and initiative. Gregg evidently represented himself to the Indians as the overall commander of the American party. Under an uneasy agreement with the Indians, Gregg then led the trading caravan across the Arkansas. Wharton at first refused to continue with the escort but was finally persuaded by Gregg, who believed the Indians intended to attack, to accompany them as far as the Cimarron. Since this was east of the supposed location of the 100th meridian, the military could cross the Arkansas without entering Mexican territory. Troops and traders parted finally on June 28. Wharton, somewhat unhappy with the venture, reported that he did not believe further military escorts were needed on the trail in United States territory. The greatest danger, he asserted, was on the Mexican side and in fact within 90 to 100 miles of Santa Fe. He recommended the negotia- tion of a treaty with Mexico that would permit a United States escort to accompany the caravans into Santa Fe and return with them. His suggestion had much merit but went totally unheeded.

Negotiations with the Mexican government during that period were virtually impossible. After the Centralists seized power in 1829, Joel Poinsett, the American minister, had been declared *per- sona non grata*. He had made the tactical as well as diplomatic mistake of supporting the Federalist cause in the power struggle of 1828–1829. Regular relations were restored when President Jackson sent Anthony Butler to the Mexican capital. Butler's understanding of Mexico seems to have been even weaker than Poinsett's, however; where Poinsett had erred on the side of ideology, Butler erred on the side of a sordid assessment of the Centralists. Butler seems to have thought that bribery and corruption were the sole forces in Mexican politics. That he had reason for such a notion is obvious, but he mistook the depths of corruption and was inept in bribery. "What a scamp," Jackson later called him. But he was probably not nearly as despicable a figure as his abolitionist and Whig political enemies depicted him.

Besides, his task in Mexico was impossible in the political climate that prevailed. Butler's primary mission was to settle the claims question between the United States and Mexico. This was a highly complex issue, subject even today to wide variance of historical interpretation. A number of financial claims against the successive governments of Mexico—revolutionary, elective, and insurgent—had been filed by United States citizens with the American State Department. Whether some of the claims were illegitimate or whether many of them were exaggerated is not germane to the central issue: that the various governments in Mexico had evaded not only a settlement but even a discussion of the matter. This was indeed one reason for Poinsett's dismissal, and the problem gave rise to the story that Jackson insulted Mexico by offering to buy Texas. Using the precedent of the Treaty of 1819 with Spain, in which Spain had swapped Florida to the United States for the claims against her, Jackson instructed Butler to attempt to trade the claims against Mexico for territory in present Texas. It was a much more logical and inoffensive gesture than deprecating historians have portrayed it.

Butler was replaced by Powhatan Ellis. More important, the Centralist government fell to Santa Anna's Federalist coalition, and the idealistic reformer Valentín Gómez Farías, elected vice-president, took office as president when Santa Anna refused to serve. There followed a series of muddled maneuverings while Santa Anna tested the disposition of the Mexican people for liberal reform. In

1834 he assumed the reins of government and by mid-1835 emerged from his false cloak of federalism as the Centralist dictator of Mexico.

The Constitution of 1824 was abrogated, and the hapless Mexican republic was converted into a dictatorship. The federal states became hierarchical departments of the central government. Elected officials, including governors, were replaced by Santa Anna's appointees. All Mexico was in a state of rebellion by the end of the year. Distant California refused to acknowledge Santa Anna's government; Zacatecas was ground under a military rule; Yucatan broke into insurgency; and Texas, as described in a later chapter, aided by American volunteers, shook itself free from the dictatorship as an independent republic in 1836.

There is little record of the reaction in New Mexico to the rise of the Centralist tyranny and the overthrow of the republic. The region had long been one of the most politically conservative areas of Mexico, remaining generally aloof even from the independence movement itself. Politics and the economy were dominated by the *ricos*—the wealthy merchants and landowners. The Centralist regime was accepted, along with its appointed minions, with seeming placidity. Any undercurrent of rebellion passed unnoticed, and the trade with Missouri continued relatively smoothly during the Texas Revolution.

But there was a flare-up in New Mexico in 1837 and 1838. Elements of the population north of Santa Fe, sneeringly referred to by Manuel Armijo, who later was governor, as nothing but poor Indians (*genizaros*—Hispanicized persons of Indian but non-Pueblo descent) arose under the leadership of self-styled Federalist "Governor" José Gonzales in confused support of the defunct federal constitution and in some imitation of Texas. The chief problem seems to have been local political turmoil in the valley of the Santa Cruz River. Following the reversal of a decision of an alcalde at La Cañada, the Centralist-appointed governor and military commander, Albino Pérez, dismissed the alcalde from office. Pérez, who had never been in New Mexico before his appointment to office, was not popular, especially with the poorer people and certainly not with those who opposed the dictatorship of the Centralist government.

On August 3, 1837, the people of the Santa Cruz area adopted a revolutionary *plan,* or declaration, and raised a motley army. Their announcement called for opposition to the Centralist proposals and particularly to new taxes. The little army marched toward Santa Fe and was met by government forces on August 8. The rebels won a victory, possibly because many of the government troops promptly defected and joined the rebels. Governor Pérez and at least a half-dozen of his minions were executed, and on August 9 the insurgents occupied Santa Fe, electing José Gonzales governor of New Mexico.

Threats of plunder and continued violence frightened many away from the cause. South of Santa Fe Manuel Armijo seized leadership of forces that were coalescing against the rebels. Armijo entered the capital on September 12 and then pursued the fleeing rebels to Pojoaque, where he routed them. Armijo then proclaimed himself "political and military chief" of New Mexico under the Centralists' departmental plan. On January 17, 1838, New Mexico was openly brought under Centralist authority when Armijo convened the "departmental junta." A new rebellion broke out in the Santa Cruz region, but Armijo had suppressed it before the month was out.

The government in Mexico City soon confirmed Armijo in office. He ruled New Mexico with a large degree of military tyranny for the Centralist regime until the outbreak of the war between the United States and Mexico, except for an interim period in 1844 and 1845. When American troops entered New Mexico, Armijo found himself utterly devoid of local support, and without the firing of a shot, the territory passed to the United States.

During this Centralist period, the trade from Missouri continued, although individual traders objected to Armijo's rule. Gregg's comments about "his majesty," as he referred to Armijo, are not kind. Among Armijo's greatest outrages were his treatment of the foreigners—Texans, Americans, and Britishers—of the Texan–Santa Fe Expedition of 1841.

CHAPTER 10

Texas and the Santa Fe Trade

Both the occasional penetrations to the west coast and the more intensive commercial developments of the Chihuahua trade had side effects of enduring significance. Mexicans were brought into contact with American ideas of political freedom and comparative economic *laissez faire*. And Americans moved into northern Mexico, first by the scores, then by the hundreds, and ultimately by the thousands. A social process was begun that finally was to result in the separation from Mexico of a vast portion of its northern territory. At no time, however, until 1846 was the process irreversible or the result inevitable. It was, as is all history, a gradual emergence from a thousand commingling factors.

One of these groups of factors is of peripheral importance to the Santa Fe trade but of central importance to the Americanization of the Southwest. Of the thousands of Americans who immigrated to Mexico before the Mexican War, the overwhelming majority went to Texas, not because of the trade but because Mexico's generous land policies attracted them as permanent settlers. Two main streams of historical development flowed from this to affect the Santa Fe trade: the independence of the Republic of Texas, which led to the Mexican War and the cession of territory to the United States, and the futile attempt by the Republic of Texas to tap the commerce of the prairies.

The initial American colonization of Texas had begun in the last year of Spanish control. After independence the imperial government of Iturbide in Mexico sanctioned the first colony, and the ensuing constitutional government of the Republic of Mexico opened wide the doors to American immigration and colonization in 1824 and 1825. Hundreds of families migrated from the United States to receive the bountiful league and *labor* grants (4,605 acres) as settlers. The successful revolution of the autocratic and generally anti-American Centralists brought this migration to an end with the law of April 6, 1830. But with the overthrow of the Centralists and the re-establishment of constitutional government by the Federalists in 1834, American immigration began again.

Then, out of the complicated turmoil of Mexican politics, as described earlier, Santa Anna created a dictatorial state, first undermining constitutional government and finally abrogating the Constitution of 1824. In name the president but in fact the head of the Centralist faction and the dictator of Mexico, in October, 1835, he replaced the constitution with an arbitrary frame of government called the Seven Laws. Angry Federalist uprisings spread across Mexico. Among these was an outbreak of fighting in Texas.

Before the end of 1835 Texas Federalists, both Anglos and Hispanics, had driven the Centralist forces out of Texas. A provisional state government was organized under the now-defunct Constitution of 1824. Centralist officers who had surrendered in San Antonio on December 10, 1835, were forced to pledge themselves not to interfere with the restoration of constitutional government in Mexico, and those troops under their command who would swear allegiance to the constitution were allowed to remain in Texas. Thus the little war that was to secure the independence of Texas began, not as a revolution against Mexico, but as a rebellion against centralism and as an attempt to help restore the constitutional government in that star-crossed country.

Having defeated rebellions elsewhere in Mexico, Santa Anna determined to suppress the Texas insurgency ruthlessly. Calling himself the "Napoleon of the West," he organized an army and marched into Texas in February, 1836. As he was invading, the people of Texas were in the process of reappraising their objectives and reorganizing their government. A convention declared the independence of Texas as a separate nation on March 2, wrote a new constitution, and established an *ad interim* government.

Santa Anna's armies, some six to eight thousand strong, overwhelmed and slaughtered the defenders of South Texas at the Alamo and Goliad, and Santa Anna set off in hot pursuit of the *ad interim*

Texas government and the little Texas army of about a thousand men. Spring floods and swollen rivers caused Santa Anna to fragment his forces, and when he confronted Sam Houston and the Texans at the battle of San Jacinto on April 21, 1836, he commanded fewer than a thousand men to Houston's eight hundred odd. Despite reinforcements of about five hundred during the day, Santa Anna was utterly defeated, due largely to the unprecedented midafternoon attack ordered by Houston. The Mexican dictator himself was taken captive in the rout that followed. Although about 80 percent of his forces were still in Texas, slowly converging on the Texans, Santa Anna was a frightened prisoner, and he hastily ordered his army south of the Rio Grande to save his own neck from the long stretch.

Had it not been for the unusual floods that separated the Mexican forces, had it not been for the incredible luck of the capture of Santa Anna, and had it not been for his officers' questionable decision to obey his order to evacuate Texas, the Texas Revolution would have been a dismal failure. But in such fashion are the realities of history frequently unpredictable and illogical.

Despite countless difficulties, the new Republic of Texas took shape and survived tenously for a decade before it was annexed to the United States. Another illogical quirk of Clio's linked the republic to New Mexico and to the Santa Fe trade. The first Texas congress, called upon to delineate the boundaries of the new nation, laid outrageous claim to the entire length of the Rio Grande, from its mouth to its source and north to the 42nd parallel and the treaty line of 1819. Although the claim was justifiable, at least by right of revolution, along the lower courses of the Rio Grande, it was hopelessly and totally unwarranted upstream from Laredo or possibly present Eagle Pass, where the Camino Real in Texas had crossed the Rio Grande. The ridiculous claim to the upper Rio Grande of course passed right through the heart of the ancient province of New Mexico and included Albuquerque, Santa Fe, and Taos. On the basis of this claim, the Republic of Texas spread across the trail from Missouri.

It was the attempt of the Texas government to establish jurisdiction in the area and to lure at least a part of the Santa Fe commerce away from Missouri and across Texas that led to the Texan–

Santa Fe Expedition of 1841. According to contemporary maps, the distance from Santa Fe to the Texas coast was about the same, maybe closer, than the overland distance to the Missouri River. Why, reasoned some enterprising Texans, could not the trade be diverted into Texas? If the overland route was shorter or more practical, certainly coastal shipping from Texas ports would be as cheap, if not cheaper, than Missouri, Mississippi, and Ohio river shipping. Besides, coastal freight to and from the eastern United States could bypass the expensive drayage over the Appalachian Mountains.

There was also a possibility of opening a direct trade with Chihuahua from Texas. A large caravan of Chihuahua merchants had made an arduous journey from Chihuahua across Texas to Arkansas and back in 1839 and 1840. With over a hundred men, protected by fifty dragoons and carrying between two and three hundred thousand dollars in specie, they reached Fort Towson, Indian Territory, only after spending weeks wandering through the uncharted plains and prairies of West Texas. They returned in the spring of 1840, passing through settlements in northeastern Texas, their ranks swollen to nearly three hundred (the increase presumably Americans), with a caravan of seventy wagons of merchandise. Dr. Henry Connelly, later governor of New Mexico, accompanied the party from Chihuahua and back. He reported that the Texans welcomed them very warmly. It is surprising that this venture was not followed by the opening of a more direct route through San Antonio to the Texas coast. Such a route was not frequented until after the Mexican War.

The Chihuahua caravan, however, must have increased interest in the project to open trade directly with Santa Fe. Mirabeau B. Lamar, who had been elected president of the Republic of Texas in 1838, had grandiose plans for the development of the republic as a powerful nation in North America. Among his many schemes was the opening of trade with Santa Fe. This would benefit Texas, not only from the flow of commerce, but also from the collection of customs duties. Many Texans, including Lamar, believed that the bulk of New Mexico's populace were opposed to Mexico's Centralist government. The unsuccessful rebellion in northern New Mexico had lent credibility to such thinking. In his 1839 message to the Texas congress, Lamar proposed a government-sponsored expedition to

Santa Fe to offer Texas jurisdiction to New Mexicans, but congress took no action. Newspapers, however, picked up the idea and through editorials tried to promote it and to persuade Lamar to undertake it as an executive project. Others joined in the cry, and when the Texas congress reassembled in November, 1840, Lamar again asked it to support an expedition to Santa Fe. A bill was introduced but died without passage when congress adjourned. On the grounds that the lawmakers had approved the principle of the expedition, however, Lamar proceeded to organize it.

Its announced objectives were to open trade with Santa Fe and to offer to extend the jurisdiction of Texas to the people of New Mexico. To fulfill the first, merchants were invited to join the caravan with pack animals or wagons of trade goods. To fulfill the second, three commissioners (William G. Cooke, Richard F. Brenham, and José Antonio Navarro) were appointed to organize a government in New Mexico, if it were indicated that the people there wanted to join the Republic of Texas. This idea was not as far-fetched as it has frequently been made to seem. Throughout Mexico, and especially in the northern provinces, there was resentment against the Centralist regime. Through American traders in Santa Fe, chiefly William G. Dryden, Lamar had been led to believe that leaders in New Mexico would be glad to unite with Texas under a republican form of government.

The call for volunteers went out, and during the late spring of 1841 they began arriving by the scores in the brand-new town of Austin, capital of the republic. Some came in hopes of profit from the trade with Santa Fe (which by this time had become considerably exaggerated); others came for adventure. Perhaps the most incongruous merchants to appear were George Thomas Howard and Tom S. Lubbock, both Texas Rangers who had taken leaves, pooled their resources, borrowed everything they could, and filled a wagon with goods they fancied would bring them a fortune in Santa Fe. Lubbock, who was only twenty-four, had rushed to Texas at the age of nineteen to fight in the Texas Revolution. Howard was three years older but possibly more of a daredevil. His exploits, such as singlehandedly leading a party of wily Comanches into ambush, had already gained him much renown. Among the other adventurers were two whose published accounts were to make the Texan–Santa

Fe Expedition internationally famous and to give it a place in North American history larger than it warrants: George Wilkins Kendall, editor of the New Orleans *Picayune,* and Thomas Falconer, a lawyer from England.

In all, the expedition was to total over three hundred volunteers, who called themselves the Santa Fe Pioneers. They were armed and organized into six military companies, including one of artillery. Hugh McLeod, a twenty-seven-year-old West Point graduate who had resigned his commission to come to Texas in 1836 and was at the time serving as adjutant general of the republic, was made commander of the expedition while on the march. The warlike aspect of the expedition provoked much comment then and later. The announced intentions of the expedition were pacific, but it headed for New Mexico armed as if for conquest. Certainly Centralist officials of Mexico declared it to be an armed invasion, and when rumors of it reached Manuel Armijo, then governor of New Mexico, he prepared to meet it as such. But this was ridiculous. How could a mere three hundred-odd men, laden with merchant wagons and over six hundred miles from their nearest supply point, constitute a serious military threat? Their armament was for hunting game for food and for protection against the Comanches whose territory they would cross. The quasi-military organization was for trail discipline across unexplored country. Even caravans traveling the well-known Santa Fe Trail from Missouri were frequently so organized and armed.

The expedition moved out in late June, 1841, optimistic, enthusiastic, and full-spirited. The air of gaiety that surrounded its departure was to be displaced by clouds of disappointment, however. Despite his military training and his rather considerable experience, for a young man, as an Indian fighter, McLeod proved to be a poor leader. Dissension appeared among the Pioneers within a few weeks and grew almost to the point of open rebellion. Furthermore, McLeod was not cautious with his supplies, which was to prove ruinous before the expedition reached New Mexico. And finally, McLeod literally did not know where he was leading the expedition. The region between Austin and Santa Fe was unexplored, and McLeod depended upon the inaccurate maps of the time, a small hand compass, the reports of a "spy" (or reconnaissance) company, rumors, vague directions from occasional Indians encountered, and the advice of a Mexican on the expedition who claimed to have once lived in Taos. Such aids to prairie navigation were hopelessly unreliable.

The stalwart and intrepid Santa Fe Pioneers got lost. They proceeded north from Austin to the breaks of the Pease River and turned westward across some of the most forbidding landscape in all of West Texas. They were harassed by hostile Indians, ran short on provisions, and suffered a severe scarcity of water. When they reached the foot of the caprock, sternly demarking the edge of the High Plains, they were desperate. They did not know where they were, how far it was to Santa Fe, or how they could cross the waterless plains. In a fateful decision, McLeod divided the command, now decimated by deaths from Indian attacks and privations (and one suicide). One hundred men, including Howard, Lubbock, Kendall, and Commissioner Cooke, were sent ahead in hopes of finding a New Mexico settlement and sending aid to the remainder of the Pioneers, who went into camp to await word. If word did not come, they would try to return to Austin.

The advance party, commanded by John S. Sutton, mounted the plains with five days' provisions and wandered for thirteen days before they struck a camp of Mexican hunters on the Canadian River in present New Mexico. According to Kendall, the Pioneers were now in truly desperate condition. Six men, including a William P. Lewis, were sent into San Miguel, about forty miles distant, to get help. The six were surrounded outside of San Miguel by an advance detachment of an army that Armijo was leading east to intercept the Texans. They were made prisoners, bound, and sent under guard to Santa Fe. On the way they encountered Armijo with about a thousand men. Lewis, however, went with the New Mexicans as interpreter.

He served not only as interpreter but also as devil's advocate. When Armijo's troops encountered the Sutton-Cooke party, Lewis artfully persuaded his comrades to lay down their arms. They were promptly made prisoner and bound together in groups of six or eight by Mexican lariats. Lewis's perfidy outraged the Texans, but they were helpless. Lewis later was rewarded with a share of the booty Armijo got from the Texan caravan, went to Chihuahua, then to Guaymas, then to the Sandwich Islands, and was swallowed up in obscurity, apparently never daring to return to Texas or any place in the United States. The Sutton-Cooke advance party was marched to Santa Fe and then to Mexico City via Chihuahua, every torturous step on foot.

Meantime, McLeod and the main party, having received a message from Cooke sent before Lewis's treachery, had started across from the Llano Estacado. Armijo and his troops rode eastward to meet them. On October 5, 1841, near present Tucumcari, hopelessly outnumbered, McLeod and his emaciated men turned over their arms and surrendered. They too were marched off on foot to Mexico City. All the goods, wagons, teams, and mounts of the Texans were confiscated by Armijo, much of the proceeds from which undoubtedly found its way into his private coffers.

The trek of the two contingents of prisoners under the bayonets and muskets of their Centralist guards was unnecessarily cruel and harsh. A number died of privation and many were exposed to smallpox. Little respite was given the sick or the lame, a few of whom were killed in cold blood. The misery of the hapless prisoners aroused sympathy not only among Americans and Europeans living in Mexico but also in the hearts of many Mexicans. Under diplomatic and domestic pressure, the government released the prisoners in June, 1842. Thus ended Texas' first attempt to capitalize on its spurious claim to New Mexico.

The next attempt came in 1843 and was a direct menace to the Santa Fe trade. During 1842 relations between the Republic of Texas and the Centralist government in Mexico had worsened. A state of war (or rebellion) still existed because of the government's adamant refusal to recognize Texas independence. In the spring the Texas navy, under a lease agreement, joined with the rebellious Federalist government of Yucatan to harass the Centralists. Twice during the year Santa Anna ordered token invasions of Texas, under Rafael Vásquez in March and under Adrian Woll in August, which penetrated as far as San Antonio. The Texas congress voted a declaration of war, and although Houston vetoed it, the whole of Texas was in an uproar over the invasions as well as over the treatment of the Santa Fe prisoners.

There followed a number of rather silly actions by Texas, some

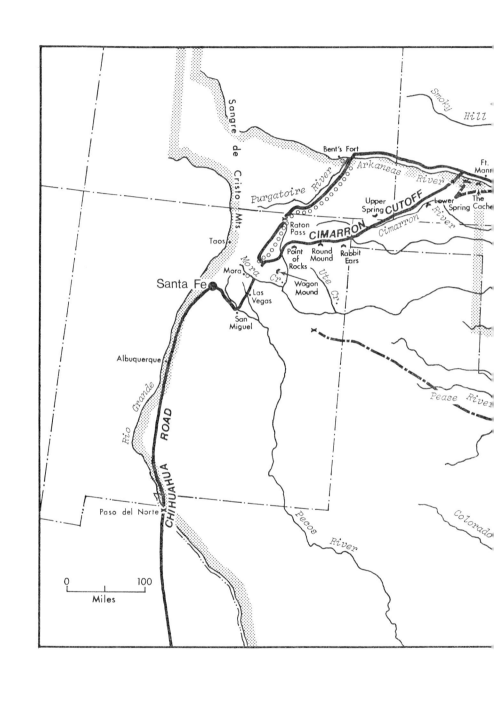

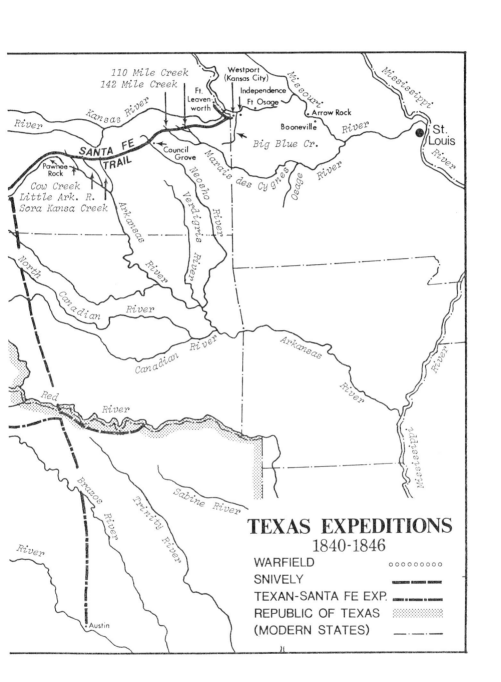

110 Mile Creek
142 Mile Creek

Westport
(Kansas City)

Independence

Ft.
Leaven-
worth

Ft Osage

Missouri

Mississippi

Kansas River

Arrow Rock

Booneville

Big Blue Cr.

River

St.
Louis

River

SANTA FE
TRAIL

Council
Grove

Pawnee
Rock

Cow Creek
Little Ark. R.
Sora Kansa Creek

Arkansas

River

Neosho River

Verdigris River

Marais des Cygnes

Osage River

North

Canadian

River

Canadian River

Arkansas

River

River

Mississippi

Red

River

Brazos River

Trinity River

Sabine River

River

Austin

TEXAS EXPEDITIONS
1840-1846

WARFIELD ○○○○○○○○○
SNIVELY
TEXAN-SANTA FE EXP.
REPUBLIC OF TEXAS
(MODERN STATES)

of which affected the Santa Fe trade. The congress passed a new boundary statute annexing all the territory south of the 42nd parallel to the Pacific coast; President Houston vetoed it. Apparently without Houston's knowledge, Secretary of War George W. Hockley authorized one Charles A. Warfield, a Missouri fur trader and resident of New Mexico, to raise a force of eight hundred men for retaliatory raids on New Mexico. And, possibly to prevent any further such extralegal activities, Houston authorized a respectable Texas citizen, Jacob Snively, former paymaster general of the Texas army, to raise another somewhat similar force whose character and objectives were substantially different.

Warfield received his commission in August, 1842. It empowered him to levy contributions on Mexican settlements in the name of the Republic of Texas and to capture Mexican property. One-half the spoils were to be turned over to the government. At best, the Warfield expedition was a shady affair. He gathered only twenty-four men, who, like himself, were mountain men and non-Texans, at Bent's Fort on the Arkansas and made one raid, in May, 1843, on Mora, New Mexico. In a brief skirmish they killed five Mexican soldiers, took eighteen prisoners who were released the next day, and captured about seventy horses. Mexican troops then stampeded the horses, including the expedition's own herd, captured five of Warfield's men, and forced the remainder to withdraw on foot back to Bent's Fort. The escapade was purely and simply a reckless filibuster by unprincipled men. But it was done in the name of the Republic of Texas and cast a very long shadow over Texas–New Mexico relations for many years to come. And it gave an unsavory smell to Jacob Snively's fiasco, which followed.

Snively's proposal, made in January, 1843, before the Warfield group had even assembled at Bent's, had a much greater aura of legality about it; the commission he requested was not totally unlike the letters of marque issued to privateers on the high seas. Snively wanted to raise an expedition to capture Mexican caravans plying the Santa Fe Trail across territory claimed by Texas. Houston authorized him to raise three hundred volunteers to operate in that area and empowered him to confiscate Mexican commerce in the name of Texas, provided that half the spoils were turned over to the government. "The merchandise and other property of all Mexican citizens will be a lawful prize," read Snively's commission, which was issued in February, 1843. He was warned to be most careful not to infringe on United States territory north of the Arkansas, as "the object of the expedition is to retaliate and make reclamation for injuries sustained by Texas citizens."

The enterprise attracted perhaps two hundred volunteers who rendezvoused near the western outpost on the Red River known as Coffee's Station in April, 1843, to carry, as one historian wrote, "their letters of marque and reprisal across a sea of grass." They set out in late April, reached the Arkansas River in May, and by June took a position that enabled them to command the Cimarron cutoff. There the "Invincibles," as they vaingloriously called themselves, awaited the passage of a Mexican caravan. And there they were joined by Charles A. Warfield and a few of his men.

Meantime, probably unknown to Snively and possibly unknown to Warfield, a tragic attack had been made on a small Mexican caravan in United States territory by a brigand who later declared he had authorization from Texas through Warfield. This was John McDaniel, who with about fifteen followers left Westport, Kansas, in April and fell upon Antonio José Chávez on the Little Arkansas. Chávez, an Albuquerque merchant, had left Santa Fe with a few friends and servants, carrying a reputed $12,000 in specie to purchase merchandise and equip a return caravan. He and several of his party were brutally murdered, and McDaniel and his men stole the funds. Fortunately the attack was quickly discovered, and McDaniel was apprehended.

He said that he had been authorized by Warfield to enlist volunteers in Missouri in the name of the Republic of Texas and that he was on route to join Warfield at Bent's Fort when he came across the Chávez venture. His claimed affiliation with Texas was widely publicized, although it was without any support, and it would be fatuous to believe that he thought he was in Texas territory when he made the unprovoked attack. However, his activities, together with the Warfield raid and rumors of the Snively expedition, led the United States Army to send a detachment of troops to patrol the Arkansas for the protection of travelers in American territory.

At the same time Governor Armijo dispatched a Mexican force of about one hundred men to repel the Texans. The Mexican soldiers proceeded up the trail along the Cimarron cutoff and late in June were discovered by Snively's forces. A battle ensued. Snively reported no Texas losses and eighteen Mexicans killed, eighteen wounded, and sixty-two taken prisoner. How many escaped in the melee is unknown. The prisoners were soon released to make their way back to the Rio Grande settlements. The booty was disappointing—only a few Mexican weapons and a small amount of ammunition.

Many of the Invincibles became discouraged and wanted to return home. A week after the battle, seventy-six men elected Eli Chandler their leader and split off from the Snively command. On June 30 Snively's group encountered the United States Army troops from Fort Leavenworth. The American detachment, about two hundred strong, was commanded by Phillip St. George Cooke. Cooke had been sent out to give protection to a wagon train of Mexican merchants headed from Missouri to Santa Fe, and to this purpose he was patrolling the Arkansas.

At the encounter, the Americans were on the north side of the Arkansas, and the Texans under Snively, fewer than a hundred men remaining, on the south side. Both raised flags of truce. After a parley, Snively crossed over to confer with Cooke. He was forced to surrender his arms, and then Cooke and his men crossed to the Texas side and demanded that the Texans give up their weapons. They were allowed to keep ten guns for the lot of them for hunting purposes and were required to return home. The Texans, somehow anticipating this demand, had hidden their own arms and surrendered those they had taken from the Mexican soldiers. Satisfied, Cooke withdrew the following day, taking with him to the United States some of the Texans who wished to go.

Cooke's actions were certainly moderate and circumspect, considering the circumstances, but the question looms whether the confrontation and Texan surrender was within the limits of the United States, as set by the Treaty of 1819. In this area the treaty specified the 100th meridian to the Arkansas River and thence up the Arkansas. Cooke had crossed to the south side of the Arkansas. Was he east of the 100th meridian and still on United States soil? The Texans did not believe so, being confident that they were at least forty miles *west* of the dividing meridian. They based their location on the inaccurate Melish map of 1819, which had been referred to in the treaty. Cooke, on the other hand, probably had more up-to-date and reliable information about the location of the line. However, he could not have been sure. In point of fact and actually unknown to either party, the Texas camp at a place called Ferguson's Grove was about ten miles east of the 100th meridian as it was later (in 1896) located. But if the matter had been taken to an international court of law, Snively could have put up a very strong argument that Cooke had assaulted Texas troops on territory claimed by Texas.

Snively's command marched back to a small tributary of the Arkansas a few miles away, where they reunited with the men under Chandler who had not yet departed for home. Dissension arose again. Some still wanted to return, but some wanted to lie in wait for a caravan Cooke had been protecting after it clearly had crossed the treaty line. Snively resigned, the Texans divided and some left for home and the remnant, now reduced to about seventy, elected Warfield to command and moved south along the tracks of the Santa Fe trail to the Cimarron. Near a place identified by the Texans as Wagon Bed Springs (probably the Upper Cimarron Springs), they cut the sign of a large body of mounted men. A Mexican guide with them said it was the tracks of Governor Armijo himself with eight or nine hundred men. Warfield accepted this rather intuitive insight and peremptorily ordered the Texans to withdraw. The tracks they saw, however, were not those of an army under Armijo but of a relatively small body of Mexican hunters. The next day, July 14, Warfield resigned, and Snively was re-elected. He led the dejected Invincibles back into Texas and disbanded them at Bird's Fort on the upper Trinity River.

Thus, in three attempts to establish some kind of jurisdiction in New Mexico and reap some sort of profit from the Santa Fe trade, the Texas expeditions had only suffered defeat and ignominy and had left a heritage of bad feeling between Texas and New Mexico, further tainted by the wholly uncreditable attack of John McDaniel on Antonio José Chávez. Except for that, the trade between Missouri and Santa Fe was undisturbed by the Texas ambitions.

This commercial relationship continued to prosper and expand during the years preceding the outbreak of the war between the United States and Mexico, although the trade was affected by increasingly cumbersome regulations and by changes in the Mexican political scenery. Santa Anna had climbed back to power by 1841, following his heroics at Veracruz during the "Pastry War," the French attack of 1838.

CHAPTER 11

The Mexican War

1844. In Mexico Santa Anna's second dictatorship came to an end. His treasury was drained, many of his supporters became disillusioned, and others grew dissatisfied with his vain and faltering leadership. It was almost as if his wooden leg, the result of his heroism in the Pastry War of 1838, had somehow become symbolic of his stance as Mexico's chieftain. Once he had stood with one foot in the Federalist camp and the other in the Centralist. In 1835 he had deserted his Federalist following; in 1844 the Federalists moved out from under him. And he fell. A moderate leader named José Joaquín Herrera garnered support from both disillusioned Federalists and disaffected Centralists. In December, 1844, Santa Anna found valor in discretion, surrendered to Herrera's forces, and accepted exile in Cuba as the price of his life. Neither he nor the hardcore *santanistas* expected it to be permanent, and it was not.

1844. In the United States one of the most important elections in American history took place. The Whig general, William Henry Harrison, had died in office and had been replaced as president by his vice-president, apostate Democrat John Tyler. The Whig leadership split apart. The cabinet, save for Daniel Webster, who lingered a while longer as secretary of state, resigned as one man. And after the Webster-Ashburton Treaty with Great Britain had been concluded, Webster also resigned. Tyler made a strong bid to annex Texas to the Union, but the treaty that had been negotiated with the Republic of Texas failed of ratification in the Senate. This issue, then, became the central theme of the Democratic presidential campaign that year. A candidate, whom historians invariably refer to as a dark horse and whose character and later administration have been grossly maligned, was found in Tennessee Democrat James Knox Polk. To the annexation of Texas, the Democrats added the acquisition of Oregon as a campaign issue. It has been called an expansionist platform, but it was more acquiescent than aggressive in nature. Texas was pleading on bended knees for admission, and the unnatural joint occupation of the Oregon country with Great Britain had to be brought to an end. Polk was elected with a fair majority but with little to prepare him or the nation for possible wars with both Britain and Mexico.

1844. On the Santa Fe Trail there was little noticeable reaction to American politics. No comment has been found in Missouri newspapers on the annexation of Texas—made probable by the results of the election—or on the effects that republic's pretentious boundary claim might have on the trade with Santa Fe. Politics in Mexico, however, had marked effects on the trade. On August 7, 1843, Santa Anna issued a decree closing the northern boundaries of Mexico to American commerce. Some of the traders believed this was a retaliation for the Texan–Santa Fe Expedition. Then came a later regulation heavily taxing the exportation of bullion, which took the profit out of the sale of goods already in New Mexico and Chihuahua. A somewhat exaggerated story in the St. Louis *Democrat* the following spring said that every trader in Mexico was forced to close his business on short notice and that the merchants were forced to dispose of the goods they had on hand at distress prices.

The ban on trade was unpopular in the northern Mexican provinces, and even before the overthrow of the Santa Anna government, it was ended, rescinded by the government on March 31, 1844. Trade was resumed in April, and the caravans began to roll again in the summer of 1844. According to one report a hundred wagons and some two hundred men made the now-familiar trek in the last half of the year, exporting goods to the total value of $200,000.

1845. In Mexico Herrera appointed a moderate cabinet of mixed political persuasion and called back to Mexico City the delegates, most of them Federalists, to the last elected congress, which Santa Anna had peremptorily sent home in the summer of 1842. The Herrera government hoped to repair Mexico's wrecked finances, stabilize its unsettled domestic politics, and resolve its foreign problems, especially those with the United States. But moderation is

"The Santa Fe Trade," a painting by Frederic Remington. (Courtesy, Kansas State Historical Society, Topeka.)

Left. As a young officer, William H. Emory spearheaded the exploration of New Mexico. During the Civil War he rose to the rank of brigadier general. *Right.* As a captain assigned to frontier duty in Kansas in 1829, Bennet Riley furnished military escorts for traders who plied the Santa Fe Trail. (Courtesy, Kansas State Historical Society, Topeka.)

The Last Chance Store at Council Grove, Kansas, offered various commodities to traders bound west for Santa Fe. (Courtesy, Kansas State Historical Society, Topeka.)

Mexican traders with an *atajo* of pack mules on the Santa Fe Trail. (From Josiah Gregg, *The Commerce of the Prairies*, Dallas, 1933.)

A Santa Fe trader from a print of 1835. (From Ralph Emerson Twichell, *The Leading Facts of New Mexico History*, vol. II.)

"March of the Caravans." Here Santa Fe traders are crossing the plains four abreast, a frequent practice. (From Josiah Gregg, *The Commerce of the Prairies*, Dallas, 1933.)

Above. The Taos Pueblo Indian village at Taos, New Mexico, as it appeared in the nineteenth century. Sibley and his men wintered at Taos in 1825–1826. (From Chas. S. Gleed, *Overland Guide from the Missouri River to the Pacific Ocean via Kansas, Colorado, New Mexico, Arizona, and California*, rev. ed., Chicago, 1883.)

Below. Arrival of a caravan at Santa Fe. (Courtesy, Kansas State Historical Society, Topeka.)

Unloading Missouri trade wagons in Santa Fe. (From Chas. S. Gleed, *From River to Sea: a Tourist's Guide from the Missouri River to the Pacific Ocean via Kansas, Colorado, New Mexico, Arizona, and California*, Chicago, 1882.)

The east side of the plaza in Santa Fe, showing the oxen-drawn wagons of Missouri merchants. (From J. H. Beadle, *The Undeveloped West; or Five Years in the Territories.*)

Sibley's journals from his winter in New Mexico in 1825–1826 are filled with such comments as "I was at the Wedding & Ball last night till after 12. . . . The Priest gave a Fandango, to which I went & Staid till 12." (From J. H. Beadle, *The Undeveloped West; or Five Years in the Territories.*)

Prairie schooners at the Dock, a stopping point for travelers along the Santa Fe Trail in its latter days. (From A. A. Hays, *New Colorado and the Santa Fe Trail,*, New York, 1880.)

The Governor's Palace, Santa Fe, New Mexico. (Courtesy, Kansas State Historical Society, Topeka.)

The rear of the mission of San Miguel, Santa Fe. Note the twisting streets, the adobe houses that abut one against the other. (Courtesy, Kansas State Historical Society, Topeka.)

Left. Christopher ("Kit") Carson, explorer and Indian fighter. *Right.* William Bent, co-founder of Bent's Fort on the Arkansas River. (Courtesy, Kansas State Historical Society, Topeka.)

Cyrus K. Holliday, founder of the Atchison, Topeka, and Santa Fe Railway. (Courtesy, Kansas State Historical Society, Topeka.)

Stock certificate for the Wichita and Southwestern Railroad, a tap line promoted by Wichitans and later absorbed into the Santa Fe system. (Courtesy, Kansas State Historical Society, Topeka.)

A work crew on the Santa Fe Railroad west of Dodge City, Kansas. (Courtesy, Kansas State Historical Society, Topeka.)

"Uncle" Dick Wooten's home at the entrance to Raton Pass. The Santa Fe Railroad's roadbed can be seen just beyond the house and the barn. (Courtesy, Kansas State Historical Society, Topeka.)

Atchison, Topeka, and Santa Fe train at Lamy, New Mexico, 1879. (Courtesy, Kansas State Historical Society, Topeka.)

Santa Fe Trail ruts, visible today along the main Cimarron branch near Fort Union. (Photo by Seymour V. Connor.)

rarely an effective antidote to the toxin of radicalism. Through the British diplomatic corps Herrera notified Polk that he was willing to resume diplomatic relations provided the United States sent a minister with "full powers to settle the present dispute." What "full powers" and "present dispute" meant has boggled the interpretive geniuses of scores of later historians. Did Herrera mean only the claims issue—those unpaid debts of various Mexican governments to American citizens? Or did he mean the claims plus Texas?

His foreign minister, Manuel de Peña y Peña, told the Mexican congress that Texas was lost to Mexico, that failure to accept this reality was absurd, and that Mexico had more to gain by recognizing the independence of Texas and negotiating with it than by watching in sullen hostility as the United States absorbed it. A pair of British diplomats, Lewis Pakenham in Mexico and Charles Elliott in Texas strove earnestly to bring about a treaty between Mexico and Texas. The British Foreign Office infinitely preferred an independent Texas to an enlarged United States. And so did calmer and wiser men in Mexico.

1845. In the United States a joint resolution offering annexation to the Republic of Texas was pushed through Congress by the departing President Tyler. A joint resolution—of questionable constitutionality at best—required only a simple majority in both houses rather than the two-thirds Senate vote necessary for the ratification of a treaty. Juan N. Almonte, who represented the now-fallen Santa Anna's Centralist government in the United States, took this occasion to depart before he could be fired by Herrera. And he made his departure a political bombshell in Mexico by crying that the proposed American annexation of Mexican territory (the Republic of Texas) was an act of hostility. This—just as Herrera was preparing to recognize the independence of Texas and settle the long-standing difficulties with the United States! The quick popularity of Almonte's jingoism was to be Herrera's undoing.

But will he, nill he, the annexation process moved on slowly and inexorably. A Texas convention accepted the offer in July, 1845, and it was ratified by popular vote in October. Polk posted General Zachary Taylor with a few hundred troops to Texas with vague orders to take a position from which he could defend the Rio Grande if need be. The preposterous Texas boundary claim to the Rio

Grande, from its mouth to its source, was embarrassing to Polk, as it surely was to many Americans who believed that the Nueces River was Texas' proper southern line. Contrary to the belief prevalent today, Mexico was not troubled by this issue. No Mexican government had ever recognized the existence of the Republic of Texas, and consequently no Mexican government nor any official of Mexico had ever made any statement about the Texas boundary. Mexico claimed all of Texas to the Sabine. Had the Herrera government not been mousetrapped by Almonte's posturing, Herrera would have had to face the issue of the boundary when he negotiated with Texas. But that never happened.

Polk, responding to Herrera's invitation, sent John Slidell to Mexico with plenipotentiary powers and instructions that suggested an unseemly acquisitiveness on the part of the United States. If Herrera would accept the Rio Grande as the southern boundary of Texas, the United States would assume payment of the pesky claims; if Herrera would accept the river as the western boundary, ceding half of New Mexico, Polk would pay an additional five million dollars; if Herrera would sell California north of Monterey Bay, Polk would pay another five million; and finally, Slidell was to offer twenty-five million for the whole of the present American Southwest. Such obvious eagerness to acquire territory from Mexico added fuel aplenty to the chauvinistic fires ignited by Almonte and spread by his Centralist cohorts in Mexico. For Polk, however, Slidell's instructions were dictated not so much by disguised imperialism as by his diplomatic problems. William A. Shannon, the last United States minister to Mexico, had left, saying that the claims issue could not be settled without force; Almonte had stormed out of Washington threatening that annexation meant war with Mexico; and Britain, whom Polk neeeded to dislodge from Oregon, appeared instead to have its eyes on California. Franklin D. Roosevelt, writing in 1939 as president of the United States, said bluntly that as the American president, Polk was forced to consider the British interest in California as a violation of the Monroe Doctrine and to take measures to prevent it.

Contrary to today's popular belief, Slidell's instruction were innocuous, if not innocent of imperialistic motive, were flexible, and, to Polk, were a basis from which United States–Mexican difficulties could have been resolved. But in Mexico they were inflammatory. Popular pressure, generated by Centralist leaders over the American annexation of Texas, forced Herrera to reject Slidell entirely. Too late. The very arrival of the American minister kicked off an uprising led by the ranting Mariano Paredes. On December 14, 1845, he issued a manifesto declaring that Herrera had failed to protect the integrity of Mexican territory, that he had prevented a patriotic Mexican army from attacking the Americans who had invaded Texas (Taylor was then encamped on the Nueces), and that he was even preparing to negotiate away the birthright of every Mexican. On December 29 Paredes and his militants marched into Mexico City and Herrera surrendered without resistance. War was now inevitable.

1845. On the Santa Fe Trail the reaction in New Mexico to the annexation of Texas began to flow toward Missouri. There was virtually no anxiety expressed over the Rio Grande as the Texas boundary, but there was concern that possible hostilities might interrupt the rejuvenated trade. The St. Louis *Missouri Reporter,* quoting a Santa Fe correspondent, said, "The spirit prevailing [in New Mexico] may prevent any cessation of intercourse with it, even if Mexico should assume a hostile attitude toward the U. States." The *Western Expositor* said, "The governor of New Mexico avers that hostilities of any character between the U. States and [the rest of Mexico] shall never prevent the admission of goods from hence entering his domain as usual." A letter from a correspondent in Taos who signed himself CORTEZ [could it have been Charles Bent?], quoted in both the *Reporter* and the *Expositor,* implied that New Mexico, like Texas, wanted annexation: "The glorious spirit of annexation is spreading like a prairie fire up the Rio del Norte and rattling the dried bones in New Mexico. . . . Two thirds of the people demand annexation as the only means to escape from avarice and tyranny. Both Americans and Mexicans are making large purchases of land upon streams running into the Rio del Norte and the Arkansas, anticipating annexation."

While such statements might not be wholly accurate in depicting sentiment in New Mexico, there is no question but that the trade, revived during the last part of 1844, continued to thrive. In January, 1845, the St. Louis *Reporter* optimistically estimated that receipts in specie for the year 1845 would top $500,000 for the first time in the history of the trade. In March Congress passed a much-desired and long-needed "Drawback Act" to help the Santa Fe traders. Much of the merchandise carried to Santa Fe had originally been imported into the United States from Europe. Thus, American customs duties had been paid on it. American merchants exporting this merchandise into Mexico were then liable for the payment of Mexican customs on the same goods—double duty. The Drawback Act allowed the Santa Fe merchants to claim a remittance of the amount of the American tariff on goods taken to Santa Fe and points farther south. This would allow American imported goods to compete at par with European goods imported directly to Mexico. Ostensibly, this would give the Santa Fe traders a slight advantage; actually, since they had been profitting for years on such imports, it would enhance their yields. And if they could evade Mexican customs or bribe their way through, so much the better.

Whether the half-million dollar prediction of the *Reporter* came true is not known, but the trade did prosper during 1845. Unsettled conditions in Mexico and rumors of a forthcoming war spurred the merchants to frantic activity. Caravan after caravan, according to newspaper reports, rolled out of Independence. A September report from Owen's Landing at Independence gave the number of vehicles loaded there in the 1845 season as 117 with a total value, goods and wagons, of $383,345. Another report for the whole year 1845 stated that 141 wagons, 21 carriages, 1,078 oxen, 716 mules, 30 horses, and 203 men had trekked to Santa Fe. The total cost of goods was $342,530 and the cost of the outfits was $87,790. The same report said that the traders paid over $100,000 in duties in New Mexico.

1846. In Mexico war with the United States seemed inevitable in January. Indeed, to the Paredes government a state of war had existed from the time of the passage of the joint resolution of annexation (according to Almonte) or from the moment of Taylor's "invasion" of Texas (according to Paredes). In January, 1846, shortly after his overthrow of the Herrera government, Paredes had ordered the army reorganized and all forces mobilized for action against the enemy. Almonte was rewarded with the post of secretary of war. The Mexican people were subjected to a vitriolic stream of anti-American propaganda. Paredes really believed that he could defeat Taylor's army, recapture Texas, and perhaps even occupy New Orleans. There was a general belief in Mexico that Mexican arms (imported from Europe) were superior to those of the United States and that Mexican regular troops, seasoned in countless revolutionary campaigns, were better soldiers than American Indian fighters. Almonte convinced Paredes that abolitionist sentiment in the United States was so strongly against the annexation of Texas that the country's division would prevent it from making war. And others told him that the Oregon question had so antagonized Britain that Mexico could expect substantial aid from that quarter.

In February Paredes told his country that a state of war existed. In March Zachary Taylor moved the American army to the mouth of the Rio Grande. On April 4 Paredes ordered his troops massed at Matamoros to attack, but they did not, and he replaced the commanding general there. On April 23 he issued a proclamation of war, saying that hostilities had been commenced by the United States. On April 24 General Anastasio Torrejón crossed the Rio Grande and attacked a company of about sixty dragoons commanded by Captain William Thornton. In the light of these events in Mexico, it is witless of historians (or worse, polemic) wholly to blame the United States for a war that could have been avoided by Mexican willingness to negotiate and that was initiated by an illegal Centralist government in Mexico City. (In terms of "consent of the governed," there had not been a legal government in Mexico since the failure of the election of 1828.)

1846. In the United States word of the attack on Thornton reached President Polk on May 9. The following Monday, May 11, he told Congress, in an interesting parallel to Paredes' war message, that a state of war existed by act of Mexico. Two days later after much debate Congress insisted on the formality of passing a declaration of war. Although as yet unknown in Washington, by that time Mexican forces had twice more crossed the river to attack Taylor at the battles of Palo Alto and Resaca de la Palma.

A virtual torrent of criticism against Polk, Texas, and the war began to flow from abolitionists in the United States. In quantitative terms, antiwar publications of the time greatly outnumbered those supporting the conflict—a smoke screen that has blinded or obfuscated countless historians who have evaluated the war as if the entire nation opposed it. In point of fact, there was solid support for Polk and the war; it just was not accompanied by such frenzied screams as those of the antiwar propagandists. Volunteer units were easily raised in all parts of the country, even in deepest New England—and certainly in Missouri.

1846. On the Santa Fe Trail, prior to the outbreak of fighting along the lower Rio Grande, there had been an unusual amount of winter activity. At least a half-dozen large outfits and several smaller ones arrived in Missouri during the first three months of the year, according to stories in Missouri newspapers. Partially quoted abstracts from these newspapers tell the story best. *Jefferson Inquirer,* January 9, 1846: Mssrs. Webb and Pruett with four others arrived in Independence. The trade in Santa Fe was dull; weather was severe. *Daily Missourian,* February 13: American merchants are safe in Santa Fe. People of Santa Fe are expecting American occupation and many desire it. *Jefferson Inquirer,* February 18: Mssrs. Houck and Hicks left Chihuahua December 1, 1845; passed through Santa Fe January 1, 1846; arrived in Independence February 3. Had $35,000 with them, seven men, and three mule teams. Another company will leave about February 1, and another about March 1. The possibility of traveling the plains at any time of the year is now demonstrated. *Missouri Reporter,* March 4: Isaac Pearsons arrived in Boonslick from Chihuahua City. There the only result of the Paredes revolution was the appointment of a new governor. Trade is off. *Missouri Reporter,* March 20: Norris Colburn is to leave Santa Fe for Independence soon. *Jefferson Inquirer,* March 21: Mssrs. Armijo [the nephew of the governor] and Elliott arrived at Independence. They were robbed of their horses by Pawnees and walked the last two hundred miles. *Missouri Reporter,* March 26: The Spanish company consisted of A. Armijo, James Florris [Flores], and Mr. Lussard. They are on their way to New York to purchase goods. *Jefferson Inquirer,* April 1: Norris Colburn had Indian trouble on the way and lost some mules. *Jefferson Inquirer,* April 1: E. and F. J. Leitensdorfer [said to be the largest wholesalers in New Mexico] with three wagons and about a hundred mules came by way of Bent's and St. Vrain's fort. The doctor has his family with him in one wagon; in another, corn; and in another, his baggage and ammunition. *Missouri Reporter*, April 18: Mr. Leitensdorfer, his lady, and Mssrs. Estes, Goldman, and Peters arrived from Santa Fe. Suffered innumerable difficulties with snow storms and bad weather. *Missouri Reporter*, May 18: Word has reached this place [St. Louis] of an attack on the troops of General Taylor. Much concern is being voiced here about the Santa Fe trade. *Missouri Reporter*, May 20: U. Skillman and Francisco Algier arrived from Chihuahua with $67,000 in specie on the way eastward to purchase goods. They state that Chihuahua and New Mexico are in favor of a more liberal government.

There was clearly some ambivalence among the men involved in the Santa Fe trade about the outbreak of war. Some were fleeing New Mexico; others were rushing to bring in more goods to sell. In Santa Fe the venerable Donaciano Vigil, a prominent elder statesman in New Mexico, made an important address to a special assembly on May 16. He expressed little alarm about the outbreak of fighting but considerable anxiety lest hostilities should interfere with the trade with Missouri. Among other topics, he urged a repeal of the ban on the importation of firearms. Before long, rumors were rife that the Santa Fe traders were smuggling gunpowder baled as dry goods into New Mexico. Such activity was probably more rumor than reality, but in at least one instance a party of traders headed by Albert Speyer, a German immigrant (called by some a Prussian Jew), cared more for potential profit in arms than he did for patriotism. He left Independence the last week in May with twenty-two wagons, many of them alleged to have been laden with powder. According to the *Missouri Reporter*, June 15, 1846, Speyer had with him ten kegs of powder and six boxes of guns that had been legally ordered by Governor Armijo from Samuel C. Owens in Independence. With him was Frederick Adolphus Wislizenus, a well-known German naturalist, whose account of his travels with Speyer and later with the Doniphan expedition has become a southwestern classic. The group departed Independence just days before the news of the declaration of war arrived in Missouri and with it a fever of excitement that swept across the Missouri frontier.

Colonel Stephen Watts Kearny, a thirty-year veteran of the Indian frontier and then commander of the First Dragoons at Fort Leavenworth, was designated to lead an expedition to New Mexico and California. His forces were soon to be termed the Army of the West. The governor of Missouri had been authorized to enlist one thousand men into federal service and place them under Kearney's orders. Enlistments were rapid in what was called the First Missouri Mounted Volunteers; Missouri attorney Alexander Doniphan was elected their colonel. In addition, Kearny, who was soon promoted to brigadier general, was to recruit as many men as he could among the Santa Fe traders. The Mormons volunteered to raise a battalion with its own officers to be led by a commander chosen by Kearny. Captain, later Colonel, James Allen was appointed to lead them from from their rendezvous at Council Bluffs to New Mexico. He died en route and was replaced by Phillip St. George Cooke. And finally, a unit of the Corps of Topographical Engineers under Lieutenant William H. Emory was attached to Kearny's command.

Kearny quickly dispatched a guard of eighteen dragoons to catch Speyer's wagon train before he could deliver the arms to Armijo. Speyer was moving as rapidly as his wagons could roll over the prairies, but the dragoons finally caught him. He was informed of Kearny's orders to return with the guns to Missouri, but he drew up his men, about forty in number and all armed, and declared his intention of fighting. The dragoons, who had not been prepared to fight, were greatly outnumbered. They sent a messenger back up the trail requesting further orders, and of course Speyer pushed on toward Santa Fe. Kearny's forces were unable to overtake him again, for he quickly headed south to Chihuahua.

While the Army of the West was enlisting troops, gathering supplies, and preparing to begin what was a hellish march from Fort Leavenworth, Manuel Armijo found himself in a dilemma in New Mexico. His own loyalties, other than such homage as an opportunist pays to his ambitions, were (and remain) an enigma. He was a Centralist appointee, but he had been considered by many to be pro-American (even if corrupt). He had been ruthless in his treatment of the Texan–Santa Fe Pioneers, but his nephew was then in New York buying goods for the trade. And the governor himself had ventured into the commerce in earlier years. In the long run he was to give up New Mexico with only the appearance of resistance, and some believed that he had accepted an American bribe to do so. Be that as it may, the people of New Mexico did not support him

or offer any significant resistance to the Americans. Armijo requested the governors of Chihuahua and Durango to send reinforcements and issued a call for volunteers in New Mexico. When this
failed, he ordered conscription and by midsummer had garnered
about three thousand unreliable and for the most party unwilling
troops. Armijo's underlying problem was that the Americans were
generally popular in New Mexico. The trade with Missouri had
brought with it a general prosperity, hitherto unknown, to almost
all classes in the province. Furthermore, scores of men were disgust-
ed with the instability of the government in Mexico City, and not
a few resented the usurpation of power by the ultra-Centralist
Paredes.

Reports embellished and flavored by rumors about the situation
in New Mexico trickled up the trail to Missouri. Of more concrete
value was information given Kearny on July 19 by George Thomas
Howard, who was returning from Santa Fe to Washington. Howard, under direct orders from Secretary of War William L. Marcy,
had been to Santa Fe as a secret agent, a sort of one-man fifth column. A remarkable and daring man, Howard had been one of the
original six captains of the famed Texas Rangers which was organized in 1837. He had accompanied the Texan–Santa Fe Expedition as a merchant, had been taken prisoner and marched overland to Perote Prison in Mexico City, and in company with another
former Texas Ranger, Tom S. Lubbock, had escaped from that impregnable fortress and returned to Texas. Howard, who was visiting
Washington when war broke out, had been rushed to Missouri by
Marcy and Polk to warn the traders along the Santa Fe Trail. He
was ordered to proceed to Santa Fe spreading alarm along the way,
at the same time propagandizing among New Mexicans on behalf
of the United States. His report to Kearny was that all but a small
minority of *ricos* in New Mexico were disposed to accept American
occupation without resistance.

Kearny and the Army of the West, having covered the march
from Fort Leavenworth under the most trying circumstances, were
encamped on the Arkansas when Howard reported. They proceeded
on up the river to Bent's Fort, which they reached during the last
week in July. There, at this frontier monument to pioneer enterprise, were gathered several caravans of traders. The Army of the

West consisted of fewer than 2,000: two companies (about 250 men) of light artillery, an infantry battalion (about 150), Kearny's own First Dragoons (about 300), a volunteer company from St. Louis (about 100), and Doniphan's Missouri Volunteers (about 850). Another regiment of Missouri troops was being organized, and the Mormon Battalion was on the march.

James W. Magoffin, one of the leading Santa Fe traders, and his brother Samuel arrived at Bent's Fort as the army was straggling in. With Sam Magoffin was his bride, several months pregnant, who suffered a miscarriage in one of the upper rooms of the fort. Though she lost her baby, her diary of this trip is one of the important documents of southwestern history. James Magoffin, after a Washington conference with Senator Benton, President Polk, and Secretary Marcy, had been commissioned to precede the army into Santa Fe and then into Chihuahua, and like Howard—but perhaps more effectively since he was better known—to smooth the path of conquest for Kearny. Kearny gave the Magoffin party an escort of a dozen dragoons headed by Phillip St. George Cooke, and they left for Santa Fe on July 31.

The Army of the West resumed its march on August 2, and, crossing Raton Pass, reached Las Vegas on August 15. There Kearny made his first important contact with the citizens of New Mexico. The next day he reached San Miguel, where Cooke reported to him on Magoffin's mission in Santa Fe—a qualified success only. Armijo was still preparing to try to defend New Mexico. On August 16 the governor occupied Apache Canyon on the road to Santa Fe but abandoned it the next day and fled to Chihuahua with a personal bodyguard—and, according to unsupported legend, a valise of gold that Magoffin had slipped to him under the conference table a few days earlier. Kearny entered Santa Fe on the eighteenth just before dark and raised the American flag. Thus, without a shot fired in resistance and indeed with some cheers and encouragement from the populace, most of today's Southwest passed into American control.

There was no question here of greedy Yankee imperialism or of an American theft of Mexican territory. Centralist tyranny in Mexico had already lost the area, for it already had been peaceably conquered by American men of commerce. The Army of the West simply made formal a *fait accompli.*

Without a clear authorization to do so, Kearny established a civil-military government in New Mexico. A body of laws—the famous Kearny Code—was promulgated, and the general appointed Charles Bent the territorial governor of New Mexico for the United States. Then Kearny divided his army into three groups. Doniphan and the First Missouri Mounted Volunteers were sent into Chihuahua where, after many exciting adventures, they joined General John E. Wool. Kearny himself would lead the First Dragoons to California, guided by Christopher ("Kit") Carson, whom they encountered on the route. And Colonel Sterling Price, with the newly arrived Second Regiment of Missouri Mounted Volunteers, would be left to protect New Mexico and support the administration of Governor Bent. Soon after Kearny left, the Mormon Battalion arrived in Santa Fe. Phillip St. George Cooke, replacing Colonel Allen who had died on the march, led them on to California by a different route than Kearny had taken.

If Price and his men cursed their fate that they would miss out on all the excitement, they were soon proved to be wrong. In part, by their boisterousness they brought the trouble on themselves. A number of disaffected New Mexicans organized a conspiracy to overthrow American rule. Some joined because of their unhappiness over the undisciplined behavior of Price's men; others, rankled by what seemed to them to be the dishonorably easy conquest by the Americans, wanted to avenge Hispanic honor; the ringleaders, especially one Diego Archuleta, felt cheated that they had not been given a part of New Mexico to rule. Their position was that the territory east of the Rio Grande belonged to the United States by right of the claim of the Republic of Texas—which Kearny had averred several times—and that the country west of the river had been surrendered with the implied promise that Archuleta would be named governor.

Price and Bent learned of the conspiracy and arrested many of the leaders in Santa Fe on December 15. Governor Bent issued a proclamation calling on the people of New Mexico to reject the conspiracy and give their allegiance to the new administration. Since the vast majority of New Mexicans were at least friendly, if not yet loyal, to the American government, Bent had every reason to believe the trouble was ended before it had started. After all, the governor had spent years in and out of Santa Fe, Chihuahua, and Taos and knew the region's people well, both individually and collectively. Then, believing that the arrests and his proclamation had solved the problem, Bent went to Taos to visit his family.

It was there that an uprising broke out. In all probability it had only vague connections with the earlier conspiracy. The leaders of the Taos plot were Pablo Montoya, a malcontent with apparently paranoid delusions, and Tomasito Baca, a Pueblo Indian. On January 19, 1847, followed by a small band of insurgents, they fell on Governor Bent's house in Taos and killed and scalped the governor. They proceeded on a path of undirected murder, killing in all twelve Americans, and then holed up in the mission at the Taos pueblo, from which they were finally routed on February 5. There was an associated skirmish at the village of Mora on January 25 and an encounter a few days earlier at Santa Cruz. Except for the death of Charles Bent, the uprising was, in perspective, relatively minor. By no means did it indicate any general dissatisfaction by New Mexico as a whole with American occupation.

CHAPTER 12

Santa Fe, Texas

General Stephen Watts Kearny's occupation of New Mexico had numerous ramifications. Obviously, it signalled the beginning of American control over the erstwhile Mexican province. It also afforded the United States government its first opportunity to assess the region realistically, to ascertain its economic potential. Surely the isolated area would become more than merely a commercial outpost of Independence merchants. And, whether he intended it or not, Kearny again opened the door to a jurisdictional dispute, leading some to wonder if Santa Fe were not a part of Texas.

As General Kearny was organizing his Army of the West at Fort Leavenworth in 1846, the Topographical Corps saw an excellent opportunity to add valuable knowledge by attaching a unit to the expedition. Existing maps of the region south and west of the Arkansas, in Mexican territory, were abominably poor, so inaccurate as to be dangerous to any wayfarer foolish enough to trust them. Similarly, army engineers—already looking toward development of the American West—wished to assess the region's economic potential. Hastily, the War Department ordered a small detachment to gather scientific instruments and, within twenty-four hours, to proceed to Leavenworth to join Kearny.

Leader of the party was William Hemsley Emory, an 1831 graduate of the United States Military Academy who had received his appointment to West Point from Senator John C. Calhoun—when Emory was merely eleven years of age. His grandfather and father had served with distinction in the Revolutionary War and the War of 1812, respectively; both had been leaders among Maryland's landed gentry. Young Emory counted among his friends Jefferson

Davis, Joseph E. Johnston, and Henry Clay, Jr. His wife, Matilda Bache, was the daughter of Alexander Dallas Bache, a founder of the National Academy of Science. Through the Baches Emory had gained entrées to three powerful families. The Baches, of course, had been prominent in Philadelphia since Richard Bache, during the seventeenth century, had established a flourishing mercantile trade with the West Indies. Richard had also married Sarah Franklin, the daughter of Benjamin Franklin. Among Richard and Sarah's sons were Benjamin Franklin (named in honor of the patriot and an influential newspaper publisher in his own right) and Alexander Dallas (named in honor of the Dallas family, to which the Baches were also related and which included George M. Dallas, Polk's vice-president). Emory had excellent connections.

The young graduate of West Point also had intelligence, which naturally had led him toward science. He was well acquainted with the leading mathematicians, geologists, and astronomers of America: William Bond of Harvard, John Torry of Princeton, and Spencer Baird of the newly created Smithsonian Institution. He had assisted Major James D. Graham in surveying the American-Canadian boundary in the Northeast in 1843–1844 and in compiling a reasonably accurate map of Texas in 1844. First Lieutenant Emory was among the best choices for the task at hand—to map and survey the Mexican Northwest.

Accompanied by three junior officers and two civilians (a statistician and a landscape artist), Lieutenant Emory joined Kearny's force in early summer, just as it was making final preparations to march out along the Santa Fe Trail. Not until the army had reached Bent's Fort on the upper Arkansas did Emory begin to describe in detail what he saw and to map the terrain through which the expedition was passing.

His observations, which continued all the way to California, fell into two categories: economic and anthropological. He saw little hope for commercial agriculture in the whole of New Mexico, save for those narrow strips of land that bordered flowing streams. Rainfall simply was not sufficient. Consequently, he speculated that slavery would never penetrate into the desert Southwest; the return to investment would be insufficient to justify the intensive application of labor that slavery implied. As did others, he believed that a

wine industry, based on the excellent vineyards he saw along the
Rio Grande, could be developed. He noted that outcroppings of
bituminous coal abounded but worried that they lay too far from
population centers to be feasibly exploited. An abandoned copper
pit at Santa Rita del Cobre, which had been worked by frontiersmen Sylvester and James Ohio Pattie during the 1820's, suggested to
Emory that other valuable mineral deposits lay undetected throughout the rugged, forbidding desertland, but again isolation seemed
to preclude exploitation. If there were any realistic economic potential in the hostile, uninhabited country through which Emory
passed, he thought it would be along the Gila River. There a transcontinental railroad could be built.

Emory was far more fascinated by the ancient ruins encountered by the Army of the West. At first intoxicated by the excitement of seeing the silent Indian ghost towns and no doubt influenced
by historian William Prescott's accounts of Cortés in Mexico, the
lieutenant believed that he had stumbled upon the origin of the
Aztecs. Further observations, especially at Casa Grande on the Gila
River, however, convinced him that these ruins were precursors of
the existing Pueblo culture like that at Taos. He still wondered
about these prehistoric peoples: Why had they left? Where had
they gone? His questions opened a chapter in American anthropolo-
gy and archaeology.

He did more. His map and accompanying report supplied the
first detailed, reasonably accurate picture of the remote Southwest.
True, Emory and his men had little time to scout far afield of the
line of march. The cartographic chart he prepared barely scratched
a narrow line through the vast wilderness. But it was a start. Tag-
ging along with Kearny, Emory trod where only intrepid mountain
men and nomadic Indians had passed. Countless gold-seekers, who
soon rushed westward to California over the Kearny extension of
the Santa Fe Trail, owed their lives to Emory's map, whether they
knew his name or not.

Emory's report was supplemented by the findings of yet another
topographical expedition. During the summer of 1848, citizens of
Fort Smith, Arkansas, were petitioning the government to open a
practical overland route between their community and Santa Fe;
their proposal pointed to Josiah Gregg's return journey of 1839 along

the Canadian River, which the frontiersman had asserted was ideal-
ly suited to wagon traffic. Arkansas congressmen echoed the sentiments of their constituents, Senator Solon Borland officially
requesting that the secretary of war direct the army to survey such
a roadway, which Borland hoped would supplant the Independence–
Santa Fe route.

Nine months passed before the War Department implemented
the request by instructing Captain Randolph B. Marcy to lead two
companies of infantry and one of dragoons westward through Santa
Fe to California. Marcy's command was to escort an emigrant train
then gathering at Fort Smith, to locate the most practical overland
route to Santa Fe and beyond, and to placate any Indians encountered along the way. Almost as an afterthought, Lieutenant James
H. Simpson of the Corps of Topographical Engineers was attached
to the expedition as cartographer. By the time Simpson arrived in
Fort Smith in early April, Marcy already had departed for the
Canadian River, and the lieutenant was hard-pressed to overtake
the emigrant train and begin his map.

Marcy had marched twenty-eight miles from the Arkansas River
community when Simpson reported for duty, eager to chart the path
to California. Marcy immediately informed the cartographer that
new orders instructed his command to proceed only as far as Santa
Fe; apparently the military had decided that Emory's survey of the
Gila Trail would suffice for the trek further west.

Disappointed though both of the young officers must have been
over the curtailment of their mission, they set to the task at hand.
Marcy steadily guided the emigrants along the south bank of the
Canadian River, over a natural roadway they both described as
excellent. Marcy was so enthusiastic that he suggested that the flat
tableland, uncrossed by any major streams, could be used by expanding railroads at minimal cost. Simpson, though equally impressed by the lack of natural obstacles along the route, accurately
forecast that twenty years would pass before any railroad would
extend its tracks across the plains and into the mountains. The raw
materials (coal, timber, gravel) were readily available, he admitted,
but the area lacked a sufficient population base and corresponding
economy to make such a project financially feasible.

Three months after they had departed Fort Smith, the party of soldiers and emigrants arrived safely at Santa Fe, uniformly enthusiastic about the new path they had blazed. Reports by Marcy and Simpson were forwarded to Washington, and the two officers bade their farewells. Simpson remained in Santa Fe, attached to the army command there, and Marcy marched out of the capital to return to Arkansas. While Simpson began preparations to explore and map much of northwestern New Mexico, Marcy's command proceeded through Albuquerque toward El Paso. The officer planned to blaze yet another trail to Fort Smith, this one across the uncharted plains of Texas. His route took him past the Kearny-Emory Gila Trail and on to Doña Ana, a few miles north of El Paso. There he turned eastward, passed through the rugged Guadalupe Mountains, skirted the southern edge of the forbidding Llano Estacado, and continued northeastward across Texas to Arkansas. Even though one of his party was killed by a hostile band of Kiowas at Big Spring, Marcy proclaimed his return path superior to the Canadian River route. It was better watered, had more timber, and provided a more direct link with Emory's Gila Trail to California.

Both new routes experienced moderate use. While some Fort Smith merchants did seek to make commercial connections with Santa Fe by following the Marcy-Simpson path that bordered the Canadian River, they were unable to challenge seriously the established Independence–Santa Fe trade. Moreover, those emigrants who used the Arkansas River community as a jumping off point for California generally followed Marcy's advice and his route to Doña Ana. Independence's domination of the trade with Santa Fe remained unchallenged.

But another challenge was surfacing, the old Texas claim to all of New Mexico east of the Rio Grande. Austin politicians had not forgotten their state's aspirations, ludicrous though they might have been. The memory of the Santa Fe Pioneers was still fresh in the minds of many. As late as 1843, Texas had attempted to exercise some control over New Mexico when forces under Charles Warfield and Jacob Snively raided into the area. And the state's boundary claims remained unsettled in 1845 when it abandoned its sovereignty and entered the Union. The joint resolution of Congress that paved

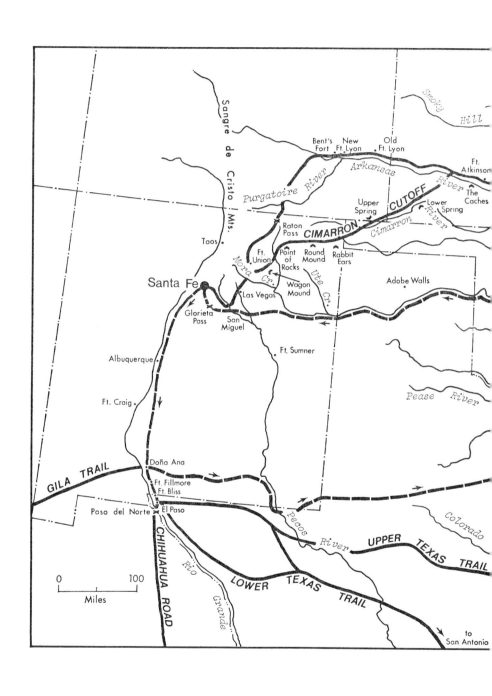

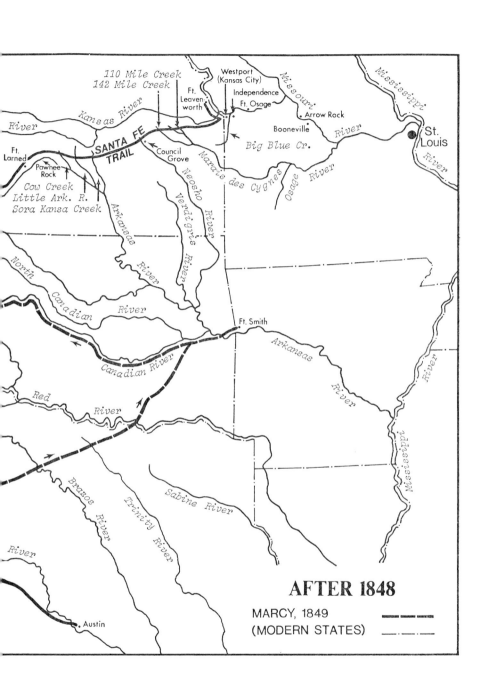

110 Mile Creek
142 Mile Creek

Westport
(Kansas City)
Independence
Ft. Osage
Ft. Leaven-worth

Arrow Rock

Booneville

Big Blue Cr.

St. Louis

Missouri River

Mississippi River

Kansas River

River

SANTA FE TRAIL

Council Grove

Ft. Larned

Pawnee Rock

Cow Creek
Little Ark. R.
Sora Kansa Creek

Arkansas River

Neosho River

Verdigris River

Marais des Cygnes

Osage River

North Canadian River

Canadian River

Ft. Smith

Arkansas River

Red River

Mississippi River

River

Brazos River

Trinity River

Sabine River

River

Austin

AFTER 1848

MARCY, 1849
(MODERN STATES)

the way to annexation vested in the government at Washington the authority to adjust "all questions of boundary that may arise with other governments." Implied in that statement was official willingness to negotiate a settlement with Mexico to avoid war; when such a peaceable solution did not materialize, Texans undoubtedly believed that, once Mexico was soundly defeated, their claims to the entire Rio Grande would be upheld. Of course, that included control of the valuable Santa Fe trade.

Ironically, when the Army of the West invaded and occupied New Mexico, neither local residents nor Texans were entirely pleased with what transpired. On August 18, 1846, even before his troops had taken possession of Santa Fe, General Kearny issued his code, in which he declared New Mexico to the Rio Grande to be part of the United States in accordance with Texas claims to the region. The following day, after having occupied Santa Fe, Kearny declared himself military governor of New Mexico and officially repeated his assertion of August 18. Thus was eastern New Mexico declared an extension of Texas, which did not please local residents, and Texas authority over the region thwarted by Kearny's unilateral assumption of civil control.

Kearny's contradictory actions, widely reported in the Texas press, appeared to assert federal claim to New Mexico as a conquered country. Texas Governor J. Pinckney Henderson on January 4, 1847, sought clarification from Washington. He wrote Secretary of State James Buchanan, protesting any action on the part of the army that infringed upon the rights of Texas. But, in a moment of candor, he added:

> Inasmuch as it is not convenient for the State [of Texas] at this time to exercise jurisdiction over Santa Fe, I presume no objection will be made on the part of the government of the State of Texas to the establishment of a territorial government over that country by the United States, provided it is done with the express admission on their part that the State of Texas is entitled to the soil and jurisdiction over the same, and may exercise her right whenever she regards it expedient.

President Polk, eager to placate the Texans, responded that the actions of Kearny had been necessary to preserve order; martial law and federal supervision would cease with an end to hostilities with

Mexico, which of course would include a mutual recognition of international boundaries.

Henderson and Polk's exchanges served merely to confuse the issue further. Sterling Price, who was promoted to brigadier general in 1847 and by 1848 served as the military governor of New Mexico, probably inferred that Henderson would acquiesce to the formal creation of a Territory of New Mexico. Accordingly, in February, 1848, two months before the United States and Mexico exchanged ratifications of the Treaty of Guadalupe Hidalgo, Price called for a territorial convention in which New Mexicans could ask Washington for "the protection of a government which imposes no bonds upon the conscience, which will protect . . . [New Mexicans] in the unmolested enjoyment of your personal, political and religious rights, under the regulation of equal laws." Eight months later, when the convention met, New Mexicans formally petitioned the federal government for separate territorial status. "We respectfully but firmly protest against the dismemberment of our territory," they pleaded, "in favor of Texas or from any cause."

Reports of Price's call for a convention and rumors of what that body would ask of Congress were circulating in Austin long before the New Mexico session of 1848 had met in Santa Fe. As long as Texas had the assurances of President Polk, who promised a withdrawal of federal control once a peace treaty with Mexico was signed, the state had no immediate reason to press its claims. But with the impending convention in Santa Fe, which undoubtedly would embrace an antislavery stance and thereby gain northern support for its separate territorial status, officials in Austin believed that the time for action was at hand.

Moreover, many Texans predicted that Zachary Taylor would run for president that year and, as a military hero, would be swept into office overwhelmingly. Taylor was known to hold a low opinion of Texas and Texans. Perhaps "Old Rough and Ready," as the general was called in the Monterrey campaign, still stung from the bitter exchanges between himself and Governor Henderson during the war; perhaps he equated all Texans with the undisciplined detachment of Rangers who had served with him and who flagrantly thumbed their noses at military courtesy; or perhaps he just disliked the harsh Nueces country where his troops had camped for so

long before the outbreak of war. Whatever the cause for his hostility, he was distrusted by Texans, who wished to see the matter of
jurisdiction settled before Zachary Taylor had a chance to enter the
White House.

On March 2, 1848, George T. Wood, who succeeded Henderson
as governor of Texas, issued a special message to his state legislature. He noted that General Price's action had set into motion the
process by which New Mexico's separation from Texas could be
accomplished. Had Texas militiamen occupied Santa Fe, the territorial convention would never have been called. The government in
Austin had been far too passive in representing its claims, and the
time to assert Texas authority was at hand. He urged the Texas
delegation in Congress to protest the usurpation of the state's authority over her own territory, and he called upon legislators in
Austin to take such action as necessary to establish Texas' jurisdiction over the Santa Fe region. Thirteen days later the legislature
authorized the creation of Santa Fe County.

While the new county encompassed all the state's western
claims from the Pecos River west and the Rio Grande north to its
source, the city of Santa Fe was the prize, the principal point of
Texas interest. The government in Austin also provided for control
of the militia at Santa Fe, authorized citizens of that county to send
one representative to the state legislature, and established the
eleventh judicial district, whose court would sit twice annually to
minister to the legal needs of Santa Fe, Texas.

At the same time the Texas legislature had enacted specific
laws designed to establish civil machinery in Santa Fe, it had also
passed a joint resolution expressing dismay that the residents of the
upper Rio Grande valley were proceeding to establish a separate
government, which violated the territorial integrity of Texas. Governor Wood simultaneously wrote President Polk, asking that the
actions of the United States government not prevent his state from
exercising her "rightful jurisdiction." When seven months passed
without a reply, Wood again wrote to Polk to assert Texas authority
over Santa Fe. Though the governor did not yield any portion of
Texas' claim over the region, he admitted that the state must rely
upon the sale of its public domain to retire the revolutionary war
debt; for the federal government to seize New Mexico without just

compensation would be unacceptable. This addendum later provided the means for compromise.

Whether or not the state of Texas by October, 1848, was earnestly seeking a negotiated settlement, it continued to press for what it believed were its rights in New Mexico. The previous May, Governor Wood had appointed Spruce M. Baird as judge of the new eleventh judicial district. Baird was instructed to organize Santa Fe County under the laws of Texas. The judge, in the company of James W. Webb, who had been appointed district attorney for Santa Fe, departed in that month; their journey by way of the Mississippi and Missouri rivers to the Santa Fe Trail (at that time no established overland routes from Texas to Santa Fe existed) took six months; news of their coming preceded them by several weeks.

Santa Feans, no doubt encouraged by the military government, were determined to retain their independence of Texas. In October a convention had requested that Congress authorize the creation of a territorial government for New Mexico, and local newspapers echoed the sentiment. In anticipation of Baird's arrival, the Santa Fe *Republican* in the fall asserted (as quoted in Texas newspapers such as the Nacogdoches *Times* of May 17, 1848):

> . . . there is not a citizen, either American or Mexican, that will ever acknowledge themselves as citizens of Texas, until it comes from higher authority. New Mexico does not belong, nor has Texas even a right to claim her as a part of Texas. We would advise Texas to send with her civil officers for this county, a large force, in order that they may have a sufficient bodyguard to escort them back safely. . . . Texas should show some little sense, and drop this question, and not have it publicly announced that Texas' smartest men were tarred and feathered by attempting to fill the offices assigned them.

Baird's mission had little hope for success.

By the time Baird and Webb arrived at Santa Fe on November 10, Baird found that Colonel John M. Washington had succeeded to the post of military governor. Twelve days passed before Baird could secure an audience with Washington, and that meeting left little doubt as to the judge's local authority. Baird presented his credentials, asserted Texas jurisdiction over Santa Fe and its environs, and argued that the Treaty of Guadalupe Hidalgo technically ended martial law and the military government in the area. The colonel responded that the code, which Kearny had announced in 1846, had been endorsed by President Polk; in short, the Texan had no authority whatsoever.

The following day Washington returned Baird's credentials with a note that they would be presented to the proper authorities at an appropriate time. The judge had little choice but to wait. He spent his time asking local newspapers, which were government owned and controlled, to publicize his mission. The requests were met by rebuff after rebuff. He surveyed the economic potential of the area, especially trade and commerce and mining, the latter of which he believed held great promise; he himself bought some land near Santa Fe. He estimated the region's population at seventy thousand, only twenty to twenty-five thousand of whom were permanent residents. He suggested that direct land routes from Texas proceed along the Pecos River.

Unknown to Baird were orders from Secretary of War William L. Marcy, dated October 12, 1848, which had instructed Colonel Washington to aid and assist Texas officials. Instead, the military governor, a Whig, sought to pacify Baird, to thwart his efforts to establish a civil government under Texas laws, at least until the Whigs under Zachary Taylor, he hoped, entered the White House in 1849. Washington's faction was well entrenched in Santa Fe, and it had no intention of losing power to Baird, Webb, and a host of other functionaries sent from Austin. And there is considerable evidence that the Whigs in Santa Fe were encouraged and aided by northern free-soilers, who hoped to prevent the extension of slavery into the area.

Throughout the spring and early summer of 1849, Baird probed for an opening that would allow him to fulfill his instructions. Once, when incorrect reports of congressional action that appeared to validate Texas claims to Santa Fe reached him, he informed Colonel Washington that he would organize the county immediately. The military governor persuaded Baird to wait until official word arrived. When it did, it reported that Congress had been unable to reach a decision as to Texas' claims to Santa Fe. Again the judge was thwarted.

By July, 1849, Baird believed that he could do no more and decided to return to Austin for consultation with authorities there. He notified Colonel Washington of his decision, and the military governor assured him that he would allow no action to infringe upon Texas claims during Baird's absence. The judge departed Santa Fe on July 4, arriving in Austin six months later.

While the Texas jurist traveled, several events transpired. First of all, Lieutenant Colonel Benjamin L. Beall, who acted as military governor while Washington was away from Santa Fe, authorized yet another territorial convention to meet in September. When the assembly convened, nineteen delegates representing virtually all of the region north of El Paso voted to petition Congress for territorial status. It also elected Hugh N. Smith, a Texan, as its official representative to Congress. The effort, however, came to nothing. Colonel Washington, upon his return to Santa Fe, refused to recognize officially the actions of the 1849 territorial session, and when Smith arrived in Washington, Congress by a vote of 92 to 86 refused to seat him as a delegate.

And as Texans expected, Zachary Taylor, who had been inaugurated as president on March 4, 1849, was unsympathetic to their claims to Santa Fe. In his state of the Union message of December 4, 1849, Taylor announced that the people of New Mexico would soon ask Congress for statehood. The issue of a Texas–New Mexico border, he insisted, should be left to the courts. One month later, answering a request from the House of Representatives for information on both California and New Mexico, Taylor again repeated his view that New Mexico should be accorded statehood, or at the very least separate territorial status. The matter of conflicting land claims, he again stated, should be decided by the judiciary.

Texas officials were understandably miffed at the high-handed treatment of their representatives in Santa Fe and realistically suspicious of President Taylor's motives. Governor Wood, no doubt summing up the majority sentiment in his state, in November, 1849, told the legislature that Texas was determined to establish its jurisdiction over the upper Rio Grande. Soon thereafter, Texas lawmakers redrew the map of Santa Fe County by cutting its size drastically. They also created three new counties—Presidio, El Paso, and Worth—to embrace most of the region between the Pecos and Rio Grande rivers as far north as Sabine, New Mexico. If Santa

Feans would not respond to reason, perhaps they would respect a diminution of their county's size. On January 4, 1850, the legislature authorized the appointment of a commissioner to organize the four counties.

Peter H. Bell, who had succeeded Wood as governor of Texas, appointed Robert S. Neighbors to the post and instructed him to proceed with dispatch to carry out the laws of Texas with respect to the establishment of civil government in West Texas. While Bell admonished Neighbors to act with firmness, he also told him to be courteous so as to "inspire confidence and esteem" among the people of the area.

Neighbors was an outstanding choice for the mission. He was a veteran of the Mexican War, having served in the Texas Rangers, and had just returned from opening a practical overland route to El Paso. On January 8, Neighbors departed Austin along the road he had recently laid out, for he planned to organize El Paso County first. The Texas official arrived at present El Paso about the middle of February and made his headquarters at the trading post John Wiley Magoffin had recently established. Neighbors told the citizens of the half-dozen small settlements that lay across the river from Mexican Paso del Norte that they were Texans and could organize a local government. Military forces there offered no interference, and in March Neighbors reported to Bell that local elections had been held. El Paso County was functioning! The ultimate significance of that fact can hardly be measured.

Rather than proceed next to the organization of either Worth or Presidio counties, Neighbors decided to go directly to Santa Fe. Without a large military escort, he believed it would be impossible to go to Presidio, for the Indians in that area were hostile to whites. Too, he logically thought that the successful organization of Worth hinged upon his reception in Santa Fe. But Neighbors was pessimistic. For one thing, he was running low on funds. For another, the issue of valid land titles was of uppermost concern. Already some Texans had moved into northern New Mexico, located on property legally owned by others, and prejudiced long-time residents of the region against Texas and Texans. He asked Bell to reassure Santa Feans.

Commissioner Neighbors also wrote Colonel John Munroe, the new commanding officer and military governor at Santa Fe. He advised Munroe that he was traveling to northern New Mexico to organize a county government. Upon his arrival in April, Neighbors secured an interview with the military governor, at which time Munroe informed him that he had ordered his troops to maintain strict neutrality in the dispute. Moreover, the colonel stated that he had no authority to abolish martial law, to suspend officials appointed under the auspices of the United States government, or to recognize the validity of any elections that Neighbors might hold.

Under the circumstances, Neighbors believed that any attempt by him to establish Texas authority would be useless. Judge Jacob Houghton, a superior court magistrate under the military government and a leading Whig, had openly advised residents to boycott any election held by the Texas commissioner, insisting that the New Mexico delegate to Congress would secure enabling legislation for territorial status. More pointedly, he once threatened to jail for contempt of court anyone who assisted Neighbors. The Texas commissioner advised Governor Bell that one solution would be for Bell personally to lead Texas militiamen to Santa Fe. That might neutralize Whig opposition.

Not long after Neighbors had arrived in Santa Fe, President Taylor directed Munroe to assist New Mexicans in organizing their own state government. The colonel complied on April 20 by issuing a call for a constitutional convention. Neighbors protested vigorously, insisting that such action not only violated the joint resolution for the admission of Texas to the Union but Article Four of the Constitution itself. Munroe was not dissuaded.

On May 15, while Neighbors, dismayed, departed for Austin, New Mexicans met and drafted a constitution. The liberal document, which prohibited slavery, was undoubtedly modeled along the lines of those of most newer states. It was also practical, for it assured New Mexicans of the validity of their land claims issued under Mexican authority. Moreover, it asserted that the proposed state embraced all lands between the 100th and 111th meridians— or the whole of the Texas Panhandle westward to Tucson. A month later, New Mexicans adopted the proposed constitution and simultaneously elected a slate of statewide officers. On the first of July, in anticipation of being admitted to the Union, the legislature met and elected two senators to represent it in Washington.

Texans were outraged. By the time Neighbors arrived in Austin and reported to Governor Bell, the details of the New Mexican actions had been publicized. Mass protest meetings were held throughout the state during the early summer. Hotheads called for secession. Not much more peaceful were those who urged military action designed to bring recalcitrant Santa Fe under Texas authority. For his part, Governor Bell wrote to President Taylor, demanding to know if Colonel Munroe's call for a constitutional convention was authorized by the White House. He also called for a special session of the Texas legislature on August 12, so that the state could take whatever action might be deemed necessary.

By the time Bell's letter arrived in Washington, Zachary Taylor had died, probably of typhoid fever, and a decidedly cooler head held executive power. Millard Fillmore had succeeded to the presidency. Although Fillmore was a northerner and had held antislavery views when elected vice-president on the Whig ticket, he was also a moderate. As the presiding officer of the Senate, he had listened intently to the encompassing debate over Texas land claims, New Mexican and Californian statehood, and slavery in the territories. He apparently believed that a compromise had to be forged to save the Union, which meant that Texas had to be placated.

Fillmore directed his new secretary of state, Daniel Webster, to respond to Bell's inquiry. Webster acknowledged that Colonel Munroe had acted upon the authority of President Taylor, but he assured the governor that such did not infringe upon Texas' land claims. Pointing to the joint resolution of Congress that had admitted Texas to the Union, Webster noted that only Congress had the authority to define the state's boundaries. Moreover, the secretary stated that any people have the right to petition their government for laws, which would include a request for statehood. In short, the state of Texas was as impotent as the presidency in settling the dispute. The solution lay in Congress.

And Congress was well aware of the problem, for it had debated the same issues for two years. As early as 1848 both houses had wrangled over the western limits of Texas, a matter that had soon dissolved into a sectional squabble over slavery. The North sincerely feared the spread of the South's "peculiar institution," and in 1846 discussion of excluding it from any territory taken from Mexico in war had been widely debated in Congress. Defeated again and again in the Senate, the Wilmot Proviso embodied the sentiments of free-soilers; it proposed to limit slavery to where it then existed. For Texas to expand to the Rio Grande would merely extend the hated labor system. The South was determined to support Texas' claims and to throw open the West to slavery. Too, there was the question of California. Would it enter the Union as a free or as a slave state? What of Utah, where Mormons had settled? A crisis that could have precipitated the Civil War was at hand.

Fortunately for the Union, Representative Henry Clay of Kentucky, although old and infirm, still held considerable influence in Congress. Working with others, such as Senator Stephen A. Douglas of Illinois, who wished to see bloodshed avoided, he began structuring a compromise that, even if it would not satisfy all parties concerned, would defuse an explosive situation. Clay hoped that his proposal would restore peace and harmony to the United States for another thirty years, the period in which the Missouri Compromise had endured as the answer to slavery in the territories.

His was truly an omnibus bill, which proposed to compromise every outstanding sectional question then facing the nation. First, California would be admitted to the Union as a free state. Second, the Mexican Cession would be divided into two territories, New Mexico and Utah, and the issue of slavery therein would be determined by a popular vote of the citizens of each upon entry into the Union as a state. Third, as sops to both sides of the burning issue of the time, the slave trade in the District of Columbia would be abolished and a more stringent fugitive slave law would be enacted by Congress.

As to the state of Texas, Congress would appropriate $10 million earmarked to pay the state's debts arising from its war of independence. In return, Texas would agree to a boundary between itself and New Mexico. The Omnibus Bill of 1850, with some minor modifications, was accepted and forged into law.

Ultimately, the limits of West Texas were drawn to exclude

claim to any portion of New Mexico. Commencing at the inter-
section of the 100th meridian with 36°30′ north latitude (a token
genuflection toward the northern limits of slavery as described by
the Missouri Compromise of 1820), the border proceeded westward
along that latitude to the 103rd meridian, turned southward to the
32nd parallel, and projected westward to the Rio Grande. North
and west of the 32nd parallel and the 103rd meridian lay New Mexico; south and east was Texas. El Paso, the gateway to Mexico, lay
firmly in Texas control, however, a result of Neighbors' action in
organizing the county.

For its part, Texas surrendered its claims to Worth and Santa
Fe counties. It also cleared a huge public debt that could have
strapped its citizens for years. But then Texas' interest in Santa Fe
had always been pecuniary. In 1841, when the Santa Fe Expedition
had marched westward, it had been to bring the lucrative Santa Fe
trade under Austin's control. And when, between 1848 and 1850,
Texas reasserted its tenuous claim to the region, it still saw Santa Fe
as a financial windfall. Perhaps the final irony of the story is that,
while New Mexico gained its independence from Texas, Texas also
benefitted financially. Such was the value of Santa Fe.

CHAPTER 13

Consolidation of American Control

Santa Fe—mysterious, remote Santa Fe—had intrigued Americans at least since 1821 when William Becknell had opened it to trade from Missouri. Twenty-nine years later the stars and stripes flapped in the breeze above the governor's palace, a low-slung adobe structure in the heart of the city. And yet Santa Fe remained every bit as fascinating to the new swarm of traders and visitors as it had been to those first bullwhackers from Missouri who had trudged into town three decades before. Santa Fe's charm, in part, was its alien culture, its decidedly different architecture, its people. But too, it was what the former Mexican outpost represented. Except for the taciturn mountain men who had crossed and recrossed New Mexico's uncharted peaks in pursuit of furs, no American knew what treasure trove lay beyond the next hill. During the decade that preceded the Civil War, an earnest attempt to assess the value of the region was made.

For one thing, the government of the United States had no idea of the territory's population. Estimates as to the indigenous Indian tribes were left to James S. Calhoun, the area's first Indian agent, who had arrived in Santa Fe in 1849. He had been instructed to locate the principal tribes, to estimate their numbers, and to propose guidelines for establishing federal control over them. Calhoun reported in 1850 that there were twenty-two known pueblos, but he vacillated time and time again when attempting to fix a population figure for these reasonably tame, agrarian peoples. After revising his figures at least three times, he finally struck upon the number 7,867, which was probably far too few. As to the "wild Indians," those tribes that ranged as far west as the Colorado River, he could do no better than repeat the guesses of others, such as Governor Charles Bent. Calhoun theorized that 45,000 nomadic Indians inhabited the territory.

The enumeration of the "civilized population" was easier, for the majority of the Mexicans and Anglo-Americans who resided in the territory lived in towns and villages along the Rio Grande. The census of 1850 reported that 61,547 people lived in New Mexico, which, until 1863, included present Arizona. Of that total, 61,525 were identified as white, the remaining 22 as "free colored." Approximately 8 percent of New Mexico's population, or 4,846 persons, lived in Santa Fe County, the majority of these in the twisting, narrows streets of the capital.

The plaza, upon which the governor's palace faced, was at the heart of the community. The dusty road that bounded it connected to others that radiated, one way or another, toward the outskirts of the village. Near the plaza was the expansive home of Don Miguel Sena; its rambling, adobe style and its central location had made it since 1840 the social center of the community. To the south of the plaza lay a tiny stream with a grandiose name—Río de Santa Fé. Along its banks modest, one-story mud-brick structures abutted one upon another, sheltering family after family. Near the river was the mission of San Miguel, which had ministered to the needs of Santa Feans virtually since the days of Juan de Oñate. Most streets, many of which were hardly a dozen feet in width, were alleyways barely suitable for more than foot or cart traffic. Visitors variously described the city as picturesque and as a collection of hovels, depending upon their own particular sense of aesthetics.

Without a doubt, Santa Fe was filthy. Chickens ran free throughout the city, squawking to one another and pecking at bits of food that had been dumped just outside virtually every door in town. Goats and pigs wandered about unmolested, scavenging for food and drinking from the numerous little garden-plot irrigation canals that lined almost every street. A generous supply of dung could be seen everywhere. But Santa Feans were equally uninhibited. As late as 1879 it was relatively common for residents to relieve themselves wherever they happened to be, a practice Americans soon emulated. That year, city officials ordered citizens and visitors alike to refrain from urinating or from defecating, during daylight hours, on any of the community's thoroughfares. Few Anglo-Americans had ever seen anything like Santa Fe, and they uniformly were intrigued with its relaxed, almost blasé atmosphere.

American men were even more captivated by its women. Young Mexican females were lovely creatures. Visitor after visitor described their raven-black hair, their dark, dancing eyes, their slender, trim figures. The typical peasant blouse, the *camisa*, worn by so many women in Santa Fe, was a low-cut garment that exposed far more of the female anatomy than the typical American was accustomed to seeing, casually. Were that insufficient, women as well as men unabashedly relieved themselves in the open, without apparent regard to the fascinated gaze of astounded newcomers. And while working in the fields, young women often disrobed to the waist on warm and balmy days, an act that was guaranteed to attract a crowd of Anglo-American men.

This casual behavior had other manifestations. Young women openly smoked, drank, and discussed sex with men. The Mexican culture, especially among the peasant class, simply did not have the taboos so common east of the Mississippi River, and American visitors to Santa Fe loved its free, comparatively licentious lifestyle. Single women bestowed their favors indiscriminately, and even young matrons were known to scramble into bed with fair-skinned Americans, who, to the Mexican women, were undoubtedly equally exotic. It was a small miracle that traders, bullwhackers, soldiers, and transients who plied the trail and who paused to dally in Santa Fe ever left.

A contemporary report in the *Niles Register* of December 4, 1841, insisted:

> The ladies certainly are far more beautiful in this [New Mexico] country than those of the same rank in America; their jetty black eyes, slender and delicate frame, with unusually small ankles and feet, together with their gay winning address make you at once easy and happy in their company. Perhaps no people on earth love dress and attention more than the Spanish ladies, and it may be said of truth, that their amorous flirtations with men are matters to boast amongst themselves. They work but little; the fandango and siesta form the division of time. The fandango is a lascivious dance, partak-

ing in part of the waltz, cotillion, and many amorous movements, and is certainly handsome and amusing. It is the national dance [of the Mexicans].

Indeed, had not service and money pulled them away, many more Anglo-American males probably would have made Santa Fe their home. Others, unaccustomed to easy and casual sex, fled in fear. Jacob Fowler, an early visitor to Santa Fe, described an episode in which three of his acquaintances were exposed to the advances of a mother and her two daughters:

> Now the Haveing of but one Beed in the House and that So large as to be Cappeble of Holding the Three Copple of poson—there Ware all to lodge to geather and the mother of the daughters being oldest Had a Corse the ferst Chois of Bows and took pall [a blackman] for Hir chap takeing Hold of Him and drawing Him to the beed Side Sot How down With Hir arms Round His Sholders and gave Him a Kis. . . . [She] Sliped Hir Hand down Into His Britches—but it Wold take amuch abeler Hand than mine to describe palls feelings at this time being naturly a little Relegous modest and Bashfull. He Sot as near the wall as Was Poseble and it may be soposed He Indevoured to Creep Into it for Such Was His atachment to the old lady that he kept His [eyes] turned Constantly up to the trap door and to His great Joy Some person oppened it to Come In to the Same Room—but Pall no Sooner Saw the light [from the trap door] than He Sprang from the old lady and Was out In an Instent and maid to our lodge-ing as fast as Poseble Wherare the other two [men] Soon followed and told what Head Happened to Pall.

Perhaps the most revealing fact is that prostitution in Santa Fe was virtually unknown until American control over the region had been consolidated.

But the principal appeal of Santa Fe and the New Mexico Ter-ritory continued to be the profit potential that its relative isolation afforded American merchants. Had Santa Fe, Taos, Paso del Norte, and Ciudad Chihuahua been less remote, traders from Missouri would have had little incentive to haul their assorted goods south-westward, for the prices these wares would have commanded would have been little different than those charged at Independence, Mis-souri. But the Mexican War and the early years of American occu-pation of New Mexico threatened to disrupt the profitable commerce of the prairies, much to the consternation of western American businessmen.

Even before the Mexican War had officially begun, traders at Independence theorized that their livelihood would be greatly imperiled if hostilities between the United States and Mexico erupted. They could easily find themselves in enemy territory, either at Santa Fe or Ciudad Chihuahua, and suffer the confiscation of their goods. To avoid such a possibility, one wagon train of merchants set forth for Santa Fe about the first of May, 1846, and by traveling at maximum speed, reached Santa Fe in forty-five days. Official news of the war's commencement had not yet arrived, and the situation in northern New Mexico was peaceful. Rumors of conflict were discussed openly, but sales were brisk. After a few days of rest and marketing, the party hitched up its wagons and moved southward on the road toward Ciudad Chihuahua, where profits were expected to be even greater. By the time the traders arrived there, news of the war had preceded them, and they were detained by government officials and their commodities seized for good measure. One American businessman immediately passed himself off as a teamster and had Albert Speyer pose as the merchant. The ploy worked, for by then almost anyone received more favorable consideration than a *gringo* in that provincial capital.

Two other Independence merchants, James Aull and Samuel Owens, as mentioned previously, were far less fortunate. They had recently formed a partnership when Aull, previously in partnership with his brother Robert, had transferred his merchandise from his three stores in Lexington, Liberty, and Richmond, Missouri, to facilities he owned at Independence; Owens, who had been selling goods on credit to Santa Fe traders for years, joined with Aull because of continuous cash-flow problems. It simply took too long to collect from the traders, and, with his own line of credit stretched to the limit, he needed some method of replenishing his stocks of merchandise. Thus, in 1846 Aull and Owens joined forces. They also decided to venture $70,000 worth of assorted goods by trading directly with Santa Fe and Ciudad Chihuahua, Mexico.

In late May, 1846, Aull and Owens, in the company of a large group of merchants, departed Independence. Three hundred miles to the southwest, near Pawnee Rock, the party was overtaken by an advance detachment of General Kearny's Army of the West and ordered to halt until the main force of the military arrived. They were to be escorted to Santa Fe. The businessmen protested. It would be an unnecessary and costly delay. The officer in charge repeated his instructions, adding that the traders might suffer the confiscation of their wares in Santa Fe unless they had the protection of the army. The War Department in Washington had decided upon the policy, and it would be carried out. When Kearny arrived at the junction of the Pawnee and Arkansas rivers, where the businessmen had camped, the traders dutifully, albeit grudgingly, fell in behind the troopers and, with what must have seemed to the Missourians to be undue caution, slowly made their way to Santa Fe.

The situation in the New Mexico capital was hardly conducive to profitable commercial arrangements when, on August 18, Kearny's Army of the West and Aull and Owens' party arrived. American and Mexican businessmen there reported that the war had greatly upset the local economy. Few buyers had been willing to part with their money or trade goods since official news of the conflict had been made public a month before. Perhaps conditions were more settled toward the interior of Mexico. At least, that is what Aull, Owens, and the three hundred businessmen and teamsters in their party apparently surmised, for almost immediately the traders proceeded southward. Almost halfway to Paso del Norte, the wagon train stopped and camped at the ruins of the Val Verde pueblo; they remained there two weeks, hoping to learn of conditions to the south.

Before they could decide whether or not to push on, the group was again overtaken by the United States Army, this time by an advance scout of Colonel Alexander Doniphan's Missouri Volunteers. Again, the businessmen were ordered to wait for military protection. By then the traders feared attack by the Mexicans and, without much serious protest, complied with the instructions. Once Doniphan arrived, he organized them into a "Traders Battalion," which was used effectively by the colonel when he captured Paso del Norte in January, 1847. Owens died in the skirmish.

Aull and his companions continued southward with Doniphan's expedition—Owens' body placed in a gunny sack and laid on one of the wagons, to be buried in Ciudad Chihuahua. Once the provincial capital was captured on March 1, Owens was interred with all the pomp of a military funeral, and Aull set forth to accomplish his mission—trade for a profit with the local residents. Sales were brisk, and on March 3 Aull was able to send $15,000 by military courier to a correspondent in Santa Fe, E. W. Pomeroy, with instructions to forward the money to his brother in Independence, who managed the store there. But rumors of Doniphan's imminent departure for the eastern front to link up with General Taylor's command circulated freely in Ciudad Chihuahua. What were the traders to do without military protection? Doniphan tried in vain to negotiate an agreement with Mexican officials whereby the captured capital would be declared an open city and thus of course afford American merchants some security as they transacted their business. Finally, in late April Doniphan's command marched out of Ciudad Chihuahua to join Taylor, and the traders were left to their own devices.

As the Missouri Volunteers marched eastward toward Saltillo accompanied by a large band of camp followers, a frenzy of activity at the other side of town announced the hasty departure of most of the traders, as they scurried back toward the relative safety of Santa Fe. A few, including James Aull, refused to be stampeded, objected to sacrificing their merchandise at a fraction of its cost or even to hauling it back north, and remained in Ciudad Chihuahua. At first Aull's decision appeared both wise and profitable, for every few days he was able to dispatch several thousand dollars to his correspondent in Santa Fe. Then, on June 23, he was murdered by four Mexican robbers in the small store that housed his wares; the culprits were soon arrested, and most of the goods and money they had stolen were recovered. Mexican authorities then placed Aull's property in a "depository," rental on which was fixed at twenty-five cents per day, and appointed a John Mandri as a receiver for the estate. Mandri maintained meticulous records, which showed that by August he had sold $4,323.19 worth of Aull's trade goods. His accounts payable column, the cost of legal documents, translations, customs, and so forth, amounted to $4,323.19. Indeed, when Aull's associate in Santa Fe, E. W. Pomeroy, arrived in Ciudad Chihuahua that month to take charge of the estate, he found virtually nothing but the meticulous records remaining. After totting expenses— $70,000 in trade goods plus approximately $30,000 in transportation costs and incidental business disbursements—Pomeroy guessed that the defunct firm of Owens and Aull had barely broken even in the trade with Mexico.

The travail of Owens and Aull, though undoubtedly one of the more extreme cases of business disaster during the Mexican War, had its parallels. Traversing the plains of Kansas and the mountains of New Mexico was hardly a safe undertaking for employer or employee. Risks were omnipresent. Potential profits, however, were sufficient to cause cautious merchants to accept the uncertainty. No doubt the widely discussed lifestyles of Mexicans in Santa Fe and Ciudad Chihuahua encouraged many young, adventurous men to risk their lives for thirty dollars a month and the mere chance of revelry at the end of the trail. And nominal American control of New Mexico did not automatically diminish the dangers.

An immediate threat to those who followed the Santa Fe Trail were the plains Indians, who continued to be as much of a problem as they had been in the 1820's and 1830's, swooping down on both military convoys and unprotected bands of traders. Robert Morris Peck, an enlisted man attached to the First Cavalry regiment at Fort Leavenworth who occasionally drew patrol duty on the trail, recalled his first impression of the path to Santa Fe in 1856:

> Frequent graves were to be seen along the roadway, many of them marked with rude wooden crosses. Such almost invariably indicated the last resting place of some Mexican, who is always Catholic. I had noticed, too, but thought it the result of carelessness in placing the crosses on the graves, that nearly all of these cross-pieces were in a slanting position, but on mentioning this peculiarity to one of the old soldiers, he informed me that when the horizontal piece was slanted it meant, "died with his boots on," or a violent death—usually killed by Indians—and that where the cross-piece was fastened at right angles to the upright (and there were few, for people seldom died of disease on the plains), it signified, "died on the square," or a natural death.

Although Private Peck was obviously prone toward sweeping, probably exaggerated generalizations, his account, published in 1904 by the Kansas Historical Society, does summarize rather well the popular attitude toward travel on the Santa Fe Trail. It was dangerous.

In the dozen years that preceded the Civil War, during which the American army sought to establish firm control over the vast

Southwest, conditions did not improve appreciably. According to an anonymous report in the June 3, 1848, issue of *Reveille,* an army publication, virtually every wagon train, military and private alike, had been attacked as it sought to cross the plains between Independence and Santa Fe. Those that ventured westward to Bent's Fort, one contemporary observer insisted, could count on the "Pawnees . . . playing the deuce with the provision wagons." Perturbed by the situation, the unnamed witness to depredations openly hoped that the bloodbath on the frontier would propel "Uncle Sam, that old fool, [to] punish these Indians who have so long committed outrages upon the traders with impunity." Comanches, who frequently raided the trail between the Arkansas and Cimarron rivers, sacked trains to obtain horses, mules, and other goods that they exchanged with New Mexican *comancheros,* traders who cared very little how the Indians obtained the wares they exchanged for guns, ammunition, and fire water. Colonel William Gilpin, attached to the command at Fort Leavenworth, estimated that 47 teamsters had been killed, 330 wagons looted and destroyed, and 6,500 head of livestock seized by the plains Indians in 1847 alone.

An obvious solution was to patrol the region more intensively, a need that was made even more pressing in 1849, once traffic along the road increased because of the gold rush to California. In southwest Kansas, three temporary military encampments were established to provide a modicum of protection for travelers: Mann (1845–1848), Atkinson (1850–1854), and Mackay (1850–1851). The army in 1853 also established Fort Riley at the point where the Santa Fe and Oregon trails bifurcated in order to provide patrols for both overland routes. In the West, the War Department literally had to establish a command organization. That territory added to the United States since 1845 was divided into military regions: Departments 8 (Texas), 9 (New Mexico), 10 (California), and 11 (Oregon). The expense of garrisoning the West was appreciable. During fiscal year 1849–1850, expenditures for Departments 1 through 7 (in essence, the settled United States) totalled $2.4 million; Departments 8 through 11 required an appropriation of $7.4 million.

In the Ninth Military Department, army facilities proliferated. In 1849 the army occupied seven more or less permanent posts with a complement of 987 troops, an average of 141 per encampment.

Ten years later, the department counted sixteen such places, a total of some 2,000 soldiers being stationed in New Mexico. And yet the average garrison had been reduced in size by 16 men. The number of troops was obviously insufficient to eliminate the threat of Indian attack, but the problem was national in character. The army was under strength, for, following the Mexican War, recruiters had been unable to meet their quotas. Too many young men preferred the comparative quiet and far more lucrative prospects of civilian life to the uncertainties and dangers of soldiering.

But the army in New Mexico tried desperately to patrol the area. Of the sixteen posts that had been established in the New Mexico Territory by the time of the Civil War, only seven were significant. In northern New Mexico was Fort Union, which served as the principal supply depot for the Ninth Military Department. Along the Rio Grande, protecting the route from Fort Bliss at El Paso, were Forts Craig, Fillmore, and Marcy (at Santa Fe). Southeast of the river, nestled atop a plateau in the White Mountains, lay Fort Stanton, on guard against the Mescalero Apaches who roamed nearby. In present Arizona, a part of the department, were Forts Defiance and Buchanan.

At best the Ninth Military Department fought a holding action against the Indians during the dozen years that followed the Mexican War. A large part of the responsibility for the army's failure to bring hostiles under effective control can be traced to Washington, where consensus as to policy failed to crystallize. During the first seven years of American control of New Mexico, the federal government seemed convinced that Indian agents and treaties could bring peace to the New Mexican frontier. Apaches and Navajos most definitely did come to terms with the representatives of the Great White Father in Washington, but as often as not they abandoned their promises as soon as they encountered targets of opportunity. Troops again would take to the field in pursuit of the raiders, skirmish with them, and, if fortunate enough to escape with their lives, see the nomads vanish into the rugged mountains. It was like chasing smoke.

About 1853, authorities in Washington ordered some changes in policy. First of all, General John Garland was named commander of the department and assigned three hundred fresh troops to strengthen existing garrisons. Patrols were ordered to increase their sweeps across the deserts and in lush mountain valleys. Congress also appropriated $30,000 with which to negotiate new treaties with hostiles, to buy their peaceable relations. But nothing much changed. Mescaleros raided unsuspecting wagon trains along the lower Rio Grande, ambushed military patrols, and occasionally even harassed army garrisons. Navajos were hardly more tractable. The army almost continuously for ten years fought these masters of the desert Southwest, until the Civil War forced an understaffed and distracted army to retrench.

Unsuccessful though the initial American occupation of New Mexico might have been from the military point of view, it did have its brighter side. The search for elusive Indians did allow troopers to chart the region and thereby afforded the United States a far better idea of the region's resources. The army, for example, discovered that the mountains contained literally millions of board-feet of lumber, valuable raw material that awaited only the axe and the saw. Soldiers camped along countless unnamed streams dreamed of riches such as those discovered in California and panned for gold. A few even found traces of the yellow mineral, much to their excitement. Businessmen in Albuquerque and Santa Fe were hardly unaware of the reports of mining opportunities, and many doubtlessly laid plans to exploit the possibility once a definitive answer to the Indian problem had been found. And too, there were those businessmen in Missouri who for so long had profited from the trade with Santa Fe and who continued to reap financial rewards, especially from the sale to and supply of the military garrisons of Department 9.

While it is doubtlessly true that the majority of the trade and commerce with New Mexico continued as it had begun thirty years before, the scope of profitable ventures had broadened. In addition to freighting assorted wares to Santa Fe and farther southwest, Missouri merchants during the late 1840's and throughout the 1850's discovered that the United States Army at Fort Union needed a wide range of supplies and was willing to pay premium prices for them. Joseph Murphy, a St. Louis wagonmaker, enjoyed brisk sales because of the army. Murphy was an adaptive entrepreneur who, when the Mexican governor of New Mexico once had slapped an exorbitant tax on each American vehicle entering Santa Fe, had simply designed a bigger one, which held more trade goods and which, even after the levy, afforded traders a reasonable profit. And when the Mexican War began, the Missourian's shop opened early and closed late to assemble as many vehicles as possible. The military demanded them, and Murphy was happy to fill any and all orders. Even after the conflict ended, he continued to sell his sturdy "Murphy wagons" to the government, which needed to transport supplies westward. Between 1847 and 1852, his factory marketed $12,263.52 worth of rolling stock to the army.

Murphy was far from the only Missouri businessman to capitalize upon the military bonanza. The army needed food for men and animals, bedding, clothing, and other staples. Storekeepers from St. Louis to Independence readily filled the demand. Freighters just as eagerly ferried the goods westward. In 1848, James Browne, an Independence teamster, agreed to haul 200,000 pounds of military supplies to New Mexico at a cost of $11.75 per hundredweight. Browne was soon joined by William H. Russell, who a few years afterward developed the Pony Express, and the two transported goods wherever the army needed them. Depending upon the distance to be traversed, the relative danger, and the time of the year, the Independence firm of Browne, Russell & Company charged the government between $7.875 and $14.333 per hundredweight of cargo. The smaller fee moved goods to Fort Union in the spring, the larger to El Paso in the winter. The company's 135 wagons reportedly were always on the trail, going to one place or another. And it was not unusual for the freighters to include a few wagonloads of trade goods in a military convoy whenever one of their trains departed Independence for points southwest.

After all, the Santa Fe trade was still reasonably profitable, even after the American occupation of the territory. To be sure, the character of the commerce continuously underwent change during the 1850's, but an enterprising businessman could expect a profit if he were resourceful.

The New Mexican economy was still primitive by any standard of measurement. The region was sparsely settled, there was almost no local production of trade goods (except for a few handicraft items), and local consumers had become accustomed to rely on wagon trains from the east to supply their needs. As late as 1850, agricultural production—both that of the Mexican population and the indigenous, "tame" Indians—was barely at a subsistence level. Mexicans constantly faced the problems posed by "wild" Indians, who took great delight in stripping fields bare and running off domesticated animals. Docile Pueblo Indians, who had farmed along the Rio Grande for centuries, saw little value in producing consistent surpluses. They grew only what they needed from year to year, and no American Indian agent could persuade them to cultivate their lands more intensively and to sell their excess corn crops.

What livestock there were in New Mexico in the 1850's, according to contemporary observers, fell into two categories—poor and sheep. "Poor" embraced the horses, cattle, and mules that were usually emaciated because local strains of grasses were sparse and provided an inadequate diet. The sheep, of course, foraged far more efficiently, and they provided both wool for export to Missouri and, later, to California, as well as meat for the local populace.

Handicrafts included a wide variety of undertakings. Carpenters constructed wagons, carts, and spare parts. Wool and even some cotton were woven into fabrics by local Indians, the Navajos already gaining some reputation for the quality of their blankets. Mexicans usually made clothing, such as *serapes*, some of which were traded to Anglo-Americans for other wares. Goldsmiths and silversmiths hammered out fine pieces of jewelry that were widely demanded. Josiah Gregg insisted that these artisans of northern New Mexico were as skilled as those anywhere.

Milling industries, until the time of the American occupation, had revolved totally about grain crops, cornmeal being the most popular flour in the region. The mills were primitive devices, relying primarily upon animal power or occasionally upon water to turn the grist wheel. Once Americans arrived in considerable numbers and had surveyed the tree-lined mountains that overlooked the Santa Fe valley, a few primitive lumber mills were established. By the early 1860's, local board production afforded some export for the Santa Fe trade.

One New Mexico endeavor—the making of wines and brandy—greatly intrigued Americans who visited the area. For example, John T. Hughes reported that the wines produced in the area were equal to those of the Rhine valley in Europe. Unfortunately, there was hardly enough of the light elixirs to satisfy local demand, much less provide the basis for profitable exportation. Such was the problem with the New Mexican economy. The fur trade, which had provided much of the original impetus for trade with Missouri, had begun to wane. And although there undoubtedly were valuable minerals in the numerous mountain chains that ranged the full length of the territory, no glory hole on a scale with that of California, Nevada, or Colorado had been uncovered in New Mexico by 1860.

The trade with New Mexico continued to be profitable for Missouri businessmen for two reasons. First, as noted, the United States government paid premium prices for supplies with which to support troops in the region; moreover, freighters reaped a profit from ferrying the wares westward. And second, New Mexicans by the 1850's were accustomed to American products and continued to demand them. That each year they apparently paid ever higher prices, in terms of the commodities they swapped, apparently bothered them little. After all, they liked the foodstuffs, bolts of cloth, whiskeys, machine goods, and other wares hawked so eagerly by traders who often stood atop their wagons to attract a crowd. Too, New Mexicans had little choice but to pay increasingly higher prices, for by the 1850's they were bidding against a horde of wealthseekers bound for California and the gold fields. And the new party of immigrants seemed willing to pay any price for supplies, just for the chance of scratching about in the rich soil of the Pacific coast. But it probably delighted New Mexicans to sell their bony animals to California-bound travelers, especially when they collected three, five, and even ten times the livestock's local value.

The trade with New Mexico during the 1850's was changing, however. The usually high profits of the pre–Mexican War era were no longer being made by businessmen from the East. Those who continued to extract excellent returns were those who relied upon sales to the government, who freighted supplies for the army, or who refurbished migrant wagon trains headed toward the gold fields. If any entrepreneur engaged in the Santa Fe trade seriously worried about the future of the commerce of the prairies, however, he kept it to himself.

CHAPTER 14

The Rumble of Cannons, the Crack of Muskets

While Americans prepared to cast their ballots during the fall of 1860 in what was to be the most crucial election of the nineteenth century, New Mexicans watched with quiet indifference. The issues of slavery and states rights hardly affected them, even though the territory had welcomed a considerable number of both northern and southern sympathizers. True, the territorial legislature in 1859 had enacted a slave code, thereby tacitly approving that labor system for New Mexicans, but the census of 1860 reported only eight-five Negroes in the entire territory, all of whom were described as "free colored." Probably of far more significance was the fact that the law also dealt with "servants," those peons who were bound by contracts or debts or both to aristocratic *ricos*. Numbering into the hundreds, these people virtually were indentured servants, their station little better than that of the African slaves to the east. And the ongoing debate over states rights was of little consequence to an area that had yet to achieve the lofty status of statehood.

But the election and its consequences were far more important to Santa Feans and their neighbors than they realized. They were tied economically to Missouri by the trade and commerce of the prairies, and the response of that state to the secessionist movement might well force even blasé, bucolic Santa Fe to action—action that would drag the remainder of the territory into the conflict. Too, there still was Texas, which bordered New Mexico on the east and south. Few knowledgeable observers seriously doubted which way that state would jump, even though General Sam Houston, the governor of Texas, was an ardent supporter of the Union. Once Texas linked up with a southern confederation, it would be merely a matter of time before officials in Austin again would cast a covetous eye toward the west. And if war between the North and South actually erupted, New Mexicans could expect to see their already understaffed military garrisons depleted by the conflict in the East. Indian raids undoubtedly would escalate, thereby endangering life, limb, property, and the Santa Fe trade.

Probably as much as any other area of the country, New Mexico had a vested interest in peace, but most of the Anglo residents of the sparsely settled territory, caught up in the emotional campaign rhetoric of 1860, tended to gravitate toward either a northern or southern position. The Hispanic population, on the other hand, yawned from the boredom of *gringo* politics. It was many months after the southern states had seceded from the Union and the shooting had begun before the reality of the Civil War reached remote Santa Fe.

Toward the end of January, 1861, an extralegal gathering of Texas politicos, elected by county voters, met in Austin to decide the fate of their state. By a vote of 152 to 6, the secessionist convention recommended that Texas withdraw from the Union, a position the electorate endorsed by a 2-to-1 margin a month later. In addition to suggesting a formal break with the government in Washington, the secessionist convention named two commissioners to travel to New Mexico and invite that territory to join the Confederacy. One of them, Philemon T. Herbert, a lawyer then residing in El Paso, immediately authored an open letter to residents of the Gadsden Purchase area, which had been acquired from Mexico in 1853, and asked them to merge their fate with "those who have ever sympathized with you." Secessionist conventions soon were held in southern New Mexico and at Tucson, and both declared their respective areas to be free of "northern tyranny." Considering the fact that northern New Mexico, especially Santa Fe, refused to follow suit, those actions south of the Gila River were of little long-run consequence.

Santa Fe's recalcitrance surprised many contemporary observers. While the pivotal city had been decidedly northern in attitude in 1850, it had undergone significant philosophical changes during

the ensuing ten years as more and more southerners had migrated
there. The territory's slave code of 1859 seemed to predict that,
were the Union dismembered by secession, New Mexico would drift
southward.

What many failed to perceive was the smoldering distrust, in
some cases outright hatred, of Texas and Texans. Twice before the
aggressive peoples to the east had attempted to annex New Mexico,
and residents of the upper Rio Grande valley had not forgotten.
There was an abiding distrust, perhaps even fear, of the more dense-
ly populated area east of the 103rd meridian. Yet it was not until
Texas troops actually invaded New Mexico that the moderately
strong prosouthern sentiment dissolved in a torrent of activity to defend the territory. New Mexico's part in the Civil War thus was less
a manifestation of the antislavery impulse than an anti-Texas bias.

Miguel A. Otero, New Mexico's delegate to Congress, suggested
that the territory turn its back on both the North and the South.
Probably expressing the views of most of the region's Hispanic population, which saw the crisis of Union as ephemeral to their inter-
ests, Otero proposed that New Mexico lead the West to form a
confederation of Pacific states, with whom New Mexicans had been
historically tied. But the territory's residents of Mexican and Indian
descent were more inclined to ignore the bloodbath to the east,
apparently hoping it would never progress as far west as the Rio
Grande valley. Californians were much more receptive to Otero's
scheme, but even there no ground swell of public support forced
action.

Otero's Pacific confederation notwithstanding, the pressing issue
was the South's secession and the armed conflict in the East. How
long could New Mexico remain aloof? To soldiers stationed in the
Ninth Military Department the issue was crucial. Those with a
southern background understandably worried that if they remained
on duty in New Mexico they might be faced with a terrible dilemma: a Confederate invasion of New Mexico would force them either
to stand and fight men with whom they were philosophically
attuned or to desert, which for officers would be tantamount to
dishonor.

For three of the department's highest ranking officers, resignation was the only solution: Colonel W. W. Loring, who commanded

the army in New Mexico; Lieutenant Colonel George B. Crittenden, Loring's chief-of-staff; and Major Henry Hopkins Sibley, considered by many to be the brightest tactician in the Ninth Military Department. After posting their letters of resignation, the three made their way southward to Texas to join the Confederate army, Sibley, a graduate of West Point, immediately being commissioned as a brigadier general and ordered to San Antonio, where he was to raise whatever size force he deemed necessary to wrest New Mexico from Federal control.

While Sibley struggled in San Antonio during the summer of 1861 to recruit an entire brigade of troops, no easy undertaking, Confederate forces in Texas already were preparing for the inevitable invasion of New Mexico. When the Texas secessionist convention had met in January to endorse separation, it had also authorized the creation of two cavalry regiments. One, under the command of Colonel Ben McCulloch, was to secure the surrender of all Federal forces in the relatively settled portion of Texas east of the San Antonio River. A second force was divided in two, one detachment under Colonel John S. ("Rip") Ford being dispatched to the lower Rio Grande valley and the other, under Colonel John R. Baylor, marching westward to occupy the region and military garrisons west of the Pecos River, most important of which was Fort Bliss at El Paso. It would serve as a staging point for any invasion of New Mexico.

While Sibley sought recruits in San Antonio, Baylor decided to strike. Confederate sentiment was notoriously strong in southern New Mexico, as illustrated by the recent secessionist conventions there, and Baylor proposed to march northward and capture Fort Fillmore, located about forty miles north of El Paso on the Rio Grande. Although he was outmanned (258 Confederates versus 550 Union troops), the element of surprise, Baylor believed, rested with the South. On July 24, Texans occupied the town of Mesilla, just across the river from Fort Fillmore, and began surveying the situation. Major Isaac Lynde, commanding at Fillmore and having reconnaissance reports of Confederate movements, almost immediately demanded that Baylor surrender to his superior force. The Texan replied that his men were there for combat, not cowardice.

Lynde accepted the challenge and ordered an attack. He would have been better advised to have remained at Fillmore, where he could have repelled the expected Confederate advance. Union troops understandably approached Mesilla cautiously, preferring that artillery reduce the village to rubble before they charged. But the cannon had to be moved by hand, an arduous task made even more difficult by soft sand that seemed bottomless under the weight of the field pieces. When the artillery was finally moved into place, aimed, and fired, the shells exploded prematurely in midflight. The Texans hooted with amusement, suggesting that Johnny Rebs could do more damage with hand-thrown stones. Citizens of Mesilla, sympathetic to the South, climbed atop houses and hurled insults at the embarrassed Yankees. As the Federal force continued its slow advance, the Texans commenced a withering fire, the first volley of which reportedly downed two officers. Lynde decided to withdraw, leaving the town to Baylor.

The major contemplated his next move. Fort Fillmore would be impossible to defend if the Confederates laid siege to it, for its water supply was more than a mile away. Spies from Mesilla reported to Lynde that Baylor was receiving reinforcements from Fort Bliss and that volunteers from the nearby community had swelled the Rebel force to more than seven hundred men. Baylor awaited only the arrival of artillery pieces from Bliss before he attacked the fort, and if Lynde advanced on Mesilla before they arrived, the Confederate officer was prepared to divert a portion of his force to occupy Fillmore in Lynde's absence. Lynde decided to abandon the fort and to march either toward Fort Craig on the Rio Grande or Fort Stanton in the White Mountains. In either case, there would be safety in numbers.

On July 26 the major ordered burned all stores that could not be transported, and in the predawn hours of the twenty-seventh, he directed his men to march toward Fort Stanton. Lynde's decision was incredible, for he had no knowledge of the route across the desert to the mountains; moreover, he did not even know the precise distance to St. Augustine Springs, a vital waterhole on the road to Stanton. And he exercised less than effective control over his command, for many Union soldiers emptied their water canteens and refilled them with whiskey, a liquid the troopers believed to be far more vital to survival. Little wonder that during the ensuing two-day forced march Baylor, who pursued Lynde, was able to track his quarry by the bodies of heat-prostrate Yankees who littered the roadway. Lynde himself became a victim of the searing desert sun, possibly suffering a mild heatstroke.

When Baylor's force of 162 men overtook the numerically superior Federal force on the twenty-ninth at St. Augustine Springs, Lynde simply surrendered. His men were in no condition to resist. Union resolve elsewhere in southern New Mexico was equally questionable. News of Lynde's capitulation caused immediate panic at Fort Stanton; the commander there ordered his men to beat a hasty retreat westward to Fort Craig on the Rio Grande. Southern New Mexico, then popularly called Arizona, had fallen to the Confederates with relative ease. Could the remainder of the territory long resist?

While he savored his victory and awaited reinforcements from Sibley, Baylor began organizing a temporary government for the "Territory of Arizona." On August 1 he announced that the new Confederate province embraced all that area bounded by the Texas and Mexican borders on the south, the Texas Panhandle on the east, the 34th parallel on the north, and the Colorado River on the west. A week later, a convention in Tucson elected Granville H. Oury, an erstwhile Texan, as the territory's delegate to the congress in Richmond. By the time Oury arrived there, a bill to organize Arizona under the laws of the Confederacy had been introduced, and on January 18, 1862, President Jefferson Davis signed it into law. The land mass of the Confederate States of America had expanded, and officials in Richmond asserted that "New Mexico," then described as that area north of the 34th parallel, soon would be annexed.

Meanwhile Sibley had begun to move. Leaving San Antonio in November with three regiments, he arrived at Fort Bliss on December 14. While there he assumed command of all southern forces in West Texas, Arizona, and New Mexico, recognized Baylor as the civil and military governor of Arizona, and by proclamation invited the people of New Mexico to join the Confederacy. Sibley then ordered his troops northward to take New Mexico from the Federals. At Mesilla he diverted a small detachment of his force westward to Tucson as a token of his authority.

But Sibley's immediate objective was Fort Craig, a garrison approximately halfway between El Paso and Albuquerque. The Union post was of considerable significance to the Confederate officer. First of all, he knew it had been reinforced by troops that had abandoned Fort Stanton in the wake of Baylor's victory at St. Augustine Springs. Second, it controlled the road between Texas and the north; it had to be taken if Albuquerque and Santa Fe were ever to fall to the Stars and Bars. And third, Craig was commanded by Colonel E. R. S. Canby, Sibley's brother-in-law.

Three thousand, five hundred soldiers in the Confederate Army of New Mexico marched out of Mesilla in early February, 1862, and followed the Rio Grande northward toward Fort Craig, where 2,065 Federals prepared for their arrival. Canby had no intention of allowing his brother-in-law to assume the offensive, and the Union commander crossed to the east bank of the river. He selected the small village of Val Verde in which to make his stand, for he believed that it would be far more difficult for the Confederates to assault than the fort. On February 20, Sibley's force arrived and prepared to attack Val Verde.

Sibley was less than an effective leader in the battle that followed. The general suffered from dipsomania to the extent that his men derisively referred to him as "the Walking Whiskey Keg," and on the morning of February 21, as his regimental commanders readied their men, Sibley apparently began to drink. As the battle of Val Verde commenced about eight o'clock in the morning, Sibley mounted his horse to watch the engagement. All morning and into the afternoon the Federals outmaneuvered, outflanked, and outfought the Rebs—Sibley becoming increasingly distraught with each setback. About midafternoon, the general declared that he was too exhausted to sit a saddle any longer, told one of his regimental commanders, Colonel Tom Green, to direct the remainder of the battle, and retired to his tent, roaring drunk, according to one eyewitness account.

Green, a veteran of the Texas Revolution and the Mexican War, was no tactician. But, like U. S. Grant, whom critics have charged with the same failing, he grasped the potential of one basic battle stratagem—the hell-bent for leather charge. Green ordered an all-out attack, and the Federal picket line almost immediately broke and ran for the protection of Fort Craig. Had one detachment of the

Texas volunteers been able to hold its position against the near-hysterical retreat of the Union troops, Green might have been able to capture Canby's entire force then and there. The temporary commander then turned his attention toward Fort Craig, which he proposed to take at once. It was about then that Sibley recovered sufficiently from his "exhaustion" to resume command, and he ordered a cease-fire. Following a consultation with his staff, Sibley decided to leave Canby in the garrison—it would be too costly and time-consuming to dislodge him—and to continue on northward to bring New Mexico under total Confederate control.

On his march to the north, Sibley left his wounded at Socorro and then proceeded on to Albuquerque, which the nervous Yankees had abandoned on hearing of the Rebel's approach. Captain H. M. Enos, who commanded a small Union detachment at Albuquerque, had elected to retreat to the relative protection of Fort Union once he learned of Colonel Canby's plight. Enos knew that he could not resist a superior force, and he believed that, rather than attempt a futile delaying action, tactics demanded that he burn what stores he could not transport and move on. When Sibley arrived in Albuquerque in early March, he occupied it without difficulty. After assigning a token force to occupy the city, he made preparations to continue on northward to Santa Fe, which he had decided would serve as a staging point for his assault on Fort Union, the final campaign designed to wrest control of the territory for the Confederacy.

As Sibley marched toward the north, incomprehensibly burning abandoned Union supplies as he went, the Yankees prepared a counteroffensive. The governor of Colorado, William Gilpin, had raised a force of 1,300, placed it under the command of Colonel John Slough, and ordered it to run the Confederates out of New Mexico, for their proximity was a real threat to Colorado. Slough had marched southward to Fort Union, where he procured materiel, and, despite apprehensions of the Yankee commander there (who undoubtedly wished that the "Pikes Peakers" would remain at Union to help defend the fort), immediately headed southward to engage the enemy. Meanwhile, Sibley had his forces trudging along the Santa Fe Trail to attack Fort Union. The two forces met at Glorieta Pass on March 28.

During the two-day battle that followed, the Rebels were totally routed. Unable to proceed through the mountain gap, Sibley's force sustained concentrated fire from the Colorado volunteers, designed to pin down the Confederates, while a segment of the Pike's Peakers crossed the mountains to encircle the enemy. Led by Major J. M. Chivington, who two years later would gain infamy as the leader of the Sand Creek Massacre, the Yankees harassed Sibley's force unmercifully, destroying in the process most of the Confederates' meager supply of rations and ammunition. At the end of the second day, Sibley decided his position was totally untenable and ordered a hasty retreat from New Mexico.

The march southward for Sibley was more a hysterical flight than an organized retreat. The Colorado volunteers continued to pressure him on the north, and Colonel Canby, having learned of his brother-in-law's defeat at Glorieta Pass, finally decided to leave the safety of Fort Craig to join in the affray. Meanwhile, a column of volunteers from California had marched eastward, captured Tucson from the Confederates, and prepared to cut off Sibley as he approached El Paso. Adding to the urgency of flight were the hundreds of Apaches who, observing the situation from afar, decided to join the fracas, not necessarily on the side of the Union but in general harassment of any vulnerable whites. Sibley's retreat soon became a mad dash for safety, wounded and dead soldiers being abandoned in the process. Wagons were set afire so that their slow, arduous progress would not impede the pell-mell rush for El Paso. By early May, more than two thousand Rebels were scattered out all the way from Doña Ana to El Paso. Sibley had lost almost half his command.

It was mid-June before the Confederate brigade, or what was left of the 3,700-man force, could muster the energy to continue the retreat to San Antonio. Sick, footsore, thirsty, and hungry men made their way eastward, the line of march stringing further and further apart with each mile traveled. On August 9 Sibley finally arrived in San Antonio. Three months had passed before the last straggler joined him. By then, substantially more than half of Sibley's brigade had been captured or lay dead in forgotten graves along the Rio Grande. Santa Fe and New Mexico remained under the Stars and Stripes, and the third and last Texas challenge to the independence of the region had ended.

But the era of warfare and bloodshed in the vicinity of the Santa Fe Trail and trade was far from over. The Civil War, which merely touched New Mexico during its earliest stages, had a serious effect on the territory, for the slow progress of a decade toward control of the indigenous population—the Indians—was wiped out in a few months. Indeed, from Kansas southward along the course of the Santa Fe Trail, hostile bands of Indians sensed the impotence of the government in Washington to control them, and their attacks on the unguarded frontier escalated markedly.

In New Mexico, the Apaches and Navajos were the principal threat. Already understaffed military garrisons were drained of manpower by the demands of the war, and these frontier posts invariably received inadequate allotments of replacements and supplies for the duration of the conflict. While the decision of the Lincoln administration to deemphasize control of the territories—given the exigencies of the war that was tearing the nation apart—can easily be understood, it nevertheless caused grief and suffering in the West. Far from being naive savages, the Indians realized their time to strike had come.

Federal forces had barely evacuated Fort Stanton in 1861 when White Mountain Apaches took to the warpath. Raiding eastward onto the plains, the marauders swooped down on unsuspecting ranches, killed whomever they found, ran off livestock, and set the torch to what remained. By 1862, the area's whites had virtually abandoned the region to the Indians. To the northwest the Navajos were equally determined to oust settlers. And the military, reeling under the initially vigorous Confederate offensive, was in no position to prevent the Indian uprising. Once Sibley had retreated to the safety of Texas, however, the situation changed.

Brigadier General James H. Carleton during the fall of 1862 was ordered to New Mexico to relieve Colonel Canby of command of the department, for Sibley's brother-in-law had far from distinguished himself in the recent campaign. Carleton appraised the situation. Rebels from Texas were unlikely to pose another threat to the territory immediately; thus, he could concentrate his manpower in an effort to stabilize the frontier. He was to order three major campaigns to quiet the Apaches, the Navajos, and the Comanches. It was the Comanches, with their Kiowa allies, who most plagued the Santa Fe trade. Rather than split his forces and engage all the hostiles simultaneously, the general decided to subdue the Apaches first.

Carleton's strategy was simple and unyielding. He ordered Colonel Christopher ("Kit") Carson to lead five companies of New Mexico volunteers toward the White Mountain stronghold of the Mescaleros and to show them no quarter. Braves were to be slain, squaws and children captured. Once the Apaches had had a thorough taste of Yankee resolve, Carleton was convinced, they would sue for peace. Following several engagements with Colonel Carson and the deaths of scores of Mescaleros, Apache leaders capitulated just as Carleton had predicted. They agreed to move to Bosque Redondo at Fort Sumner on the Pecos River, where they were to be watched by the military. Some four hundred Apaches had surrendered to authorities at Fort Sumner by the spring of 1863, the remainder fleeing to remote mountains in the territory. The immediate threat to the southern half of New Mexico had been removed.

General Carleton then repeated the tactic in the northwest against the Navajos. His scouts informed the Indians that after July 20, 1863, all members of their tribe who had failed to submit to relocation at Bosque Redondo would be treated as hostiles and every male capable of bearing arms killed on the spot. A few Navajos gave up, but most retreated into the forbidding mountains in the northwest corner of the territory. Again Carleton sent Colonel Carson to round up the hostiles. In early 1864 Carson engaged a large force of Indians at the Canyon de Chelly, where his force killed twenty-three Navajos and captured thirty-four others. Upon witnessing the battle, two hundred more Indians laid down their arms. Though sporadic fighting continued throughout the northwest for the next several months, the back of Navajo resistance had been broken. By the end of the year, more than seven thousand members of the tribe lived at Bosque Redondo.

Not until the fall of 1864 was the military prepared to continue the offensive, this time against the elusive plains Indians. Carson was ordered to lead the expedition into the Texas Panhandle, to locate and destroy the winter quarters of the Comanches, and to bring peace to the Santa Fe Trail. Carson's command of some four hundred cavalry and infantry troops marched eastward along the course of the Canadian River, carrying with them supplies for forty-five days and two mountain howitzers. The colonel planned to make Adobe Walls, the ruins of a trading post operated by William Bent during the 1840's, his headquarters; he was a few miles west of his objective on the evening of November 25 when he made camp at Mule Springs. His Indian scouts soon informed him that a large body of Indians had established villages in and about Adobe Walls.

Early the next morning Carson ordered a cavalry attack against a Kiowa village, routed the Indians, and moved on to the ruins of Adobe Walls, which he made his fort. Meanwhile his infantry and supply wagons moved cautiously to join him. The frightened Kiowas soon regrouped and, with Comanches who had camped within a mile of Adobe Walls, assaulted Carson's position. The Indians numbered between three and seven thousand and probably would have overwhelmed the soldiers had Carson not brought with him his ordnance; the field pieces greatly disconcerted the Indians, blunting the edge of their superior forces. All day the battle raged, neither side gaining an advantage.

As night fell, Carson ordered his men out of Adobe Walls to link up with the supply train, which understandably hesitated to run the gauntlet to reach the ruins. While one detachment set fire to the Kiowa camp as a diversion, Carson's main force headed toward Mule Springs to rendezvous with the supply train. Reunited, the military camped for the night, and on the morning of November 27 retreated toward New Mexico.

While the battle of Adobe Walls was far from decisive, Carson traditionally is credited with a victory. More important, however, was Carson's assessment of the situation. He later insisted that it would take a thousand troops and an extended campaign to end the plains Indian menace. To be certain, the Comanches and the Kiowas, unlike the Apaches and Navajos, had not been even temporarily subdued and placed on a reservation. Indian wars were far from over in the Southwest.

The attempt to civilize the Navajos and Apaches by confining them to the reservation at Bosque Redondo was an utter failure. The two tribes quarreled incessantly, making life on the reservation less than peaceful. And too, the Navajos were inept farmers, much preferring the raising of sheep to the growing of corn. But grasses along the frequently dry Pecos River were inadequate for grazing. The military was soon hard-pressed to prevent the Navajos from starving. Confined and malnourished, their spirit was soon broken and communicable diseases ravaged their camps. Were these problems insufficient, plains Indians—Comanches and Kiowa Apaches —frequently raided the reservation, running off the Navajos' livestock. Where Kit Carson had been so effective against hostiles in the mountains, he was virtually incapable of dealing with the swift, mounted raiders of the plains.

Fortunately for the Navajos, the federal government had authorized a peace commission empowered to secure new and lasting treaties with the western tribes. Led by General William T. Sherman, the delegation from Washington met in June, 1868, with the Navajos, who wished only to return home. The government agreed to allow this, gave them a reservation in the northwest corner of the territory, and promised them assorted material assistance—livestock, seeds, schools—designed to make them more tractable. And, even though Washington largely failed to meet the terms of the treaty with respect to subsidies, the Navajos were happy. They were allowed to return to the ancestral homes and freed to resume their nomadic life. The tribe thereafter remained generally peaceful.

A solution to the Apache problem was not so easily devised. Angered at having to share Bosque Redondo with the Navajos and frustrated in dealing with Indian agents of questionable ethics, the Apaches had fled the reservation in 1866. They were determined not to return. Skirmishes and pitched battles ensued for the next several years, the Apaches in the process gaining a reputation second to none in the Southwest for brutality. Occasionally federal authority would assert itself, as when in 1873 the Mescaleros were again confined to their traditional haunts in the White Mountains near Fort Stanton. Seven years later they were joined by the Jicarilla Apaches, a smaller, less formidable branch of the tribe. Nevertheless, the two bands launched sporadic raids into the surrounding countryside, harassing ranchers, farmers, and miners.

As affected as any Anglo-American endeavor by Apache belligerence was a minor, albeit lucrative variant of the commerce with Santa Fe—the cattle-trailing industry. The commerce driving of livestock from Texas to New Mexico, especially to Santa Fe, to army posts, and to Indian reservations (either under contract or for spot sale), had begun almost as soon as the Civil War had ended. Texas cattlemen, oversupplied with rangy longhorns, looked for markets of opportunity, and northern New Mexico was one of those immediately discovered. In 1866, Texans Charles Goodnight and Oliver Loving drove a herd of mixed beeves along the Pecos River to Fort Sumner for sale to the army, which needed to feed itself and Apaches and Navajos. The Goodnight-Loving Trail was born. Eventually extended through Raton Pass and into Colorado, it proved to be the most dangerous of all the post–Civil War cattle trails.

Loving himself was killed by Apaches the following year while driving a herd to Fort Sumner. Goodnight, who during the late 1860's was the principal contractor using the Pecos River route, then associated with West Texas rancher John S. Chisum, who agreed to transport his livestock to Goodnight's Bosque Grande ranch for further distribution and sale throughout New Mexico. During the four years that followed, Chisum lost two entire herds to the White Mountain Apaches who swooped down on the cattle trail, stampeded the animals, and drove them off toward the foothills. Even those drives that arrived safely at northern New Mexico markets were considered successful if only a dozen head had been lost to Indian harassment. So dangerous was the cattle trail that in 1871 Goodnight abandoned it. But for those drovers who continued to use the Goodnight-Loving Trail, the risks were everpresent. The Coggin and Parks Cattle Company of Central Texas estimated its losses on the trail between 1871 and 1874 at a quarter of a million dollars. It abandoned the trade with Santa Fe and northern New Mexico as too costly.

Meanwhile, the Chiricahua Apaches had been placed on the Ojo Caliente Reservation in present Grant County, New Mexico, much to the consternation of settlers at Silver City. Continuous protests from local citizens, who understandably feared the Apaches and their charismatic leader, Victorio, prompted the government in 1877 to remove the chief and most of the Chiricahuas to the San Carlos Reservation in Arizona; the Apache leader protested and twice attempted to flee San Carlos, only to be captured and returned. Two years later Victorio, determined to drive the whites from the Southwest, declared war. Joined by renegades from the

Mescalero reservation, he pounced upon the military detachment stationed at Ojo Caliente, killed the guards, stole 45 horses, and recruited 150 braves to follow him. Raiding relentlessly throughout the region, Victorio attacked remote settlements in Arizona, New Mexico, Texas, and Mexico, all the while being pursued by troops from two nations. Finally trapped by Mexican regulars in Chihuahua in 1880 while American troops across the border in Texas stood ready to prevent his retreat, Victorio was killed in battle. Though occasional problems with the Apaches continued to arise in New Mexico even after the death of the Chiricahua leader—as when the White Mountain Apaches erupted into violence in 1882 and when Geronimo led the Chiricahuas on their last warpath in 1885—the Indian wars in New Mexico had virtually ended, much to the glee of settlers who wished to exploit the region's many economic potentials.

To the northeast, along the route of the Santa Fe Trail, the story had been much the same. Since the outbreak of the Civil War, hostile Indian tribes had been on the offensive. By 1864 the situation along the wagon road was so serious that the military advised teamsters arriving at Fort Larned not to proceed any farther westward, for the army could not escort them through the dangerous hunting grounds that lay ahead. But wagon trains, especially those under government contract, were inclined to pay little heed to the admonitions. With the Santa Fe trade greatly disrupted by the Civil War and the concurrent Indian depredations, profits from freighting goods were few and far between, and businessmen who had the chance for profits accepted the risks, whatever they might be.

One such business operation, a wagon train owned by the Missouri firm of Stuart, Slemmons & Co. and ferrying supplies to military posts along the Santa Fe Trail, soon understood the seriousness of the army's warnings. The Stuart-Slemmons train, determined to proceed, joined with others hesitating at Larned and departed the garrison in August, 1864. Traveling along the "cut-off" road, a more direct path between Larned and Fort Dodge than that afforded by the river's twisting, turning course, the train had traversed twenty-five of the fifty miles to Dodge when Indians were sighted on the horizon. A dozen warriors rode down on the freighters' camp, running off whatever livestock they could spook. The hundred or so men in the camp immediately opened fire in the direction of the fleeing Indians, only to discover another sortie rapidly closing on their rear. Again the mounted hostiles raced through the camp, stampeding more animals. One teamster, Andrew Blanchard, mounted a horse in hot pursuit of the raiders. A hundred yards or so from the wagons, he was encircled by Indians who knocked him from his horse. One of the Indians stabbed him with a lance, dismounted, and appeared ready to lift the wounded man onto his own pony and carry him off when teamsters rushed forward to rescue Blanchard. He lived an hour. The Indians disappeared with half the wagon train's livestock.

It was during that summer that travel and communication on the Santa Fe Trail from Fort Larned westward was virtually halted. Cheyenne and Arapaho bands raided southward into the region from the northern plains. Comanches and Kiowa Apaches roamed northward out of the South Plains. In the absence of sufficient Federal forces, the entire region—western Kansas, Northwest Texas, the Indian Territory, eastern Colorado—lay at the mercy of the plains Indians.

Governor John Evans of Colorado, seeing the whole territory on the verge of collapse, was determined to do what the federal government was incapable of: institute a vigorous Indian policy. He admonished residents of the territory to pursue Indians, to kill them, and to destroy their villages. He authorized the raising of two companies of militia to guard the frontier. By the end of the summer, Evans was ready to launch a major counteroffensive. But by then the northern plains tribes were ready to abandon the warpath.

The Indians traditionally had made war during the summer when food was readily available, and, just as predictably, during the hard plains winters had settled near military posts where they were subsidized with government rations. Black Kettle, a Cheyenne chief, in late August, 1864, thus informed Evans that his warriors were ready to talk peace. Evans demanded nothing short of unconditional surrender. Understanding that Evans was bent on controlling the Indians, especially in the summer, Black Kettle instead marched his people to Fort Lyon in southern Colorado, where he submitted to federal authority. While Major Scott J. Anderson, the commander there, at first took the Cheyennes' weapons, he soon returned them, fearing that he had exceeded his standing orders.

Evans, far from satisfied with the temporary solution, ordered Colonel J. M. Chivington, who two years before as a major in the Colorado volunteers had gained fame against the Confederates at the battle of Glorietta Pass, to lead a cavalry regiment against the Cheyennes. When Chivington arrived at Lyon, he conferred with Anderson, who apparently suggested that Chivington attack Black Kettle's camp, for he, Anderson, had never given the Indians assurance of military protection. The engagement that followed on Sand Creek still remains in dispute. Some point to the fact that the Indians were armed, that depredations in the area had not abated (despite their surrender to Anderson), that fresh, white scalps hung in Cheyenne lodges. Others, including some of the soldiers who participated in the raid, noted that the Colorado militia rode down on the unsuspecting camp, that helpless men, women, and children had their skulls fractured by rifle butts, that it was wanton butchery. Whatever the correct assessment, five hundred Indians reportedly were killed. Those Cheyenne who survived and later allied with other northern groups redoubled their raids against the whites.

But not long thereafter the Civil War ended, bringing to the frontier new hope for peace. Surely troops would be diverted westward to put an end to Indian depredations once and for all. In June, 1865, General W. T. Sherman was named commander of the Division of the Missouri, through which most of the Santa Fe Trail passed, and Congress slowly began authorizing additional troops for the West. By the following summer, more than fifty thousand men were assigned to the plains region. And some of the commanders there were determined to take to the field against the Indians. General Grenville M. Dodge, from his headquarters at Fort Leavenworth, on November 1, 1865, informed his superiors that he had formulated a bold strategy designed to sweep his area clean of marauders:

> In forming my plans for the campaign my understanding was that the hostile Indians were to be punished at all hazards, and this I intend to do, knowing if I was allowed to press the campaign according to my plans that before another spring a satisfactory and durable peace could be obtained. [I shall] move with three columns against the southern Indians . . . and aid in keeping the great overland routes unobstructed.

But even as Dodge began his campaign, it was being scuttled by officials in Washington who were determined to solve the Indian problem another way.

The Chivington massacre had had severe repercussions in Washington, where Congress demanded to know why the Indians had been butchered. It sent a committee westward to investigate, and that body later reported that military abuses and excesses, such as those at Sand Creek, would forever preclude peace on the frontier. The army should be restrained, and the Indians should be restricted to two large reservations, one on the northern plains and the other in the Indian Territory, where the red man slowly could be persuaded to abandon his roving lifestyle. Meanwhile, white civilization, freed from the threat of Indian attacks, could proceed with an orderly occupation of the West. Peace treaties with the various tribes to guarantee the sanctity of their hunting grounds, the report asserted, would bring a lasting tranquility to the frontier.

Although many of the roving, southern tribes consequently signed an accord with Indian agents whereby they would accept what they had never wanted, permanent homes and a sedentary way of life, many bands of Indians never agreed to "peace." Even some of the Arapahoes, Cheyenne, Comanches, and Kiowas who did sign the Treaty of Medicine Lodge Creek in 1867 must have done so with only half-hearted sincerity, for they were soon on the summer warpath with those who had openly disdained the idea of being wards of the Great White Father in Washington. Two years later the government institutionalized the approach by developing what became known as the "Quaker Peace Policy," whereby well-intentioned missionaries served as Indian agents. To prevent the natives from being corrupted, the military was expressly forbidden to enter the reservations. Consequently, these became havens for marauders who pillaged the frontier from Texas to Kansas and who, when pursued by the army, simply raced back to the safety of the reservation. It was not until 1873 that the Department of the Interior was thoroughly convinced that pacification must await subjugation and stepped aside to allow the army an unrestricted hand.

During the three years that followed the southern plains were swept clean of the marauders who raided the Santa Fe Trail and virtually every other roadway west. The Fourth Cavalry, stationed in Texas and led by Colonel Ranald S. Mackenzie, was ordered onto the Llano Estacado, and the attack began. Joined by cavalry and infantry from Fort Dodge, Fort Sill, Fort Union, and elsewhere in Texas, Mackenzie chased his quarry relentlessly, seldom allowing Kiowa and Comanche bands a moment of rest. Even through the winter of 1875, the renegades were pursued, never allowed to flee to the sanctity of the reservation. Finally, that summer, they began straggling in to Fort Sill and surrendering. The Indian threat to the Santa Fe Trail had been ended.

For a quarter of a century the Santa Fe trade region had been subjected to almost continuous warfare. Simultaneous with the Confederate invasion of New Mexico, the Indians had rebelled. Not until the mid-1880's were the last of the Apaches captured and their leaders shipped to Florida. During that quarter-century, cattle drives from Texas, which had hoped to profit from the market opportunities of northern New Mexico, had sustained devastating losses. Freighters plying the Santa Fe Trail suffered a similar fate. The once-booming business symbolized by Santa Fe merchants ready and able to do business with any and all traders had, throughout much of the period, been brought to a virtual standstill. But by 1887 all was peaceful along the wagon road west. And well that it should have been, for by then the Santa Fe trade no longer existed.

CHAPTER 15

The Coming of the Railroad

However disrupted the trade and commerce of the plains might have been because of the Civil War and the consequent Indian uprisings throughout the Southwest, intercourse with Santa Fe had continued. Although wagon train after wagon train halted at Fort Larned or at Fort Dodge, many mustered the courage to continue the trek westward, and the volume of goods ferried over the route actually increased over the course of those years. In 1855, some five-hundred wagons carrying merchandise estimated to be worth more than $5 million had made the long journey from the Missouri River to northern New Mexico. Five years later, on the eve of the Civil War, more than three thousand wagons bounced along the trail. And, in the first year that followed the crisis of Union, the number of commercial vehicles hauling goods over the well-beaten path to Santa Fe almost doubled; the value of merchandise, in terms of war-inflated greenbacks, expanded several times over.

Enterprising businessmen heretofore not associated with the Santa Fe trade were well aware of the pecuniary potentials of the transportation frontier. Mail subsidies supported the establishment of the Butterfield overland stage route to southern California. It is worth noting that John Butterfield chose to follow a path from St. Louis across the Indian Territory and Texas that came nowhere near the Santa Fe Trail. The Butterfield road roughly traced the route Henry Connelly had once taken through West Texas, later surveyed in 1850 by Randolph B. Marcy on his circuitous return from Santa Fe. Railroad promoters were equally cognizant of the profit possibilities that followed established pathways westward; for decades Americans had dreamed of linking the mineral-rich Pacific coast to the settled, manufacturing Atlantic seaboard. Indeed, during the late 1840's Congress had toyed with the idea of building a transcontinental railroad to California to expedite the movement of gold eastward.

Original intrigue with a transcontinental railroad, however, soon dissolved in the maelstrom of states rights, secession, and Union. The North and the South had been at loggerheads for so long that no one route across the unsettled West would suffice. The nation would have to construct two roads, one for each section, or have none. As a partial consequence, the United States acquired the Gadsden Purchase from Mexico in 1853 for the South, and Congress passed the Kansas-Nebraska Act the following year to facilitate the construction of a railroad for the North. Guerrilla warfare in Kansas soon dashed the hopes of both regions for securing transcontinental tracks that would terminate in their respective areas. And even though the Congress of the United States in 1862 provided generous subsidies for the construction of a line westward that would tie Union territory together, it was not until after the Civil War that the dream of two decades became a reality.

In the relatively short span of twenty-five years following the Civil War, the West was linked to the East by steel rails. While construction on the Union Pacific Railroad did not begin in earnest until after Appomattox, roadbeds westward were prepared quickly— some critics say hastily—to connect with the Central Pacific Railroad, which was building eastward from California. In 1869, the two lines met at Promontory Point, Utah, and the first transcontinental line had been completed. By then a half-dozen other corporations had been chartered and, with varying amounts of public assistance, sallied forth to lay new track westward.

One of those lines, the Atchison, Topeka, and Santa Fe, actually had predated the organization of the first transcontinental railroad and hoped to profit from the commerce of the prairies. A precursor of the Santa Fe had been chartered by the Territory of Kansas in 1857 as the St. Joseph and Topeka Railroad, and the proposed carrier had laudable ambitions. One of its directors, Cyrus K. Holliday, believed that if his road could be extended southwestward to the capital of New Mexico, the St. Joseph Railroad would supplant totally the slow-moving, marginally efficient wagons that plied the

Santa Fe Trail. One of the firm's earliest brochures summarized his sentiments:

> . . . the greater object to be secured at present by this enterprise, is the trade to Santa Fe and New Mexico, which is annually very considerable, and will richly reward the earliest railroad communication that may be extended in that direction. This trade is increasing yearly, and is composed mainly of the manufactures of the Middle and Eastern states; all of which, in the event of railroad communication west and south of St. Joseph, must pass over roads leading from the East to that place, affording them, in itself, a source of revenue by no means inconsiderable.

Thus were the line's route and fortune entwined with the commerce of the prairies.

But the tiny St. Joseph and Topeka Railroad faced enormous financial difficulties; institutional lenders were less than enthusiastic in their support of comparatively shortline projects, given the alternative of underwriting major, transcontinental carriers. The St. Joseph's westward ambition was just that—a vague, formless dream of someday building southwestward from Topeka and tapping the potentials of northern New Mexico. Moreover, Holliday had serious doubts about the road's eastern terminus, St. Joseph. He believed that another site on the Missouri River, such as Atchison, Kansas, would have far greater commercial potential. By 1859 he was exploring the possibility of securing a charter for another railroad to run westward from the Missouri River to Santa Fe.

Holliday, born on April 3, 1826, at Kidderminster, Pennsylvania, was graduated from Allegheny College in 1852. He apparently read law and was admitted to the Pennsylvania bar; there is even some evidence that Holliday was awarded a master's degree from Allegheny College, but the date of his graduation is subject to question. In any case, he practiced law in Pennsylvania, where he was moderately successful. One of his clients there was organizing a shortline railroad and asked Holliday to draw up some necessary papers; sensing the profit potential of the road, the attorney declined to accept his usual fee for the work, asking instead for stock in the carrier. When, shortly thereafter, the shortline was acquired by the Atlantic & Great Western Railroad of New York, Holliday pocketed $20,000 from the transaction. He then decided to migrate westward to Kansas, which he believed to be a land of great opportunity. Once there, he soon became acquainted with like-minded promoters who thought that the best business prospects lay in the transportation industry. With them, he had organized the St. Joseph and Topeka Railroad. But Holliday was not satisfied, and he began to develop a new carrier.

On February 11, 1859, the Kansas territorial legislature approved articles of incorporation for the Atchison and Topeka Railroad. The firm's charter provided for a total capitalization of $1.5 million, stockholders being required to subscribe in cash 10 percent of the par value of their holdings, the remainder being on call. In addition to Holliday, the principal organizers of the line were E. G. Ross, a newspaper publisher who later served Kansas as a United States senator and New Mexico as governor; Joel Huntoon, a leading political figure in the territory; R. H. Weightman, a former attorney-general of Missouri; J. H. Stringfellow, an Atchison newspaper editor; L. C. Challis, who soon became a Wall Street financier; and Samuel C. Pomeroy, a free-soiler who had been an official of the New England Emigrant Aid Society. The company's leaders were buoyant with optimism in early 1859, convinced that, given the line's aspirations of connecting with Santa Fe, financial underwriting could easily be secured. During that summer, as Holliday began approaching eastern capitalists and asking for funds, a severe drought blanketed the Midwest. Easterners understandably became cautious, fearing for the safety of their investment in an area so subject to the caprice of weather. After all, much of the line's economic mainstay would necessarily arise from transporting farm commodities raised along its course. Crop failures due to drought thus called the project into question.

That fall, as the company began organizing officially with Holliday as its first president, leading stockholders began to reassess their line's future. Skeptical financiers had to be reassured, and they well might be if the fledgling carrier could secure aid from Washington in the form of a land grant. The federal government in 1850 had established the precedent of awarding alternate sections of land to railroad companies as a means of promoting their development. The Atchison and Topeka earnestly desired to secure such a subsidy for itself because the land would serve as security for the bonded indebtedness it proposed to float. Eastern lenders then surely would become more receptive to overtures from Topeka, the company's headquarters.

In 1860, the territorial legislature of Kansas petitioned Congress for four land grants, one of which bracketed the proposed southwestern route of the Atchison and Topeka line. But politicians in Washington were far more concerned with the state of the Union than with frontier projects, and the issue lay dormant for three years. Kansans understandably believed that their requests would never receive proper attention so long as they were represented in Congress by a nonvoting delegate. Statehood first must be achieved; land grants would follow. And once the South began seceding from the Union, the way was cleared for the admission of Kansas as a free state, which was accomplished in 1861.

Immediately the state's representatives in Congress pressed for railroad land grants. Leading the fight was Senator Samuel C. Pomeroy, who happened to serve as director of the Atchison and Topeka line. When he became convinced that his bill would be held in abeyance until Congress approved the Transcontinental Railroad Act, which would incorporate the Union Pacific Railroad, he worked feverishly for its passage, piling up political IOU's in the process. The Union Pacific bill was approved by Congress and signed into law in 1862, and Pomeroy, working with a draft resolution supplied by Holliday, introduced a land-grant bill soon thereafter. Once it had been approved by both houses of Congress, President Lincoln signed it into law on March 3, 1863.

The land grant specifically directed the Kansas railroad to build southwestward from Topeka "in the direction of Fort Union and Santa Fe, New Mexico," which, of course, was precisely where the line's promoters had projected their right-of-way. Furthermore, it awarded the railroad ten alternate sections of land for each mile of track laid in Kansas. The transfer technically went through the state of Kansas, which in turn was to award the land to the carrier by stages, title being given to the company upon the completion of twenty-mile segments of a "good and substantial and workmanlike" line. The Atchison and Topeka Railroad was also allowed to select alternative tracks of land when it faced the conflict of land titles already being held by settlers, as usually was the case in the eastern edge of the state. For all practical purposes, the line's land grants began approximately twenty miles southwest of Emporia, Kansas, and stretched westward to the Colorado border. The company was given ten years to complete its work in Kansas or forfeit whatever land it by then had yet to claim.

Thus subsidized with government aid, the railroad began to promote itself. First, the line's name was changed officially to the Atchison, Topeka, and Santa Fe Railroad, which the directors believed more accurately described the scope of their firm; moreover, it was hoped that the new name would be more alluring to eastern investors. Second, for obvious political reasons, Holliday stepped down as the carrier's president, allowing Senator Pomeroy to hold that title, while Holliday directed the day-to-day activities of the corporation from the post of secretary. Then the railroad's principal officers began lobbying with the state's legislature for an act that would permit individual Kansas counties to underwrite construction costs by approving revenue bonds. Such a measure was approved during the spring of 1864. With both federal land and local tax moneys at their disposal, AT&SF officials foresaw little difficulty in selling their firm's stock and in disposing of their own corporate bonds. Financially, they had constructed a well-lubricated corporate machine.

Holliday, Pomeroy, and associates, however, continued to have problems starting its engine. Eastern backing remained reticent, forcing the AT&SF to rely increasingly upon county bond issues for their working capital. So crucial were these funds that the road's officials in 1867 carried out a house-by-house campaign to ensure the success of a quarter-of-million-dollar bond vote in Shawnee County. Similar referendums in Atchison, Jefferson, Osage, and Lyon counties raised amounts varying from $150,000 to $200,000. Furthermore, the carrier, which still existed merely on paper, was finding difficulty in locating a competent construction company to build the road. It had signed contracts with three separate firms before the first shovel-full of dirt was turned. Holliday became so exasperated with the situation that he once proposed to organize his own construction company just to get the work started, or so he claimed. He undoubtedly also knew that windfall profits were to be made in laying track, for the Credit Mobilier subsidiary of the Union Pacific by then was widely discussed among railroaders. Its return on investment was a fantastic 100 percent.

In June, 1868, the railroad signed a contract with the Cincinnati firm of Dodge, Lord and Company, which agreed to build the railroad. Three months later ground was broken at Topeka, from which point surveys projected a southerly route for the initial thirty or so miles. It was decided to begin work on the segment toward Santa Fe first, for Topeka already had been reached by the Kansas Pacific from Kansas City, and, initially, the AT&SF could lease that carrier's eastern facilities. Moreover, valuable coal deposits in the vicinity of the state capital could be readily exploited for fuel. In the months that followed, a ten-mile stretch of roadbed was built and track laid.

Such an accomplishment required the purchase of a second-hand locomotive from the Ohio and Mississippi Railroad; shortly thereafter the firm bought one coach, borrowed another from the Kansas Pacific, and hooked up an excursion train to survey the work done. In early May, 1869, one hundred Kansans piled aboard the first Santa Fe train, which chugged along at fifteen miles an hour to the end of the line, a point little beyond sight of the city. Following appropriate orations from Holliday and other interested parties, the spectators entrained once more, this time to back all the way to Topeka. Two months later the grading had been completed to the Shawnee County line, for which feat the railroad was able to collect one-half of that county's revenue bonds. The Atchison, Topeka, and Santa Fe Railroad no longer was a thin pencil line on a surveyor's map but the proud possessor of thirty miles of track and two pieces of rolling stock.

That was scarcely enough to impress cautious eastern investors, who continued to view the project with supercilious disdain. The Atchison, Topeka, and Santa Fe Railroad, for all its ambitious dreams of supplanting the commerce of the prairies, continued to be seen by Wall Street as a local project—hardly intriguing to financiers who were sinking millions of dollars in glamour issues like the Union and Central Pacific lines. There were too few people in Kansas to make the road even marginally profitable in the short run, and it would be years before the line could expect to develop a thriving business ferrying freight between the Missouri River and Santa Fe. Moreover, some potential investors chuckled at the naivete of subcontractors who were building the line; it was widely and accurately reported that many of the AT&SF's gang bosses did not even know how to lay track on a curve. The line in 1869 was hardly worth New York's attention.

The eastern evaluation of the Santa Fe Railroad was far from unjust, for the line was experiencing numerous difficulties. After six years, it had completed only thirty miles of track. Four years remained on its government land grant; if it failed to reach the Colorado border by then, it would forfeit its claims to that portion of the public domain to which it had not yet received title. Those county revenue bonds on which the AT&SF relied to solve its short-run cash-flow problems were being discounted highly, which of course cut deeply into the firm's actual monetary receipts. And the Cincinnati construction company that was building the line had reorganized itself as the Atchison Associates, complained that its payments were in county bonds of dubious value, and later in 1869 withdrew from the project. The railroad had to assume the task of constructing roadbeds and laying track. Company officials were fortunate in pursuading T. J. Peter, chief engineer for Atchison Associates, to remain at his post to supervise the construction.

Clearly the principal problem faced by the Atchison, Topeka, and Santa Fe Railroad was in raising the funds necessary for construction. And that task had been made inordinately difficult by the line's provincial image in eastern financial circles. The railroad seemingly had little hope of establishing a profitable volume until it tapped the potentials of northern New Mexico; until it did, Wall Street financiers preferred to invest their money elsewhere. If the carrier failed to raise enough money to complete construction, it would never reach Santa Fe, and therefore it would never be profitable. Moreover, it stood in danger of losing a large slice of the public domain it had been promised. In 1870, the railroad's future was far from secure.

New, bold leadership was needed, and it came in the form of Ginery Twichell, who assumed the presidency of the firm that year. Twichell, a New England Yankee with a better than average grasp of reality, had developed and controlled several lines in the East before assuming the responsibility for the faltering Santa Fe. If money were the catalyst, then money he would have. Ordering his subordinates to sell large blocks of county revenue bonds, at substantial discounts if necessary, to secure funds, Twichell generated sufficient cash flow to speed construction across adjacent Kansas counties, which, of course, gave the company more bonds to sell on the open market. Crossties were slapped down on roadbeds and rails bolted down at a furious pace, for speed was desperately needed.

In 1871, the Atchison, Topeka, and Santa Fe Railroad proudly lay claim to 137 miles of track, and its western terminus was Newton, Kansas, still barely one-fourth of the way to Colorado. But Newton was far more important to the line than any of the other tiny hamlets served by the ambitious railroad, for it tapped the lucrative cattle trade from Texas and promised substantial revenues for freighting slaughter beeves to Kansas City. The long drives from Texas had begun the year after the Civil War, and by 1867 most cattle were being trailed to Abilene, Kansas, located on the Kansas Pacific Railroad, where Joseph G. McCoy had built stockpens. But Newton and the Santa Fe were sixty miles closer to Texas than Abilene and the Kansas Pacific, a fact that Twichell loudly proclaimed. Cattle-trailing contractors, businessmen whose profits depended upon their own efficiency, eagerly embraced Newton as the market of first opportunity, and in 1871, the initial year of the community's existence as a railhead, shipped almost 200,000 live cattle aboard Santa Fe cars. That figure represented about one-third the total trail traffic. Twichell was delighted. He waved copies of bills of lading before the eyes of reluctant investors, who began bidding up the price of Santa Fe securities. The liquidity problem was being solved.

Newton's success immediately inspired nearby communities not on the Santa Fe's projected route to petition Twichell for service. Wichita, some twenty-eight miles south of Newton and at the point where the Chisholm Trail forded the Arkansas River, asked the line to swing toward it, residents there voting a bonded indebtedness of $200,000 to fund the railroad's construction. A year before, when the carrier was experiencing extreme difficulty in raising money, officials in Topeka probably would have accepted such invitations with considerable relish, but the situation had changed. The Santa Fe already enjoyed the benefits of the cattle trade at Newton, and it had more than three-hundred miles of track to lay westward along the old Santa Fe Trail in less than two years or lose a portion of its land grant. Twichell declined Wichita's offer.

Hardheaded Wichita leaders decided to build their own spur to Newton, named the Wichita and Southwestern Railroad, with the revenue bonds. While Twichell did not openly encourage the project, there is some evidence that T. J. Peter, the AT&SF's chief engineer, served as a consultant to the tap line, which was completed in the late spring of 1871. Soon thereafter, the Wichita and South Western Railroad was sold at cost to the Santa Fe. No doubt Twichell began referring to the Atchison, Topeka, and Santa Fe "railroad system" when he discussed finances with Wall Street backers.

Time had become the crucial issue. In January, 1872, Twichell openly wondered if construction could reach Colorado in fourteen months. If the Santa Fe failed to secure title to all the land due it under the terms of the Railroad Act of 1863, then once more it would become less attractive to the eastern investors who would be so vital to the last leg of construction through Colorado and into New Mexico, where the railroad held no federal subsidy. Twichell ordered Peter to proceed with all due haste to complete the construction in Kansas. The railroad had to have that land.

Roadbeds rose like small hills above the flat Kansas grasslands as common laborers followed mule-drawn blades that piled and smoothed a mixture of rocks, top soil, and caliche. Crossties were slapped into position ever faster—some being borne by Chinese coolies recruited from the West Coast—to await iron and steel rails, both of which were used by the company. Growing ever more experienced, the crews hesitated less and less when presented with unusual construction problems, such as steep gradings and long curves. The money market was growing tighter, a strong forewarning of the eventual financial collapse of 1873, but Twichell ordered securities sold, again at substantial discounts, to raise the needed capital. All hinged upon reaching the Colorado border by March 3, 1873. More than two months before the deadline, Peter informed Twichell that the last rail had been laid and that Santa Fe tracks now extended into Colorado; the railroad's president was elated. Again an excursion train from Topeka was organized, for late December, to survey the entire route; when it returned eastward, the steam engine could have continued all the way to the Missouri River, for by then the extension to Atchison had been completed. The Santa Fe traversed the entire state. It had qualified for all of its federal land grant.

Construction then paused so that surveyors might explore feasible routes westward through Colorado and then southward into New Mexico. The rolling prairies of southeastern Colorado presented no serious obstacles to construction. The problem was instead one of markets: the AT&SF could expect precious little freight business should it select the most direct, yet most underpopulated, route toward Santa Fe. Consequently, Henry Strong, a Scot who had succeeded Twichell as president of the firm, ordered Albert A. Robinson, the railroad's chief surveyor, to choose a route westward to Pueblo, which would allow the AT&SF to exploit flourishing lumber and mining operations along the Arkansas River. For a couple of reasons, the Santa Fe decided to incorporate the project under the laws of Colorado as the Pueblo and Arkansas Valley Railroad. First, a local charter gave the Kansas subsidiary preferential tax status in Colorado; second, separate incorporation allowed the AT&SF to avoid encumbering the projected segment with the debts of the parent firm. It would be easier to raise money for the line to Pueblo.

The Atchison, Topeka, and Santa Fe was soliciting bids for the construction of the Pueblo and Arkansas Valley Railroad in the fall of 1873 just as the first shock waves from the collapse of Jay Cooke and Company were reverberating across the nation. The huge eastern banking house had overextended itself to finance the building of the Northern Pacific Railroad and was forced to close its doors. Immediately other financial institutions tightened their credit policies, especially with respect to railroads. Many carriers soon sought receivership, and even those that did not, such as the Santa Fe, suddenly found it impossible to locate investors willing to buy their bonds. Complicating the situation for the AT&SF was a locust plague that descended upon Kansas the following year. Farmers' fields were stripped bare by the hungry grasshoppers, a fact widely reported in the nation's press. The visitation made financiers wary of business ventures on the plains. Construction on the Santa Fe virtually ended for two years.

Credit finally became more readily available late in 1874, and construction resumed along the route of the Pueblo and Arkansas Valley Railroad. Track was laid at a rate of a mile a day, except on Mondays when barely half as much could be expected. The decline in productivity at the first of the week was attributed by the line's officials to the fact that laborers, released from work on Saturday evenings, rode company flatcars eastward to the first available town, where they drank and cavorted. Pounding headaches the following Monday invariably impeded progress, but there was little the construction companies could do about the situation except to station flatcars to haul lifeless bodies back to camp on Sunday evenings.

The Pueblo and Arkansas Valley Railroad was completed in February, 1876, and, according to L. L. Walters' history of the AT&SF, townspeople at the end of the line immediately laid plans to stage "the biggest drunk of the present century" in March to celebrate the coming of the Santa Fe. Dignitaries representing the company entrained at Topeka to join in the drinkfest, only to be caught in a severe blizzard near Larned, Kansas. Ever ready to pitch in, the line's construction crew eagerly volunteered to serve as alter egos for their bosses. Few sober souls were seen in Pueblo for days.

Again, construction toward Santa Fe languished. For one thing, the Atchison, Topeka, and Santa Fe Railroad felt no immediate pressure to continue its current pace southwestward. Land grants had ended at the Kansas border, and money had to be raised for the cost of laying tracks, a feat made more difficult by the dearth of population in the area. Too, freighters plying the Santa Fe Trail by 1876 were using the railroad's facilities to haul their goods as far west as La Junta, Colorado, on the Pueblo and Arkansas Valley line, and offloading onto wagons for the trip southward through Trinidad and Raton Pass. The AT&SF already was profiting from the commerce of the prairies. It was not until the Topeka-based carrier faced direct competition that it again rushed forward to lay track.

William J. Palmer, once an executive with the Kansas Pacific, had organized the Denver and Rio Grande Railroad in 1870 and projected its route along the eastern edge of the Rocky Mountains to connect the Union Pacific on the north and the proposed Southern Pacific on the south. Key among Palmer's ambitions was to beat the Santa Fe to Raton Pass, for whichever line controlled that im-

portant entrance to northern New Mexico would dominate the inter-
connecting freight business between the two transcontinental carriers. By the summer of 1872 the Denver and Rio Grande had built
southward from the territorial capital to Pueblo, preceding by four
years the arrival of the Santa Fe's subsidiary. There Palmer's road
was forced to stop while its promoter scratched about for needed
finances. It was not until 1876 that the Denver and Rio Grande was
able to extend its facilities southward toward Trinidad. That turned
out to be a costly delay.

Meanwhile, the Atchison, Topeka, and Santa Fe Railroad had
dispatched survey crews about southeastern Colorado and western
Kansas to determine which path into New Mexico would be the
most economical. While A. A. Robinson studied surveyors' reports,
corporate leadership in Topeka changed. In 1877, Henry Strong
resigned the presidency and was replaced by William B. Strong, a
native of Vermont and no relation to his predecessor. William
Strong was most interested in the railroad's route through the Southwest and even contemplated extending the AT&SF's tracks to the
Pacific Ocean. He gave the New Mexico project top priority, simultaneously determining to thwart the rival Denver and Rio Grande's
connecting link scheme.

Using the same ploy as in Colorado, Strong secured from the
legislature in Santa Fe the incorporation of the New Mexico and
Southern Pacific Railroad and laid plans to have the Pueblo and
Arkansas Valley line take charge of construction in Colorado. But it
was not until February, 1878, that all was ready and that Strong
ordered Robinson to begin work. The route selected was from La
Junta along the Purgatoire River through Trinidad and southward
to Raton Pass. But by then the Denver and Rio Grande had built to
within five miles of Trinidad and held a decided advantage. Subter-
fuge would be needed if the Santa Fe were to control Raton Pass
and, consequently, the route to Santa Fe.

On February 26, Robinson entrained for the end of the line at
Pueblo, where he boarded a Denver and Rio Grande coach for El
Moro, Colorado, located some five miles north of Trinidad. Riding
with him on that last leg of his journey was J. A. McMurtrie, the
chief engineer for Palmer's line. While the men exchanged pleasant-
ries, neither discussed his mission with the other. Had they done so,

they would have discovered their instructions to be identical: occupy and hold Raton Pass. While Robinson rented a horse that
evening to ride southward to Raton, McMurtrie decided to catch a
few hours' sleep at El Moro. Those two decisions proved fateful.

In the predawn hours of February 27, Robinson arrived at an
inn operated by "Uncle" Dick Wooton near the northern entrance
to the pass. Wooton, a colorful frontiersman, scout, and sometime
Santa Fe trader, in 1865 had secured a charter from the New Mexico
legislature to construct a toll road through the pass from Trinidad
to Red River, New Mexico, thereby providing an easier passage
through the rugged mountain gap. Once it was completed, he had
built an inn to cater to those freighters and emigrants who used the
trail. By 1878, Wooton had developed a profitable business, but he
undoubtedly knew it would die once the railroad reached Santa Fe,
which was inevitable. Thus he was most receptive to Robinson's
overtures.

The Santa Fe surveyor promised Wooton fifty dollars a month
for life, payable in goods from the railroad's stores at Trinidad, for
the frontiersman's help. Wooton needed only to grant the Santa Fe
the use of his grading through the pass (until the railroad could
tunnel through the mountain) and to assist Robinson in establishing
possession of the right-of-way. Wooton accepted and, somewhat
bleary-eyed, set about to roust from their sleep assorted transients
who were lodged in his inn. They were recruited to begin work on
the railroad's grading and, not coincidentally, to resist attempts by
any Denver and Rio Grande crew that might seek to displace them.
Before dawn Robinson had his men digging by lantern light at the
entrance to Raton Pass. Less than an hour had passed when Mc-
Murtrie arrived, eager to begin work on the Denver and Rio
Grande's proposed route. As only one railroad could go through
Raton, as the Santa Fe held the pass, and, even more importantly,
as Robinson's work force was larger than McMurtrie's, the Denver
and Rio Grande crew retreated. The Atchison, Topeka, and Santa
Fe controlled Raton, and with that possession went the right to
traverse New Mexico.

With the company in solid possession of the pass, construction
on the main line from La Junta was begun, the segment to Trinidad
being completed in September. From Trinidad southward, building

was compartmentalized. While roadbeds from Trinidad to Raton and from Raton to Las Vegas were being prepared, the New Mexico and Southern Pacific attacked the pass in two fashions. First of all, a "switchback"—that is, a series of graded, U-shaped curves designed to mount the 7,807-foot summit—was completed as a temporary method of crossing the mountains. Meanwhile, labor gangs chiseled and blasted away at solid rock to tunnel through the barrier some two-hundred feet below the pass, which would provide for more efficient service. The first train steamed into Las Vegas in July, 1879, almost a full year before the tunnel was in use. From there, the Atchison, Topeka, and Santa Fe followed the overland trail—until it turned northward to Santa Fe.

By 1879 the railroad's officials had decided that their original objective, the city of Santa Fe, no longer offered their firm the financial rewards it once had promised. The Atchison, Topeka, and Santa Fe already carried most of the commodities destined for northern New Mexico. To add thirty miles of track once beyond Glorieta Pass merely to reach Santa Fe was questionable economics. Wagons could haul those goods earmarked for the relatively remote community, as they had in the past, without jeopardizing the line's revenues. Moreover, the Santa Fe Railroad now had determined to push westward to the Pacific Ocean and become a transcontinental carrier. A route through Santa Fe would require considerable backtracking in order that the railroad might utilize a practical route through the Rocky Mountains to California. The phrase "Santa Fe" in the firm's corporate name suddenly had become superfluous.

While the trunk route swung southward through Albuquerque and eventually toward the west, residents of Santa Fe fumed about the situation. The city's newspaper, the *New Mexican,* while agreeing with the railroad's appraisal of the situation, decried the firm's decision to leave the legendary community high and dry. The paper soon endorsed a bond issue whereby Santa Feans would build their own railroad southward to tap the Atchison, Topeka, and Santa Fe. John B. Lamy, the bishop of Santa Fe, lent his prestige and considerable support to the project. Corporate officials in Topeka encouraged the idea, and the ensuing bond election overwhelming endorsed the project. On February 16, 1880, the first train steamed past "Lamy Switch," through Glorieta Pass over the shortline, and toward the territorial capital. When it arrived that day, the Santa Fe trade—the commerce of the prairies—quietly came to an end.

The arrival of that train in Santa Fe ended for all time the need for slow-moving wooden wagons, for bewhiskered teamsters who spat tobacco juice at the rumps of their mules, for jaded cavalrymen who rode pell-mell into the mountains to eject Indians who raided along the trail. It also eliminated most of the adaptive, innovative entrepreneurs who for decades had profited by risking all in outfitting trading ventures to remote New Mexico. The iron horse had arrived. All else was passé.

CHAPTER 16

The Santa Fe Trade

Commercial relations—that is, economic exchange between widely separated regions—develop because they are mutually beneficial. In the case of the commerce of the prairies, which properly should be viewed as including mercantile operations in Chihuahua, the trade originated because the inhabitants of Mexican settlements warmly welcomed American merchants and their relatively sophisticated manufactured wares. Similar goods simply were not readily available in primitive northern Mexico. Americans, for their part, desired the specie and raw materials that accrued to them in the commerce of the prairies. Both participants in the Santa Fe trade gained from the interchange.

Yet, as in the case of any ongoing enterprise, the Santa Fe trade evolved over the course of decades so that by 1880, when the Atchison, Topeka, and Santa Fe Railroad's first train steamed up the tardy spur from Lamy and into the capital of New Mexico, the exchange between the settled eastern United States and the remote, underpopulated Southwest bore little relationship to what it had been four decades before. New Mexico was being Americanized, and that had led to a perceptible change in the territory's economic base. Animal husbandry, not fur trapping, had become the principal employer of manpower. And rudimentary specialization had set in; a few of the products once imported from Missouri were being produced locally and were no longer highly prized by Santa Feans.

Although the region continued to export eastward far more raw materials than finished products, local enterprise had decreased the territory's dependence upon eastern manufacturers. Consequently, at least for the East, Santa Fe was no longer as attractive a trading partner as it had been. Eastern industries that needed New Mexican raw materials increasingly were forced to pay in cash for the supplies they required. And this diminished the need for the middle man, the Santa Fe trader, who had once bartered for these goods.

The first, timid steps toward establishing commercial ties with New Mexico during the early 1820's clearly show their experimental nature. The earliest traders risked far more than mere financial loss, for they often were subject to arrest by ethnocentric Spanish officials determined to protect the crumbling empire of Ferdinand VII from the radical ideas of Yankee democrats. Not until Mexico achieved independence from Spain were Americans greeted by anything but hostility when they entered New Mexico.

When the situation changed, traders became bold, arriving in Santa Fe as early as 1821. Traders, such as William Becknell, packed their mules with assorted wares and braved a frontier that, for the most part, was unknown. The modest volume of goods they transported necessarily limited their overall impact, and yet it guaranteed that their margins of profit would be astronomical. Bolts of cloth sold for ten times what they would have brought in Missouri; that scarce commodity, imported in a limited quantity, was in greater demand than could be satisfied. Hugh Glenn found much the same situation when he, too, arrived in Santa Fe that year. Calico, a cheaply woven fabric of decidedly plebeian character, sold for as much as three dollars a yard. The merchants probably could have made a fortune selling the cloth had they been able to import tons of it. Demand greatly outstripped supply during those initial years of commerce. Substantial profits naturally caused American importers to expand their ventures, for if a small volume brought handsome returns, an increase seemingly would make them rich. And it did—in the short run.

But short-run profit maximization, as the economist would contend, frequently leads in the long run to a restructuring of the market and consequently to the erosion of profit margins. Such was the changing face of the commerce of the prairies. As has been pointed out, initial American entrepreneurial interest in the New Mexican city arose because of that isolated outpost's disadvantageous trade relations with Ciudad Chihuahua. Chihuahua merchants, closer to a supply of finished Mexican wares, could and did gouge their countrymen to the north. Tenfold profits were not unusual for traders in Ciudad Chihuahua who supplied northern New Mexico. Americans, while admittedly extracting equally exorbitant returns on investments, nevertheless held the advantage of furnishing Santa Fe, and eventually Ciudad Chihuahua itself, with consumer goods markedly superior to those generally available in Mexico.

Historian F. F. Stephens, writing in the 1916 edition of the *Missouri Historical Review*, however, noted that even during the initial years of the trade actual returns on investments varied enormously from year to year and from venture to venture. William Becknell's second expedition reputedly earned an incredible 2,000 percent for its organizer! The estimated gross value of merchandise hauled to northern New Mexico two years later ranged from $35,000 (according to Gregg) to $52,500 (Stephens), including the cost of transportation. Once sold in 1824, its value had escalated to $200,000 in specie and trade goods. That year's commerce provided a more modest threefold return on investment. While in 1824 earnings were substantial, they in no way approached Becknell's fantastic profits of 1822, but they underscored the attractiveness of the market. One year later, Missouri traders insisted that they realized a mere $9,000 on that year's investment of $75,000, or a relatively poor profit margin of 12 percent.

But even when difficulties with the Indians were unusually severe, as in 1828, reasonable returns were the rule rather than the exception. That year businessmen plying the Santa Fe Trail reported cumulative losses of $40,000 in equipment and wares to Indian harassment. Even so, government sources suggest a net return on investment of 30 to 50 percent. As late as 1832, Secretary of War Lewis Cass, in supporting the traders' requests for military escorts, asserted that profit ranges of 25 to 100 percent were usual in economic intercourse with Mexico. The commerce of the prairies was in the best overall interest of the United States, Cass concluded, and it deserved the protection of the government.

While his general assessment undoubtedly was accurate, Secretary Cass considerably understated the case for the Santa Fe trade. He did not take into account generally ignored but substantial secondary benefits that accrued to the United States. Most of the goods imported into the United States from Mexico were in the form of raw materials, which fueled the productive process in America. Furs, especially beaver and otter pelts, increasingly were in short supply in the United States, for trappers had methodically stripped much of the frontier of these fur-bearing animals. Yet affluent Americans demanded coats and hats manufactured from the pelts; moreover, a lively export trade with Europe in finished furs and fur goods had evolved over the years, which of course enhanced America's balances of trade and payments.

Furthermore, by fashioning consumer goods from Mexican raw materials the United States gained the lucrative value-added that accrues in the manufacturing process. While it is undoubtedly true that such raw materials imported by way of the Santa Fe Trail hardly sufficed to supply the entire need of American manufacturers, they did add substantially to the flow of consumer goods being poured onto the market. A typical wagon train returning from northern New Mexico, according to Josiah Gregg, carried 50,000 to 70,000 pounds of furs and other raw materials. The "terms of trade"—that is, the value of raw materials by volume exported by Mexico relative to the volume of finished products they procured for that nation—were most advantageous to the United States.

While Gregg observed and commented upon returning American entrepreneurs as they trudged back to the United States with their trade goods, he dismissed as inconsequential this import traffic. Mexican commodities, he stated, consisted primarily "of mules and asses—some buffalo rugs, furs, and wool—which last barely pays a return freight for the wagons that otherwise would be empty." While stating the situation clearly and accurately, Gregg seemed to ignore his own observation—"*wagons that otherwise would be empty.*" Here the traders faced fixed costs in returning to Missouri, with or without the commodities they might haul eastward. By carrying Mexican wares they were able to defray a small, albeit important, portion of their overall transportation expenses. The goods imported into Missouri were as important to Santa Fe traders as they were to America's growing industrial machine.

Furthermore, from a strictly materialistic point of view, those trade goods provided American merchants in Mexico yet another advantage in the commerce of the prairies. Businessmen from Missouri obviously and understandably preferred to consummate sales in cash, which in northern Mexico meant gold dust, silver bullion, or intrinsic coins. And this presents an interesting situation. Gregg reported that between 1832 and 1835 New Mexican gold production amounted to $60,000 to $80,000 annually. If one compares the reported annual value of the Santa Fe trade with the mineral production of the area, it is immediately apparent that a significant imbalance existed.

To be certain, additional silver bullion and specie entered the trade from Chihuahua, as goods sold in Santa Fe were hawked by intermediaries further south or hauled on by American merchants. Nevertheless, it appears evident that an insufficiency of precious metals, with respect to the overall volume of the trade, existed throughout the early period of international intercourse. Had barter—the direct exchange of American and Mexican commodities—not entered the marketplace, the Santa Fe trade would have suffered.

American merchants holding fast to their prices and accepting only gold dust, silver bullion, or intrinsic coins in lieu of payment would soon have found themselves with masses of unsold goods, for the quantity of precious metals in New Mexico and Chihuahua was insufficient to sustain the level of trade that had developed by the 1830's. They would have been forced to maintain permanent stores wherever they hawked their wares, to transport back to the United States unsold goods, or even to reduce their prices. It seems entirely likely that large inventories would have forced prices down. A dearth of circulating medium, given basic principles concerning the supply of money and the quantity of goods available for purchase, could not help but have a deflationary impact—as apparently was the case in the long run.

That the price structure slowly declined rather than tumbled can be attributed largely to the barter system that developed. Whenever Mexicans found themselves short of the cash that Americans preferred, they exchanged their own goods for the finished products they desired. Without any doubt, Missouri merchants discounted greatly the value of Mexican commodities when swapping, thereby of course helping to maintain the high prices they had set on their own wares. Without this necessary trade in raw materials, American commodities would have glutted the market; the profit potential of the Santa Fe trade would have eroded overnight. Thus did the barter system aid in maintaining the artificially high prices that so richly rewarded American businessmen.

Another aspect of the specie situation afforded windfall profits for American traders. As Josiah Gregg reported, there were discrepancies between Mexican and American mint par values. Both coins struck in Mexico and bullion poured into bars there were of a finer grade than those produced in the United States. Hence gold valued (and procured) in Mexico for $15.00 per troy ounce was easily sold in the United States for $17.30 and even for as much as $19.70. Chihuahuan silver, Gregg insisted, afforded exporters a 10 percent profit merely for carrying it to the United States and trading it for American money.

The types of capital investments made by Santa Fe traders also contributed to the American economy. Missouri businessmen required pack and draft animals, most frequently mules, and wagons to move their goods southwestward, a hundred or so vehicles making the journey by the 1830's. However, on the return trip, observers such as Josiah Gregg pointed out, the volume of goods imported into the United States was barely sufficient to sustain half that capital investment. Consequently, wagons and oxen, perhaps rarely even mules, were sold in Santa Fe and Ciudad Chihuahua once they had been unloaded, the merchants retaining only that amount of equipment they deemed necessary for their return. The rapid disposal of animals and vehicles thus contributed to the stream of hard cash and raw materials imported into the United States and coincidentally greatly increased the significance of the Santa Fe trade for those who would supply it with capital goods.

Countless stockmen from St. Louis to Independence seized upon this market of opportunity and supplied traders with mules, thus forever identifying that animal with Missouri. Ironically, many of the asses and horses required by that state's breeders were acquired in Mexico through the Santa Fe trade. Vehicle manufacturers similarly benefitted: since many of the wagons were sold at the end of the trail, they could expect freighters to visit their shops year after year to buy again and again. During the early years of the trade, pack mules, two-wheeled carts, and large wagons requiring eight mules to pull them were used. By the mid-1830's, the latter vehicles, capable of transporting a thousand pounds of cargo, carried most of the wares destined for northwestern Mexico.

Then in 1839, New Mexican Governor Manuel Armijo imposed a tax of five-hundred dollars on every carrier, large or small, that entered Santa Fe. The pack mule and the two-wheeled cart immediately became unprofitable, and even those traders who used the larger vehicles found the tax burdensome. Enterprising businessmen in the United States like St. Louis wagon builder Joseph Murphy immediately began constructing larger products, capable of carrying as much as five-thousand pounds of goods, to cushion the effect of the excise. The ploy worked, for Armijo soon returned to the *ad valorem* method of assessment. The freighters nevertheless continued to use the larger vehicles for, even with a return to the old method of taxation, their unit cost of transportation was lower. And of course greater efficiency translated into larger profits.

Nor were other Missouri businessmen unaware of the possibilities of profit in the Santa Fe trade. During the initial four years of the commerce of the prairies, mercantile operations supplied the few hardy souls who braved the trek southwestward, but there is little evidence that the volume of traffic was sufficient to excite shopkeepers, to encourage their greater participation. Most transactions between trader and merchant were in cash. By 1825, however, the tenfold profits of the trade had led Missouri merchants to bid actively for the business of exporters. Newspaper advertisements announced that scores of western Missouri mercantile operations carried a wide assortment of goods "suitable for the trade with Santa Fe." Store owners, such as James Aull, readily agreed to furnish commodities on consignment for ten months, interest free. Aull's habit of marking up his wares as much as 25 and even 75 percent above East Coast prices, however, obviously served the same purpose as interest. It was years later that the Missouri businessman decided to forego the use of an intermediary and to haul his own goods to Santa Fe. Other firms, such as Marmaduke and Sappington of Saline County, employed similar techniques—high mark-ups, interest-free consignments—to lure prairie traders into their establishments.

Rarely, if ever, were the original participants in the international exchange well financed. Early ventures frequently were joint-stock operations, individual investors (who usually made the trip) providing as little as $10 worth of merchandise. Larger outlays became necessary as the trade expanded both geographically (to Chihuahua) and physically (in volume). The average investment per trader by 1826 had reached $900. As vehicles better suited to transporting large quantities of consumer goods became more readily available, individual stakes shot skyward. By the end of the decade, $3,000 worth of cloth goods and other items made up the typical proprietor's inventory; by 1839 the figure had reached $6,000, and by 1843, $15,000.

The changing structure of the trade may also be seen in its work force. During the formative half-dozen years, perhaps one-third of the 90 or so persons annually making the trek were wage earners, the balance being entrepreneurs. By 1843 as many as 175 men were hauling goods southwestward each year. Only one in ten of them were proprietors. As the volume of merchandise involved in the trade had expanded, so too had the incidence of independent backers who supplied money and wares but who remained comfortably behind in the East.

The Mexican War, of course, served as a watershed for the Santa Fe trade. For one thing, the strained relations between the United States and Mexico had led President Santa Anna in 1843 to embargo all commerce between Missouri and Santa Fe. It was not until the war erupted three years later that the interchange, as an adjunct to the American invasion of New Mexico, was resumed. Even then, the business was far from satisfactory. The disastrous experience of merchants Samuel Owens and James Aull, already mentioned, made businessmen increasingly wary. Moreover, profit margins, so high during the initial years of the international trade, naturally had begun to decline as more and more goods had been hauled to Mexico over the years. As the supply of American commodities increased with respect to a relatively fixed demand, the only possible consequence was a decline in prices.

While it is true that the trade between Santa Fe and Missouri resumed with the United States' occupation of New Mexico, it increasingly focused upon an American population that was far more discerning insofar as relative prices and quality were concerned. The dollar value of merchandise tripled between 1850 and 1860, but the population of the territory increased only by one-third. Again, the relative positions of supply and demand cut into profit margins as prices naturally declined over the years, bringing the cost of goods in New Mexico into closer alignment with that of the East. Too, the general price level for the whole United States had advanced by more than 12 percent during the period. Hence a significant proportion of the dollar increase in the trade must be attributed to inflation.

With the Civil War, the trade began to pass through a final transition. Commerce between Missouri and New Mexico increasingly fell victim to Indian harassment, which cut deeply into profits. Indeed, the war even served as an expelling force throughout the territory. New Mexico's population actually declined during the decade. While the net change was indeed small (a decrease of about 2 percent), an eroding market, given the difficulties of reaching it, could not have been very alluring to those who traditionally had plied the Santa Fe Trail.

The close of the war, of course, seemingly breathed new life into overland ventures, as freighters increasingly turned to draying supplies to the numerous military garrisons that were springing up throughout the region. Just such an increase in business, however, doomed the Santa Fe Trail, for railroad promoters also saw ample possibilities for lucrative returns. And as the Atchison, Topeka, and Santa Fe slowly snaked its way southwestward, businessmen began to use its facilities to transport commodities both for general and military consumption. Wagoners met the trains at railheads, offloaded goods onto their vehicles, and proceeded the rest of the way along a trek that was shrinking almost daily. By the time the railroad finally approached the community of Santa Fe, corporate officials had concluded that the sleepy town of six-thousand souls was hardly worth their attention or their firm's investment.

The Santa Fe Trail was blazed by profit-conscious businessmen who sought to fill an economic vacuum, a vacuum in which demand far outstripped supply. Those eager entrepreneurs annually shipped an ever increasing volume of goods along the trail to exploit this market of opportunity, only to see their own efficiency eventually erode their excellent profit margins. And finally they were replaced by the railroad, which offered more efficiency still.

A Note about Sources

No useful scholarly purpose can be served by appending a lengthy bibliography to this work because there is readily available to serious students of western history an excellent critical listing of works related to the Santa Fe trade: Jack D. Rittenhouse, *The Santa Fe trail: a historical bibliography*, Albuquerque (Univ. of New Mexico), 1971. This has become almost a sine qua non for the study of Southwestern history.

However, a selected list here of additional or supplemental books (no articles or pamphlets) might be worthwhile for readers who desire such an expanded list. Modern library style is followed in the entry format. We have made some annotations on a number of these, which we hope will add to the list's usefulness. Also, it might be worthwhile to discuss briefly some of the research problems we encountered and the sources we used in trying to resolve them. In a general way, we have tried to indicate in the text the most important sources used, especially where controversial points came up.

For the early commerce between Santa Fe and central Mexico we relied almost totally on Max Moorhead's fine book, *New Mexico's royal road: trade and travel on the Chihuahua trail*, Norman (Univ. of Okla.), 1958. The core problem in this early trade as well as in the later trade with Missouri was New Mexico's financial viability; that is, where did the people of New Mexico get the purchasing power? Professor Moorhead did not answer this satisfactorily and neither did we. For conditions in Santa Fe and New Mexico at the time of Mexican independence and the opening of the trade, we tried to look at everything, especially the Spanish Archives of New Mexico, which are available on microfilm through the courtesy of the New Mexico Department of Archives and Records. Particularly troublesome was the absence of usable quantitative data. Even the population censuses of the last years of Spanish control created as many problems as they solved because of the shifting and sometimes indeterminate use of such classifications as *gentes de razones, indios, coyotes, lobos,* and so forth.

The journals of the Missouri traders for 1821 and 1822 leave much to be desired about the opening of trade, especially Becknell's, which was fancied up and published several years later in the *Missouri Intelligencer.* The most valuable of the early journals was M. M. Marmaduke's, which along with a reprint of Becknell's can be found easily in Archer Butler Hulbert's compilation, *Southwest on the Turquoise trail: the first diaries on the road to Santa Fe,* Denver (Public Library), 1933. And like everyone else who has written about the subject, we leaned heavily on Josiah Gregg, who had secondhand information about the early years as well as firsthand knowledge of the thirties and forties.

Contemporary newspaper accounts were of great value, and for these we are under a debt that we cannot repay to the late (and great) Dale Morgan who had for years searched western newspaper files for all items related to the fur trade. True scholar that he was, he deposited copies of his typed transcripts at Huntington Library, which graciously made them available to us. The newspaper story, unhappily, is one-sided for the simple reason that there were virtually no newspapers in New Mexico, and there is no extant file of the Santa Fe *New Mexican* for the later years of the trade.

Any reliable quantitative analysis of the trade, even after it was well under way, continued to be elusive. The best source would have been customs receipts in New Mexico during the period from 1821 to 1847, but too many of the customs books have been lost for an acceptable account to be pieced together. Some fragmental records exist in the Mexican Archives of New Mexico (also on microfilm), and several were found in the Ritch Collection at Huntington. From these, at least, it was possible to get a somewhat clouded (and possibly distorted) look at the type of goods the traders brought in.

Many reminiscent accounts of the Santa Fe Trail and some business records of Missouri traders have been published. Among the unpublished materials, we found one of the most useful collections to be the letters of Thomas A. Hereford (at Huntington Library), a literate and observant physician and an in-law of the prominent Sublette family.

For the political situation in Mexico, the relations between Mexico and Texas and Mexico and the United States, and the Mexican war, we turned to our own studies, especially Connor's *Texas: a history*, New York (Thos. Y. Crowell), 1971, and Connor and Faulk, *North America divided*, New York (Oxford), 1971. The reactions in New Mexico itself to political and international developments seem to have been lethargic and certainly remain unsullied by serious historical investigation. Similarly, the only studies of American occupation of New Mexico after the Mexican War are distorted by a preoccupied emphasis on American "aggression" and New Mexican "resistance."

On the route of the trail, the definitive study is William E. Brown's theme study for the National Park Service, "The Santa Fe Trail," available in mimeograph form. In trying personally to see the sights (and sites) of the trail, we turned to the useful book by Hobart E. Stocking, *The road to Santa Fe*, New York (Hastings), 1971.

RECOMMENDED READING

Abert, James William. *Report of an expedition led by Lieutenant Abert, on the upper Arkansas and through the country of the Comanche Indians, in the fall of the year 1845.* Washington (29th Cong., 1st sess., SD 438), 1846 [serial 477]. An edited version was issued under the title, *Guadal P'a*, ed. H. Bailey Carroll, Canyon (Panhandle-Plains His. Soc.), 1941. An illustrated edition is available as *Through the country of the Comanche Indians*, ed. John Gavin, San Francisco (Howell), 1970. Abert was a member of the Corps of Topographic Engineers who traversed a section of the Santa Fe Trail from Bent's Fort south through Raton Pass to the Canadian River in 1845.

Barreiro, Antonio. *Ojeada sobre Nuevo Mejico, que da una idea de sus produciones naturales, y de algunas otras cosas. . . .* Puebla, Mex. (J. M. Campos), 1832. Trans. J. Villasana Haggard as *A glance over New Mexico*, in *Three New Mexico chronicles*, ed. H. Bailey Carroll, Albuquerque (Quivera Soc.), 1942. This is one of the very few accounts of the trade from the Mexican viewpoint.

Barry, Louise (ed.). *The beginning of the West: annals of the Kansas gateway to the American West, 1540–1854.* Topeka (Kansas State His. Soc.), 1972. This excellent collection of original narratives of Kansas history contains many accounts of the early Santa Fe trade.

Beadle, John Hanson. *The undeveloped West; or five years in the territories.* . . . Philadelphia (National Publishing), 1873. Beadle's lively narrative, which was quite popular at the time, contains an account of a stage coach adventure on a portion of the Santa Fe Trail.

Bender, Averam Burton. *The march of empire: frontier defense in the Southwest, 1848–1860.* Lawrence (Univ. of Kansas), 1952.

Bennett, James A. *Forts and forays: James A. Bennett, a dragoon in New Mexico, 1850–1856.* Ed. Clinton E. Brooks and Frank D. Reeve. Albuquerque (Univ. of New Mexico), 1948.

Bieber, Ralph P. (ed.). *Exploring Southwestern trails, 1846–1854.* Vol. VII of the *Southwest historical series.* Glendale (Arthur H. Clark), 1938. This important publication contains the journals and diaries of Phillip St. George Cooke, William Henry C. Whiting, and Francois X. Aubry, plus a bonus in the form of a useful introduction by Bieber.

Brown, William E. *The Santa Fe trail.* Santa Fe (National Park Service), 1963. This was a theme study prepared for the Park Service's survey of historic sites and buildings. It is an outstanding account of the location of the trail itself. Mimeographed versions are available.

Cleland, Robert Glass. *This reckless breed of men: the trappers and traders of the Southwest.* New York (Knopf), 1950. This excellent and readable history contains a chapter on the fur traders who entered the Santa Fe commerce.

Conrad, Howard Louis. *"Uncle Dick" Wootton, the pioneer frontiersman of the Rocky Mountain region: an account of the adventures and thrilling experiences of the most noted American hunter, trapper, guide, scout, and Indian fighter now living.* Chicago (W. E. Dibble), 1890. Reprinted Columbus (Long's College Bookstore), 1950. From 1836 to 1878, Wootton was intimately involved with the Santa Fe Trail. This is a reminiscence full of personal stories about the trade.

Cooke, Phillip St. George. *The conquest of New Mexico and California, an historical and personal narrative.* New York (G. P. Putnam), 1878. Reprinted Albuquerque (Horn and Wallace), 1964. Cooke's is the best and most literate account of the march of the Mormon Battalion, which he led from Santa Fe to California after the death of its original commander.

Davis, William Watts Hart. *El gringo; or, New Mexico and her people.* New York (Harper), 1857. Reprinted Santa Fe (Rydal), 1938; Chicago (Rio Grande), 1963. This is an amusing and observant account of the customs of the people of New Mexico as viewed by a somewhat prudish Yankee.

Duffus, Robert L. *The Santa Fe trail.* New York (Longmans, Green), 1930. Reprinted Albuquerque (Univ. of New Mexico), 1972, paperback. This has long been the standard history of the Santa Fe trade. It is quite readable.

Emmett, Chris. *Fort Union and the winning of the Southwest.* Norman (Univ. of Oklahoma), 1965.

Emory, William Hemsley. *Notes of a military reconnaissance from Fort Leavenworth in Missouri to San Diego in California, including part of the Arkansas, Del Norte, and Gila rivers.* Washington (30th Cong., 1st sess., HD 41), 1848 [serial 517]. Reprinted under the title, *Lieutenant Emory reports,* Albuquerque (Univ. of New Mexico), 1951. This is the complete report of the Corps of Topographic Engineers who accompanied (more or less) the Army of the West.

Falconer, Thomas. *Expedition to Santa Fe: an account of its journey from Texas through Mexico, with particulars of its capture.* New Orleans (Picayune), 1842. Another version under the title, *Letters and notes on the Texan Santa Fe expedition, 1841–1842,* ed. F. W. Hodge, New York (Dauber and Pine), 1930; reprinted Glorietta, N. M. (Rio Grande), 1963. Falconer was an Englishman who accompanied the Texas venture.

Fowler, Jacob. *The journal of Jacob Fowler, narrating an adventure from Arkansas through the Indian territory, Oklahoma, Kansas, Colorado, and New Mexico to the sources of the Rio Grande del Norte, 1821–22.* Ed. Elliott Coues. New York (Francis P. Harper), 1898; reprinted Minneapolis (Ross and Haines), 1952; Lincoln (Univ. of Nebraska), 1970.

Garrard, Lewis Hector. *Wah-to-yah, and the Taos trail; or prairie travel and scalp dances, with a look at los rancheros from muleback, and the Rocky Mountains campfire.* Cincinnati (H. W. Derby), 1850. Many reprints. This is a great classic of the trail by a man who made the trip in 1846.

Gibson, George Rutledge. *Journal of a soldier under Kearny and Doniphan, 1846–1847.* Ed. Ralph Bieber. Vol. III of the *Southwest historical series.* Glendale (Arthur H. Clark), 1935. Weston was a newspaper publisher, and his journal is an important source of information about the occupation of New Mexico.

Gregg, Josiah. *Commerce of the prairies; or the journal of a Santa Fe trader, during eight expeditions across the great western prairies, and a residence of nearly nine years in northern Mexico.* 2 vols. New York (Langley), 1844. Many editions available, some abridged, some paperback. This is the foundation for all study and writing about the Santa Fe Trail.

———. *Diary and letters of Josiah Gregg.* Ed. Maurice G. Fulton. 2 vols. Norman (Univ. of Oklahoma), 1941, 1944.

Gregg, Kate L. (ed.). *The road to Santa Fe: the journal and diaries of*

George Champlin Sibley and others pertaining to the surveying and marking of a road from the Missouri frontier to the settlements of New Mexico, 1825–1827. Albuquerque (Univ. of New Mexico), 1952. Carefully edited accounts of the official survey of the trail.

Hafen, LeRoy R. *Broken Hand: the life story of Thomas Fitzpatrick, chief of the mountain men.* Denver (Old West), 1931. Fitzpatrick made several trips over the trail, beginning in 1831.

————. *The mountain men and the fur trade of the far West: biographical sketches of the participants. . . .* 8 vols. Glendale (Arthur H. Clark), 1965–1970. This monumental work contains biographies of many of the most important men in the early Santa Fe trade.

Hall, Thomas B. *Medicine on the Santa Fe trail.* Dayton, Ohio (Morningside Bookshop), 1971. This is basically the journal of a physician, Dr. T. B. Lester, who was with Doniphan. Contains a good description of Santa Fe at the time.

Hughes, John T. *Doniphan's expedition; containing an account of the conquest of New Mexico; General Kearny's overland expedition to California; Doniphan's campaign against the Navajos; his unparalleled march upon Chihuahua and Durango, and the operations of General Price at Santa Fe; with a sketch of the life of Col. Doniphan.* Cincinnati (James), 1848. Several editions and reprints. This is one the classics of the American West.

Hulbert, Archer Butler (ed.). *Southwest on the Turquoise trail: the first diaries on the road to Santa Fe.* Denver (Public Library), 1933. Among others, this work contains M. M. Marmaduke's journal of his 1824 trip to Santa Fe.

Inman, Henry. *The old Santa Fe trail: the story of a great highway.* New York (Macmillan), 1897. Numerous reprints. This was the first history of the Santa Fe Trail from its beginning to the coming of the railroad. Although lively reading, it is not wholly reliable.

James, Thomas. *Three years among the Indians and Mexicans.* Waterloo, Ill. (Office of the War Eagle), 1846. Among several reprints is one with an excellent introduction by A. P. Nasatir, Philadelphia (Lippincott), 1962. Since James reached Santa Fe only a couple of weeks after Becknell, this is one of the most important journals of the trail.

Kendall, George Wilkins. *Narrative of the Texan Santa Fe expedition, comprising a description of a tour through Texas, and across the great southwestern prairies, the Camanche and Caygua hunting grounds, with an account of the suffering from want of food, losses from hostile Indians, and final capture of the Texans, and their march, as prisoners, to the city of Mexico.* 2 vols. New York (Harper), 1844. Other editions and reprint of the first, Austin (Steck), 1935. Kendall was editor of the New Orleans *Picayune.*

Lamar, Howard R. *The far Southwest, 1846–1912: a territorial history.* New Haven (Yale Univ.), 1966.

Lavender, David. *Bent's Fort.* Garden City (Doubleday), 1954. Because of the Bents' close involvement in the trade and because of Lavender's literary and historical skills, this is one of the most important books available relating to the subject.

Loomis, Noel M. *The Texan–Santa Fe pioneers.* Norman (Univ. of Okla.), 1958.

McCall, George Archibald. *New Mexico in 1850: a military view.* Ed. Robert W. Frazer. Norman (Univ. of Okla.), 1968.

Magoffin, Susan Shelby. *Down the Santa Fe trail and into Mexico: the diary of Susan Shelby Magoffin, 1846–1847.* Ed. Stella M. Drumm. New Haven (Yale), 1926. This is the delightful, poignant journal of a bride who accompanied her husband and the Army of the West into New Mexico during the Mexican War.

Majors, Alexander. *Seventy years on the frontier: Alexander Majors' memoirs of a lifetime on the border.* Ed. Prentiss Ingraham. Chicago (Rand, McNally), 1893. This is an important work on the freighting business, although only a few pages relate directly to the Santa Fe Trail.

Marcy, Randolph Barnes. *The prairie traveler: a handbook for overland expeditions, with maps, illustrations, and itineraries of the principal routes between the Mississippi and the Pacific.* New York (Harper), 1859.

———. *Route from Fort Smith to Santa Fe. . . .* Washington (31 Cong., 1st sess., HD 45), 1850; also in *Reports . . . with reconnaissances of routes. . . .* Washington (31 Cong., 1st sess., SD 64), 1850. And there is a reprint entitled *Marcy and the gold seekers,* ed. Grant Foreman, Norman (Univ. of Okla.), 1939.

Marshall, James L. *Santa Fe: the railroad that built an empire.* New York (Random House), 1945.

Meline, James F. *Two thousand miles on horseback; Santa Fe and back; a summer tour through Kansas, Nebraska, Colorado, and New Mexico, in the year 1866.* New York (Hurd and Houghton), 1867.

Moorhead, Max L. *New Mexico's royal road: trade and travel on the Chihuahua trail.* Norman (Univ. of Okla.), 1958. This excellent work contains an outstanding study of the economics of the trade as it related to central Mexico.

Morgan, Dale L. *Jedediah Smith and the opening of the West.* Indianapolis (Bobbs-Merrill), 1953.

Murray, Robert A. *Citadel on the Santa Fe trail.* Ft. Collins (Old Army Press), 1970.

Oliva, Leo E. *Soldiers on the Santa Fe trail.* Norman (Univ. of Okla.), 1967.

Otero, Miguel Antonio. *My life on the frontier, 1864–1882.* New York (Press of the Pioneers), 1935. When Otero was three years old his father moved from New Mexico to Missouri to enter the mercantile business in Westport. Although this, the first of three volumes of reminiscences, covers roughly the last decade of the trail, it does provide a Hispanic New Mexican view.

Pattie, James Ohio. *The personal narrative of James O. Pattie of Kentucky, being an expedition from St. Louis, through the vast regions between that place and the Pacific Ocean.* Ed. Timothy Flint. Cincinnati (John H. Wood), 1831. Many reprints. This edition includes "Dr. Willard's Journal of Inland Trade with New Mexico," originally published in the *Western Monthly Review.* Pattie was in Santa Fe in 1824; Willard, the following year.

Rittenhouse, Jack D. *The Santa Fe trail: a historical bibliography.* Albuquerque (Univ. of New Mexico), 1971. This was a foundation stone for the present study. The introduction and annotations are excellent.

Russell, Marian Sloan. *Memoirs of Marian Russell.* Ed. Mrs. Hal Russell. Evanston, Ill. (Branding Iron), 1954. Marian Russell began traveling the trail in 1852 and after five trips, she and her husband opened a trading post in northern New Mexico. Her reminiscences are worth reading.

Ryus, William Henry. *The second William Penn: a true account of incidents that happened along the old Santa Fe trail in the sixties.* Kansas City, Mo. (Frank T. Riley), 1913.

Sage, Rufus B. *Scenes in the Rocky Mountains, and in Oregon, California, New Mexico, Texas, and the grand prairies. . . .* Philadelphia (Carey and Hart), 1846. Also issued as vols. IV and V of *The Far West and Rockies series,* ed. LeRoy Hafen, Glendale (Arthur Clark), 1956. Sage was on the Snively-Warfield expedition of "Texans."

Stocking, Hobart E. *The road to Santa Fe.* New York (Hastings), 1971. This readable book is particularly useful because it locates the route of the trail in relation to present landmarks and highways. The author's illustrations are charming.

Sunder, John E. *Bill Sublette, mountain man.* Norman (Univ. of Okla.), 1959.

——— (ed.). *Matt Field on the Santa Fe trail.* Norman (Univ. of Okla.), 1960. This is an interesting collection of the writings of Matt Field, a journalist, about the Santa Fe Trail, but it adds little of value to the history of the trail.

Taylor, Benjamin F. (ed.). *Short ravelings from a long yarn, or camp march sketches of the Santa Fe trail; from the notes of Richard L. Wilson.* Chicago (Geer and Wilson), 1847. Reprinted Santa Ana (Fine Arts), 1936. This hopelessly syrupy account of an 1841 trip down the trail is well known, but of little value.

Twitchell, Ralph Emerson. *The history of the military occupation of the territory of New Mexico from 1846 to 1851 by the government of the United States.* . . . Denver (Smith-Brooks), 1909. Reprinted Chicago (Rio Grande), 1963.

————. *The leading facts of New Mexico history.* 5 vols. Cedar Rapids (Torch), 1911–1917.

Vestal, Stanley (pseud.). *The old Santa Fe trail.* Boston (Houghton Mifflin), 1939.

Waters, Lawrence L. *Steel trails to Santa Fe.* Lawrence (Univ. of Kansas), 1950. The best scholarly history of the Santa Fe railroad.

Webb, James Josiah. *Adventures in the Santa Fe trade, 1844–1847.* Ed. Ralph Bieber. Vol. I of the *Southwest historical series.* Glendale (Arthur Clark), 1931.

Weber, David J. *The Taos trappers: the fur trade in the far Southwest, 1540–1846.* Norman (Univ. of Okla.), 1971.

Wislizenus, Frederick Adolphus. *Memoir of a tour to northern Mexico, connected with Col. Doniphan's expedition, in 1846 and 1847.* Washington (30th Cong., 1st. sess., SMD 26), 1848 [serial 511]. Reprinted Albuquerque (Horn), 1969; Glorietta, N.M. (Rio Grande), 1969.

Young, Otis E. *The first military escort on the Santa Fe trail, 1829; from the journal and reports of Major Bennet Riley and Lieutenant Philip St. George Cooke.* Glendale (Arthur H. Clark), 1952.

Index